SLEEP, BABY, SLEEP

SLEEP, BABY, SLEEP

Jessica Auerbach

HEADLINE

First published in Great Britain in 1994 by
HEADLINE BOOK PUBLISHING

10 9 8 7 6 5 4 3 2 1

British Library Cataloguing in Publication Data

Auerbach, Jessica
Sleep, Baby, Sleep
I. Title
823 [F]

ISBN 0-7472-1122-1

Typeset by
CBS, Felixstowe, Suffolk

Printed and bound in Great Britain by
Mackays of Chatham PLC, Chatham, Kent

HEADLINE BOOK PUBLISHING
A division of Hodder Headline PLC
338 Euston Road
London NW1 3BH

To René and Mort

PART 1

Chapter 1

At first, for what she later estimated to the police must have been just under three minutes, Sylvie was completely calm. She'd been expecting her mother to come by, and she'd taken all the ingredients for their lunch out of the brown paper grocery bag. There was tortellini, marinara sauce, salad greens and dressing, and an Italian bread that she was going to slice up and try to make into super-buttery garlic toast like they served at Alfredo's. Then she went in to check on the baby.

Sylvie always started to miss Cally after about an hour or so, especially when her breasts started getting heavy, which was what was happening just then. She went down the hall toward the back bedroom (and yes, the door was closed, she absolutely remembered that she turned the knob, and how it sort of stuck a little, the way it always did). She said she was halfway across the room before she realized the crib was empty. She took a couple of steps back, like she'd seen something startling inside the crib that was there now instead of Cally. Then she stood for a few seconds, just staring at the crib sheet, and she saw how the rosebuds weren't just spattered here and there as she'd always thought, but were held fast in a rigid diagonal grid. Then she turned and walked all the way back to the kitchen, to the only phone in the apartment, and dialed 911.

The dispatcher specifically remarked on Sylvie's detached tone, saying how she made herself perfectly clear – no repetitions, no vagueness, no disjointedness. He said it was like the third-party calls they sometimes got, the ones where some outside observer calls in, or like the ones where somebody's just trying to up the ante in a domestic quarrel. The police got it on tape, because every call that comes into the station is

3

recorded. All Sylvie said was, 'My baby is missing,' and then she gave her address. The only thing that seemed a little jumpy about her was that she didn't stay on long enough to close out the call – no goodbye or the usual 'Please hurry.' You can hear the disconnect before the dispatcher has his whole sentence out about getting someone over there.

She said it was when she finished with the telephone and walked into the baby's room for the second time that she went to pieces. She walked right up to the crib and lifted the bunched-up blanket, even though there couldn't have been a baby (not even one as small as Calida) underneath. She even shook the blanket, though later, when she was questioned, Sylvie couldn't say what she thought she might have gained from such a maneuver, and that maybe she'd just lifted it. Next after that, she looked under the crib, and all over the floor and behind the baby's dresser, because she thought maybe Cally had somehow rolled out of the crib and across the floor. Then she walked down the hall toward the living room because it occurred to her that maybe she'd just had a memory lapse and had put the baby in there, in the wicker cradle, and for a second she really believed she was going to see her all curled up under the pink lacework blanket and she even started worrying about whether the police would think she was a real nut forgetting which crib she'd put her baby in, but Cally wasn't in there, either, and then she thought maybe Peter had come home and had her in another room, and so she started calling his name, but each time she did so, all she heard was an echo, no answer. Still, she checked every room, every closet – pulling things out as she went, as if it were possible the baby was stored under towels or sweaters. She checked the crib and the cradle six or seven times more, and then decided maybe she'd actually taken Cally to the store, not left her in the house, and so she went out the door (coatless though it was an unseasonably chilly day) and started off for the Grove Market, where she'd been thirty minutes earlier. She kept her eyes down toward the sidewalk as she went, looking to the left and right the way people do when they've lost a coin or a ring, and then once she was in the store, she went up and down the aisles, though she actually remembered what had happened perfectly well. She remembered looking in on Cally in her crib, deciding not to wake her for just a quick run to the market, and then leaving her. At home. In the crib.

All the witnesses said that she was hysterical by the time she reached the Grove. 'A kind of moaning and groaning mixed in with the crying,' one of them said. Tony, the manager at the Grove Market, said he watched through the front window when she went back out and that 'she looked scared to the core.' He said it brought a lump to his throat, seeing somebody so upset.

She ran the two blocks back, and the police officers who were just pulling up in front of her residence, said she tore right past their squad car and up the stairs toward her entryway. She said she didn't see them, that she was thinking about checking the crib again, thinking she'd see the baby there and that she'd still be wearing that white suit with the pink bunnies on it that she'd bought just the day before at Wee Baby, and she remembered crossing her fingers at that point, hoping and concentrating, too, as hard as she could, on how Cally looked in that suit, because it seemed so important. Like that was what was needed to get her to be back there.

The senior officer, Reynolds, said he rang the bell, even though the door was wide open, but when there was no response, he went on in. There was a tea-kettle whistling full blast. His partner, Bellarosa, made his way toward the kitchen, turned off the burner, and put the kettle in the center of the stove. Later, Sylvie said she thought she had put up a full pot of water just before she went in to check on the baby.

From the look of the place, Reynolds assumed it'd been ransacked, and that more than just the baby had been taken, which might have meant the baby was an afterthought – usually a really bad sign in terms of ever getting them back alive. But then he saw Sylvie pulling things out of a bedroom closet, so he knew he was probably on the wrong track on that one.

He had to secure the place before she completely wrecked everything, so he quickly asked her please to refrain from

5

destroying evidence, but there was no stopping her with words. She was worked up to such a high pitch, to hear her, it was like the tea-kettle had never been shut off. He and Bella knelt down on either side of her and each took hold of an arm. At first she fought them, tried to pull her arms away, but that was when Reynolds said he tightened his grip, and probably Bella did, too – it's one of those instinct things. She had hold of this yellow blanket, an old-fashioned handmade one, and when she went limp, which she did as soon as they both had a good grip on her, and let herself be steered over to the bed, she held the blanket against her chest in what Reynolds called 'a fierce way.' They were able to get her to sit down, but not to quiet down. By that time she had started screaming, 'He'll kill me,' – just that, over and over.

Reynolds tried explaining to her that he needed to know who else might legitimately have the baby (a couple of times a year, it turned out that baby-sitters had taken their charges down to the mall or over to visit their sisters, not intending any harm by it), but that was when she pulled the blanket up to her face and just bawled into it, no more words. He tried to take her hand, make her feel he understood how bad it was, but she pulled away the second he touched it.

Just before that, he'd noticed the dark, wet patches spreading across her shirtfront. It made him think of this dog, Jinx, he had when he was a kid that had a litter of just two babies, stillborn. They took the pups away, of course, and buried them, but then Jinx curled up with a little teddy bear that used to sit on his sister's bed. And she licked it all over, shined up the brown fur so it looked a lot like a newborn pup. It'd been pathetic to watch because it was so wrong, so totally screwed up. He'd had to turn away, he said, from that dog, and from this girl – she looked so young, not old enough to be a mother. No, he couldn't watch this girl, either.

He looked over at Bella and saw he was shaking his head, so he just told him to call in and get them to send Forensics down and Marty, too, if they could. 'Fast,' he said, right while Bella was on the phone trying to talk. Because if anything, she was definitely getting worse.

Chapter 2

Hannah did see the squad car when she pulled up at her daughter Sylvie's apartment house, it was just that she assumed, as people do, that the trouble was elsewhere. And anyway, she was more concerned with getting the bags and boxes that lay next to her on the passenger's seat into her arms. There were fresh-cut flowers, a box of cupcakes, a bag of baby clothes, including a pair of roll-cuff jeans that she hadn't been able to resist, and two of her oversize shirts which she thought Sylvie might find convenient for nursing. She didn't want to make two trips up the steps and front walk, so she flung her handbag over her shoulder and scooped the rest of the stuff into her arms, not being terribly careful of what got crushed into what, though she did make some attempt to keep the cake box level. She managed to lock the car door without actually dropping anything, but she had to bite onto the paper that held the flowers in order to keep them from falling.

What Hannah was expecting inside Sylvie's brick front apartment was a simple, lazy lunch, a chance to hold Cally and perhaps see her in the new jeans and tie-dye tee-shirt she now carried in her arms. The university break had just begun, so Hannah felt rich in time.

A police officer, however, opened the door to Hannah. Something – possibly simple confusion – immobilized her so thoroughly that she couldn't step over the threshold, and couldn't figure out what she needed to ask of this man. Perhaps it was the officer's question, 'May I help you, ma'am?' that made her wonder if, in her preoccupation with juggling her packages, she might have walked up to the wrong door.

Beyond the uniformed officer Hannah saw two other people,

7

one of them kneeling at the couch in front of Sylvie. She could see her daughter's shoulders shake and heave, and she could hear the sound of her sobs.

'Ma'am?' the officer repeated, and said something, more, some other question Hannah didn't hear.

'What's happened?' she demanded of the portly doorkeeper, though her eyes were seeking the answers directly from the slumped figure that was Sylvie.

'Are you her mother, then?' the figure in blue asked.

'Yes, yes,' she said, catching at the bakery box that was starting to tip and slide through her arms.

'The baby appears to be missing,' the officer said.

'Oh God, no, not the baby,' she said, and tossed the packages to the tiled floor of the entry hall, then stepped past him, one hand pressed briefly against his chest, so as to move him aside as she might have moved a door had it similarly blocked her passage. He didn't try to stop her. Sylvie lifted her head, seemed, for a second, to recoil, though by the time Hannah actually reached her side, Sylvie had extended her hand, and she was rising, but almost falling toward Hannah, too, needing to be caught and embraced. Hannah held tight to her daughter; tighter still, with each of her convulsive sobs. After a few moments, Sylvie's breathing seemed to ease, and Hannah asked, 'What happened?' but her daughter only wailed mournfully. 'Tell me what happened,' Hannah begged, her own voice as desperate, as full of panic, as her daughter's. 'Sylvie,' she pleaded, and saw, over her daughter's shoulder, a man in a tweed sports coat staring directly at her. Hannah averted her eyes, whispered to Sylvie, 'Tell me,' and wished the man – all of the men – were gone, but he was still very much there when she looked up again. He leaned closer toward her; she held Sylvie more firmly. He introduced himself, though she took no notice of his name. Hannah stroked her daughter's blonde head, then asked him, her voice trembling but coherent, 'Where's the baby?'

'We're doing our best to figure that out,' he said. 'But we need to get your daughter calm enough to help us.' He asked if she thought Sylvie would do better if she were to lie down.

8

'The baby's gone?' Hannah asked, and he nodded, just one deep, very thorough nod: down, then up. But it seemed to her that they might have overlooked the baby, the house was in such turmoil. Couldn't it be, she said to him, that they had just (here she choked down the word *thrown*) put her somewhere, and he said, 'I believe it's your daughter who's turned the place upside down, not the kidnappers.'

'Sylvie did?' she asked him, though she might have asked Sylvie herself, of course, given that she was right there. 'That doesn't make sense,' she insisted.

'Yes, ma'am, I know that. And we need to make sense of it, so we'd like to get back to talking to her as soon as we can. Do you think she'd do better lying down? I can talk to her in the bedroom, if you think it'd be better. So far we're all batting close to zero, I must say.'

'I can talk now,' Sylvie said, her voice ragged and hiccoughy.

The weeping had quieted, but Hannah saw that her eyes – her whole face – were so puffed up, so bruised-looking, she asked her, 'Did they hit you?' and Sylvie shook her head for answer.

'It'd be best if you let me ask the questions,' he said. 'We'll get there fastest that way. Time is of the essence, you know. If she's ready, that is.'

'I need tissues,' Sylvie said, easing herself back down onto the couch.

Hannah sped off to the bathroom, but once arrived in the small room, had to take hold of the cold porcelain sink to steady herself before she could reach out a hand for the tissue box. She walked back more slowly, her sense of balance tenuous, her vision as brittle as reflections in a shattered mirror.

The man's name was Martinson – Detective Martinson. He was the one all the officers hoped for when there was calming-down that needed to be done. Everybody'd seen it – he could take hysteria and turn it into peace, though nobody had quite figured out how he managed that. They could see it wasn't a laying on of hands, because he never touched; never even got close. Among themselves they said it must be something in his voice, which could be deep and smooth in a dark basso way, but

9

they kind of knew it wasn't that, either, because the wilder the person was, the more brusque Marty became. What the detective himself knew, was that it had something to do with how much he hated chaos. It made him crazy to watch people shake and scream. So what he did was he told them not to shake or scream – that was how it felt to him, anyway. He thought they felt his fear. It wasn't that they were comforted or knew that they were in good hands, it was that they picked up on how close he was, too, to going out of control if they didn't straighten up. So out of desperation, they did.

Like a twelve-year-old who feels lost when he's made to wear dress clothes instead of jeans, Martinson kept his hands in the pockets of his sports jacket a lot of the time. He let the weight of his arms ease forward so that even when the pockets were empty, they stayed as drooped and worn-looking as the ears of a weary hound. Hannah took it as a good sign that he wore running shoes, even if they were black leather and designed to make people think he was wearing real shoes, because there was at least the chance that he was a runner, or if not actually a runner, then an active person, capable of a sprint. Leather soles would not be of much help if he had to chase down a kidnapper.

Martinson was not, Hannah quickly saw, a sympathetic interviewer.. Aside from his initial suggestion that Sylvie lie down, he seemed almost oblivious to her distress. And Hannah had to look away, right at the beginning, when he pulled at the knot of his tie, a too-thick, unattractive thing of silver and blue striping. It struck her as a terrible obscenity, that loosening of his tie. He has no right, she thought, to be thinking of his own comfort when this has happened.

The pace of the interview was all his – when he chose to linger in dead air contemplating answers between questions, he did so, but then he'd follow his time-out with a relentless string of questions fired at Sylvie so quickly, she barely had time to breathe between them. There was no apparent order to his inquiries, either, but, rather, it was as though he spun the pointer on a wheel that sometimes turned up the same questions, sometimes new ones. To Hannah's mind, all he was getting was a jumble of out-of-order facts. Martinson asked about Peter, then what the baby was wearing, what time Hannah was expected for lunch, what Sylvie had purchased at the store, how long she'd lived in the apartment. Then he said, 'So, you're not married?' as though that detail, stated by Sylvie ten minutes earlier and not mentioned since, had only just sunk into his consciousness.

Martinson asked Sylvie to go back into the bedroom where Cally had been, and to place the crib exactly where it had stood. 'Did you put her down to sleep on her stomach or her back?' he asked, and then, 'Why on her back? Was her head touching the end of the crib or was it two, six, eight inches, maybe, from the end? *Think*,' he said when she hesitated, and Hannah saw Sylvie wince under the sharpness of his command. What could possibly be the importance of such niggling details? she wondered. 'Show me with your hand where the top of her head came to,' he said. Hannah saw Sylvie sway above the crib; for a moment it seemed she might pass out. Insensitive bastard! she thought. Why was he making her touch those sheets, making her go through it so closely so many times? Then he wanted to know the names of everyone who took care of Cally besides Sylvie, Peter, and Hannah. There was no one else, Sylvie told him. He wanted to know if any other clothes were missing and when she told him she didn't know, that she couldn't remember all the clothes the baby had, and besides, they were all scattered around everywhere, he stopped her mid-sentence and said, with a ferocity Hannah thought cruel, '*Think*.'

'She has attention deficit disorder,' Hannah interjected, rising, thinking to stand between this man and her daughter.

'Yes?' he asked, turning toward Hannah, his eyebrows raised in expectation – of an explanation, she supposed.

'She wouldn't be able to remember and list all that for you.'

'She'll do the best she can, then, won't she?' Martinson said, looking toward Sylvie, who nodded, then haltingly began to enumerate jumpsuits and overalls, none of which, it appeared, were missing.

Next he wanted the minutes and seconds that had passed

11

from when she put the baby down to when she realized Cally was gone. And then he wanted that time again, telling her to subtract backward this time, as though he were asking her to check a column of figures by adding it down, then up. It wasn't the sort of thing Sylvie could do on her own, at least not under pressure, Hannah knew. First she told him forty minutes, then twenty-two to twenty-five and now she was settling, possibly by way of compromise, on thirty-four. He was deliberately trying to confuse her, Hannah concluded as she watched him record Sylvie's answers in a small notebook, and clearly he was succeeding.

While they spoke, police officers were taking photographs, dusting doorknobs, bagging crib-size blankets and sheets. Some of them carried receivers at their belts that crackled out incoherent messages and to which they appeared to pay no heed at all. What they should be doing was cleaning this place up, Hannah thought, so that Sylvie could feel that something, anything, was back to normal and as it should be. Hannah'd been straightening it in her mind the whole time she'd been there, willing the clothes back into drawers, the towels back onto shelves, and the books returned to their orderly piles. And she'd even imagined Cally, gliding slowly through the still air, arms and legs moving in gentle swimming motions, back into her crib. 'Oh, put the room back together, already,' she enjoined them in silence.

And then suddenly Martinson was going at it beginning-to-end, getting Sylvie to tell what happened from the minute she woke up that morning. 'Yes,' he said, 'I do want to know if you went to the bathroom or took a shower and what you ate for breakfast. I want every detail.' And it was then that Hannah understood, for the first time, that Sylvie had left Cally alone in the house and Hannah nearly grabbed for her shoulders, wanted to shake her, to scream, 'You did what? You left that tiny little baby alone? Of course someone took her!' And Hannah remembered that she'd thought at least a hundred times, surely, that she ought to say to Sylvie, 'You don't ever take your hand off her when she's on the changing table, do you? You don't ever carry her when you're wearing that long robe that

12

you could step on and trip, do you? When you carry her down the front brick stairs, you hold onto the banister, don't you?'

But those were things she'd never said, though she'd thought about each and every one of them. And she'd never said, 'You don't leave her alone in the house, do you?' though she'd certainly thought about that as well. Was Sylvie so blind to reality that she wasn't aware that people stole children? Didn't every *child* know that? Hannah hadn't spoken up because Sylvie'd been doing pretty well, had seemed, finally, to grasp a subject, *this* subject, taking care of a child. Poor Cally, Hannah thought. I could have saved you! I knew Sylvie needed to be instructed and reminded. I ought to have advised. I ought to have insisted.

'I made a mistake,' she now heard her daughter say, her voice thickened by new sobs. 'And I'll never, ever, forgive myself. I wish I was dead.'

'Stop,' Hannah said, reaching for Sylvie's hands as though to keep her from some sudden rash act against herself. 'The important thing now is to stay calm so we can find her.'

'It was five minutes that I was gone, I swear,' Sylvie said. Her eyes were closed and Hannah remembered that those were the same words she'd said to the doctor when she'd brought her own limp and unconscious infant into his office. She'd only expected it to take a few moments, she'd said to him. She thought she'd be able to run into the pharmacy and out – better that than expose her daughter to all the sick people hovering round the prescription area, she'd reasoned. She hadn't thought she'd have to wait so long for her order. 'They can die from this,' the doctor had said, pitiless in his attribution of blame. 'They can dehydrate in minutes in a closed car in this weather.' And of course it hadn't been just five minutes, Hannah remembered. They'd had to admit Sylvie to hospital overnight, hook her up to an IV. The doctor had mentioned social workers and protective services in a long speech he'd rendered while he held Sylvie's dry hand in his and took her pulse. She'd wanted to grab the baby back from his arms, steal her away, but she was paralyzed into mute obedience, and she stood, back against the wall, crying, while he lifted the phone and called for an ambulance.

Even after Hannah brought her baby, perky and fully recovered, back home to her tiny, one-room apartment, she spent weeks starting at the sound of footsteps approaching her door. But there had been no visits from social agencies, nor what Hannah had really feared, a visit from a police officer.

Now, in Sylvie's living room, in this huge, sprawling apartment, Hannah stroked her grown daughter's hand, tried to smooth down the tight angles of her closed fist. 'You thought she was safe,' Hannah said softly.

'It was only five minutes,' Sylvie repeated.

'Shall we go on?' Martinson asked. He wanted to know how to locate Peter.

He was on a business trip to three sites in Florida, Sylvie told him. 'He's driving all over the state.' Martinson wanted the name of the hotels where Peter would be staying, but Sylvie said she didn't know where he'd be. He usually stayed in one of the chains, the cheaper places, she said.

'Is he likely to call?' Martinson asked.

'He usually does sometime while he's away.'

'Time?' Martinson asked.

'I don't know. He calls all different times. I guess it depends on when he gets a break.'

Martinson took down this information, then excused himself to consult with the other officers and to make several phone calls. Hannah and Sylvie sat in silence. Hannah was remembering, again, her child, Sylvie, strapped down in a bed, a needle leading from her arm to a bag of glucose water suspended above her head.

'Will you stay with me till Peter gets here?' Sylvie asked her mother, her voice now level but strange – something like the telephone computer voice that guided you through merchandising conflicts. 'How am I going to tell him?' She spoke quietly, to herself, seemingly. 'He'll kill me.'

'Don't say things like that,' Hannah whispered, warning her daughter. She didn't like that way the police officers seemed to lean toward their words. 'You have to remember that it isn't your fault.' Nor was it mine, with you, she said to herself. Simple miscalculations. Poor timing, bad coincidences. At least,

14

those were the ways she'd explained it once.

'It is,' Sylvie insisted, and her face started to crumple again. Hannah wanted to say, 'He won't be upset or angry, he'll understand.' Except that that was a wishful lie. You don't tell someone his child is gone and expect anything less than total devastation, do you? — and if he turned his anger against Sylvie, would that be so surprising? Wouldn't it be his right to ask, 'Would this have happened if you hadn't left her?' Could anyone be expected not to raise that fundamental question? Much as she disliked Peter, Hannah did think he was a decent father, taking time to change and feed his daughter. And Sylvie said that the other night, he'd pulled a chair up next to the crib and stared at the baby while she slept. How could he be expected to render full absolution for such a loss?

'Will you find her?' Sylvie asked Martinson when he was again in front of her, her sentence an awkward string of disconnected words.

'We'll do our best.'

Stock answer, Hannah thought. 'Do you have any ideas? Any leads?'

'We know what a typical kidnapper does, and we proceed to interview anybody who might typically be connected with this incident.'

'Like . . .?' Sylvie asked.

'Like everyone in this building and the buildings to the left and right and the ones across the street. Maybe somebody was sitting at their window and saw something. I'd like you to give Officer Reynolds a list of all the people who've been to this apartment since the baby was born — the workmen, delivery people, anybody.' And it was on the tip of Hannah's tongue, the question she wanted to ask: 'Detective Martinson, what *does* a typical kidnapper do?' but she sat in silence, and even shook her head when he asked them if they had any more questions.

There were the usual closing statements about calling if they thought of anything else, no matter how insignificant. About how he would be discussing the case with his superiors, and that other law agency officials would probably want to speak to Sylvie. He thought it best for now that it be kept out

15

of the press and he was going to put a temporary gag on all the officers involved, but they would discuss that further when Peter arrived. He wanted to hear from her as soon as Peter was located.

'Right now,' he said, 'all we know for sure is that she's gone. But we're going to do our best, I can promise you that.' Hannah saw Sylvie grab for his arm, clinging, willing him to stay.

'She's so little,' Sylvie said.

'You can believe I'll be working on it,' he said, and Hannah saw how he couldn't wait to twist his arm back out of her grip. It was all she could do to keep from pouncing on him, demanding a little human decency out of the man.

When he'd gone out the door, Sylvie, one hand clutching at the long heavy strands of her white-blonde hair, said to her mother, 'It was only five minutes.' Hannah said nothing – if she dared to open her mouth, the real words, the ones that had piled up between them the whole time Martinson had been there, were bound to force their way out: Nobody leaves a baby alone. Nobody with a brain, Sylvie, because the world is just too terrible a place.

Chapter 3

Sylvie always insisted she'd seen Peter first, though he argued it had happened the other way around. They tussled over it like puppies straining their milk teeth, pulling on opposite ends of a soft rope, this one's feet sliding out from under him for a few seconds along the slippery floor, then that one's. Sylvie and Peter invariably ended the disagreement (and most of their arguments) in a draw. One of them would say, 'All right, we saw each other at the same time, at exactly the same time.' When Sylvie posed the compromise language, it tended to be fairly overblown, like 'in one brilliant crystal moment.' Once it was settled, they inevitably moved on to kissing, or as puppies might, to nipping and tumbling.

All that, of course, was before Cally disappeared, back when the feel of the other's breath moving across their faces as they lay together in bed was all that seemed really significant. When what he said always seemed right, and what she said seemed to be important to him. But as Martinson said, these things take their toll on a relationship.

And even Martinson, when he heard Sylvie tell of that first meeting, admitted that it did sound romantic. Or if not romantic, at least, as she suggested to him, serendipitous.

How it happened was, she'd felt she absolutely had to get out of the Old Mill Medical Services building where she worked because she'd felt like she couldn't breathe anymore in that stuffy little lounge where everybody ate lunch. The room had a permanent smell of tuna fish and banana, and she hated watching them all knitting, which to her looked like an incredibly boring version of hell where you were doomed to wind yarn

17

forward and then back without stopping, day after day. So she'd headed for the mall – at least there nobody criticized the nutritional values in her lunch. Peter was the one who called the whole thing serendipitous – that they should both be there at exactly the same time and for, really, the same kind of reason, too. It turned out he'd come into the mall to escape somebody called Damien that he worked with who'd been bugging him so bad about something that Peter'd just left his desk without even signing out. So, there she'd been, just leaning into the upper railing, looking down, thinking maybe being a nurse's assistant wasn't working out, either, and wondering if maybe she'd just rather work at a clothing store at the mall, to hell with whether her mother thought that was a comedown. She was watching people walk by down below, mostly mothers and little kids, and she realized how there were two different styles: half the mothers hung on real tight to their kids and the other half completely lost track of them and had to stop and shout out their names every ten seconds. And then she'd looked up and there he'd been, across on the other side, hands on the rails, same as her, looking at her.

She turned her face away, the way you do when you look at someone and see they've seen you looking at them, felt that hot flush – part scaredness, part thrill – and then she'd waited a moment and looked again, and saw he wasn't looking at her after all. She'd kept her eyes on him, on how neat-looking he was with his yellowy hair combed up that new way, those soft-fitting dark gray pants, and then he did look back toward her, and it was like an automatic response, she turned away for two seconds, maybe, and she peeked again and he was smiling, definitely trying to catch her eye, so she let him this time, but then looked down to remind herself what she was wearing, which turned out to be all right, this faded-looking jumpsuit she had (and which was a part of the reason actually she was having trouble at work because they all wore skirts and heels and she just wouldn't do that, wouldn't be uncomfortable and encased in panty hose), and then looked up at him again, and she saw he was walking off left but still looking at her, his hand sliding along the railing. They had their eyes tight on each other – it was wild how jumpy she felt, ready to run, but not doing it.

He made his way around to where there was a cross-passage, then down along that to the other side, her side, getting closer and closer, and she could hear her heart beating, that's how insane she was, waiting for what was next. Her hands were wrapped around the railing still and she almost felt like she was paralyzed – except for her head, which she was turning so their eyes stayed together. (Like a movie scene in slo-mo, or, no, like that painting in her mother's office called *Meeting in the Park* – one of those ones where everything is soft and vague and the one thing that stands out in the dreamy haze is these two sets of eyes, his and hers, dark and intense on each other. 'That,' she remembered Hannah once saying as she pointed at the two young lovers, 'is naked sex with its clothes on.') And then he was there, next to her, introducing himself, asking her all about herself, asking, too, if she wanted an ice cream cone, and she was laughing, coming out of the paralysis, seeing, even up close like this, he was really good-looking, golden skin, tanned almost, to go with that hair, the darkest blue eyes maybe the world had ever seen, and she couldn't have even told anybody how they got to the Häagen-Dazs counter (elevator, escalator, stairs? – anybody's guess) and she was telling him about her whole life, it seemed.

They got waffle cones and he kept trying to get her to put more and more toppings on hers so that the cone ended up looking like a trick-or-treat bag and the ice cream came off almost like an afterthought – it must have cost him about eight dollars. Later she said to him, 'Best lunch I ever had, ice cream and Pepsi, I swear,' and he took hold of her hands (it was so like that painting it was *scary*) and said he'd pick her up from work, what time was she finished?

'It looks like somebody just moved out,' she said that same evening when he took her back to his apartment. A couch, a mattress, and a single barstool were all the furnishings in the cavernous place.

'Well,' he said, 'I guess that's what happened. Somebody

19

moved out and I moved in.' He'd only been there a couple of weeks, he explained.

'But you have no table or chairs.'

'I have the couch, so I can sit there. I eat at the counter, and I sit on the stool. And I can always spread a blanket across the floor if I have company,' he said as he did just that, lifting it off the arm of the couch and shaking it out across the hardwood floor. *'Voilà,'* he said, and put the bag of Chinese take-out and the liter of Pepsi down dead center on the blanket. 'And somewhere I've got cups for the soup and tea,' he informed her.

It wasn't that he was morally opposed to furniture or anything that extreme. And he wasn't into the ascetic lifestyle. It was more a matter of time and money and wanting to have the right things, not just any things – did she understand that?

'Why such a big place, then, with so much to fill up?' That, too, as he explained it, was more serendipity. The guy whose job he took over was moving to the West Coast and still had eight months on his lease. The apartment was big, yes, but taking it meant he didn't have to search all over, he didn't have to pay hotel room rates in the interim, and he got an incredible break on the rent because the guy was so glad to find someone to pick up the lease at all. But the thing was, he'd fallen in love with the place as soon as he saw it – he was crazy about the old-style brick building with the double-sided stairs leading up from the street, the courtyard garden and benches and the fountain. 'There's actually a gardener here,' he told Sylvie. 'He was out there last week, checking on things – mulch, the burlap wrappings, whatever else it is you check in winter. He told me he hooks up the fountain as soon as the danger of frost is over. The birds out there are supposed to be fabulous – he said birds come here that you don't see anywhere else in New Haven anymore.' And who needed furniture, he said, when he had all the old architectural features built right in – Doric columns in the living room rising up to the incredibly high ceilings, crenelated moldings, tooled brass knobs and hinges, six-paneled doors, glass cabinets in the kitchen, and French doors that led right out to the courtyard. In the end, he said, it was the courtyard that had clinched it; made him willing to shell out the extra money. He really liked the feeling it gave him that he wasn't in the city at all, but in some quiet little country spot. It was a very lucky find, he said. An amazing find, in fact.

What Sylvie thought was amazing was that he knew and cared about things like crenelated moldings (she didn't even know what they were till he pointed them out and named them) but that turned out to be only one of tons of unusual nuggets of information he had stored away. It made her feel a little self-conscious, though, because she wanted to be able to say interesting things back, but she couldn't. She'd never gone out with anybody this old – he was thirteen years her senior – and she kept feeling like she wasn't sure what the rules were for people his age and that he must think her incredibly stupid. 'I've got this thing called attention deficit disorder,' she blurted out at one point, and she felt her face color to say it. Like telling him that was going to help or make it all better, make him like her even though she was dumb. She knew she ought to have waited; people, guys especially, hated to hear there was something wrong with you.

'So what does that mean?' And she took a deep breath, ready to go into the explanation about motor neuron connections and birth trauma, but he continued: 'It probably means your mind wanders, right?' She nodded her head in response. 'Everybody's mind wanders, especially when you're having to hear about stuff you don't care about – in other words, the whole time you're in school, which, I'm willing to bet, is exactly where they decided you had this.'

She shrugged. 'Yeah,' she admitted. 'And my mother, too. She picked up on it.'

He told her he thought the way people labeled kids who weren't carbon copies of themselves was criminal and he passed her a pair of chopsticks. 'But somebody has to give the shrinks something to do, I guess,' he said, and laughed. 'They tried it on me, wanted me in a special class, but my parents said, "Hell no, you're not going to make him different." You can *make* a kid different that way, you know.'

'What was it they said you had?'

21

'I don't know,' he said. 'I was lucky, I never got to hear the name of it, so I never had it. Personally I think schools have way too much power. They tell you you're crazy or weird or learning disabled, like they did you, and they're the teachers, right? You believe that, just like you believe the Indians scalped the benevolent white men and whatever other crap they pile on.' He was lying on his side on the edge of the blanket opposite her, the cartons of chow mein and tangerine chicken between them. She was on her back, staring up at the elaborate circular decoration in the middle of the ceiling, thinking about asking him what it might be called, but not wanting to interrupt him. 'But hey,' he continued, 'I'm pontificating now, and I really don't mean to.'

'What's that mean?' she asked him, looking over toward him, and he was staring at her again, fixing her with his eyes just the way he had at the mall, and she saw how his hair had fallen forward across his forehead and she wanted to touch it, to feel if it was soft, if it would stay if she pushed it back over with the other hair, and she reached out her hand, which didn't get over nearly to where he was, and he shoved the food cartons clear out of the way (spilled them, too, they later discovered) and pulled the blanket with her on it, the whole thing, over to him and looked into her face again and whispered her name and kissed her and she touched his hair, which was much softer than she'd thought it would be.

Next morning she tried to remember some of the words. She got *crenelated* and *serendipity* – with their meanings – pretty quickly, but then drew a blank on the others she'd been trying to remember. 'What word?' he asked her. 'How'd I use it?' But she couldn't remember. 'Stop worrying about it,' he advised. 'I like the way you talk just fine.'

'They were always making me learn tricks for remembering things.'

'Who's they?'

'Everybody. My teachers, my mother.'

'And what kind of tricks, exactly?'

'You know, the sort of thing where you put things in alphabetical order or rhyme them with something else. Half the time I couldn't remember what the trick was, let alone the stuff I was supposed to remember.'

He turned away from his nearly empty refrigerator and put his arms around her. 'Don't tell me anything else about *them* and *they*,' he said. 'Because *them* and *they* do not give a shit about you. Start listening to what you think, because you're the only one that matters.' Her hand went for his blond chest hair where it emerged around the V-opening of his shirt, the wisps straightening between her fingers then springing back into curls as she released them. 'The power lies in you,' he continued, kissing her lightly on the mouth. 'In you.' He kissed her again, a small kiss, then another, then others, nuzzling delicately but stealing her breath somehow, too, inhaling it into his own. 'The power's in you,' he said, his words a metered counterpoint beneath her moans.

Chapter 4

It was in Puerto Blanco, in a room with a balcony facing the sea, that Cally had probably been conceived. Not in anything so deliberate as a conscious act, but as a side effect of sweet tropical flowers, gauzy white curtains in an open balcony door, and a breeze that captured the sweat from off their naked bodies.

In Puerto Blanco the sand was white and the ocean ran in alternating ribbons of turquoise and jade. Like a child's picture of paradise, Sylvie thought, only there were no Crayolas that were as vibrant as what she could actually see from her balcony room. The colors – was it because they were so very clear, or so very excessive? – brought tears to her eyes.

And then, too, they did forget to bring birth control along – there'd been so much confusion, so little time. A cold rain had been falling and freezing as it hit the pavement in New Haven. When Peter called after work, she had ranted a bit about how much she hated winter, about how she was ready to commit suicide if she couldn't see the sun. He took the whole thing a lot more seriously than she'd meant it – it was really a joke, though she *was* depressed about the cold weather, and maybe even more strung out about the bleakness. The lack of color, that's what it really was. He'd said, 'Don't do anything. I'm coming right over,' and then he'd hung up. She tried to call him back because she felt really stupid being so histrionic (another new word), but there was no answer. Then he didn't show up. More than an hour went by and she was still waiting, and she thought, Fine, what if I'd really been suicidal? I'd be dead by now, and she was furious and then the door buzzed and he was there holding out two plane tickets. She couldn't believe it –

two tickets to Puerto Blanco! 'Forget winter,' he said, taking her hand and kissing the fingertips, and the whole thing was just so wild, she started laughing and couldn't stop. It was ridiculous, like a kind of joyous hysteria, Peter said. She actually laughed till she cried. No guy had ever given her anything like that in her whole entire life and it wasn't like she hadn't gone out with a lot of guys, it was just that in her experience men didn't give presents. Unless they had specific occasions they had to do it for. And when they did give presents, what were they? Flowers or a CD, not trips to the Caribbean.

'This is completely crazy,' she said to Peter as she wiped away her tears.

He shook his head. 'Impetuous, yes. Crazy, no.'

'Overdone?' she suggested, but again he shook his head.

'Grand scale, that's all.'

And then she really looked at the tickets and saw they were for late that same night – four hours from then – and she said, 'Hey, this really *is* insane.'

'Impetuous,' he insisted. 'And a perfect cure for winter.'

Then she tried to kiss him (she loved his lips), but he held her off.

'You need to pack. My stuff is in the trunk, ready to go.'

'What am I supposed to do about my job?'

'Call in sick. It's only just the three days and then it'll be the weekend. So if you get the three days, we'll have five.'

She walked to the phone, then couldn't pick it up, didn't know what she'd say. While she stood there tying to compose her lie, she took hold of her long white hair in two thick clumps, one in each hand. 'Pigtails,' he commented, and she let the hair go. 'I liked it,' he protested, walking toward her, holding her hair now that same way, half off to each side. 'If I didn't know, I could believe you were twelve.'

'Twenty.'

'I know that. I happen to like it that sometimes you look like a little girl, and sometimes you look altogether different – sultry, seductive. I like all the things you are.' Then he was kissing her, starting with those little bites on her lips that she liked so much, sliding his mouth over her cheek. 'The tickets are non-refundable,' he whispered, 'and I really, really want to take you with me, so you need to make that call.'

'What'll I tell them?' she asked him. 'I'm a terrible liar. I always end up confessing before my lies are even half out. It's a doctor's office. If I say I'm sick, they might tell me to come and get checked.'

'It's a gynecologist's office, Sylvie, they don't want to see you for a sore throat.'

She picked up the phone. 'I'm no good at that voice-faking stuff. I won't even sound sick to them, probably. They'll know I'm lying.' She put the receiver back down in its cradle.

'So don't lie. Say you have to be out of town on personal business.' She laughed at his suggestion. He'd picked up the remote control for the television and had clicked through to the Weather Channel. The TV radar showed that the cold air mass apparently wasn't going to move off New England for several days.

'Oh shit,' she complained. 'I do want to go, you know that, don't you?' she asked, coming up behind him and encircling him with her arms. 'It's just making me really nervous. I don't know what to do.'

'Look,' he said, taking hold of her hands, 'Your office is closed now. All you'll be doing is calling the answering service, and they aren't going to do anything except take down your message, word for word. They aren't going to say, "Hey, who the hell do you think you are, saying this?" Right?' She nodded and he kissed her hand. 'You're calling the shots on this one. You're taking control.' He tugged at her arms so she came round to face him. 'Tell them that you have to leave town for the rest of the week because of a family emergency.' She scrunched her nose at him by way of response. 'Listen, that's completely legit. You're part of your family, right?'

'Ooh,' she said through a smile.

'And aren't I practically like family?' he asked, his breath warm on her neck as he leaned his body against hers. 'And don't we actually like each other better than family anyway?'

'That part's true,' she said, moving closer.

'It's all true, little girl.' And then the way he told her to think

27

about it was, if she didn't go on this trip, somebody in her family (her) would commit suicide and somebody (him) would be out almost six hundred dollars for the tickets. 'To me that's a genuine emergency,' he said, and they laughed and he ran his hands up and down her back, and then down round her bottom and said, 'Forget winter.' And then quick, she made the phone call and got a suitcase of summer stuff together.

It seemed like it took forever just to try to remember where she'd stowed her bathing suits and to begin to focus on the necessary objects for time in the sun, like tank tops, suntan lotion, and sandals. Nothing was going to match, she said to him, but even that seemed part of the pleasure. Under the circumstances, it wasn't entirely surprising that they failed to include birth control in their luggage.

Their critical omission wasn't noted till after they had arrived in Puerto Blanco, checked into their room, stripped off their clothes, and abandoned contemplative thought. Sentences like 'How do you think one would go about obtaining birth control materials in a Caribbean country in the middle of the night?' were well beyond their rational capacity by the time the discovery was made. 'I won't get pregnant,' Sylvie simply promised him, and it seemed, for that moment, that she could will it, just that easily.

Afterwards Peter said it wouldn't be bad, maybe, having a baby. And he said he had a confession: that he'd actually thought about making a baby with her because she was so beautiful and because he really felt like he was crazy in love with her. He'd never even thought about that kind of thing before, he said, not with anybody. But with her, he'd definitely thought about it, before this night, even, but hadn't wanted to mention it because he figured she'd think it was too soon, too much of a possessive thing, or maybe even a macho thing, and she cried and said, 'Yes, a baby,' though she herself had never thought about it before unless you counted thinking about preventing one. But it was on this night, Sylvie knew, when they opened themselves to the idea of Cally, that they invited her into their lives.

It was a very different kind of sex that she had with Peter in

Puerto Blanco than she'd ever had with anyone else. Before this, sex had been something she did because it felt good, like a swim on a hot, hot summer afternoon, or a fabulous dinner on a day when she'd forgotten to eat lunch. This sex had that self-indulgent aspect, but it had something else, too, and it had to do with both of them thinking – and saying to each other (that was maybe the most important part, the saying) – that they wanted to make a baby. An old-fashioned word, *union*, crossed her mind.

'That's too earthbound a word,' he argued. 'It's something much more spiritual.'

Yes, Sylvie said, she'd felt that, felt something like a shadowy white guardian who stood watch over them while they made love, whose existence came from the warmth that flowed outward from their embrace.

Even when they got back to cold, gray New Haven they didn't use birth control. They were afraid to tamper with what they had; wholly unwilling to spoil any of it. Peter said you had to go back to that night in Puerto Blanco to understand it, to remember that they had left the balcony door open while they made love. It was that symbolic gesture of opening themselves to a wider world, he said, that had created the intensity between them.

It was barely any time at all before the misty figure that hovered above them began to take the form of a baby floating beside them, just within reach of their arms. Soon enough, they began to imagine the specific shape and sound of this baby, and even to name her, so it no longer seemed as though it were an unknown for whom the door had stood open. Sylvie began to feel she knew her, and that she knew her very well.

Chapter 5

Sylvie might have told Peter she was pregnant after she was wakened at five a.m. by a strange tingling ache that traveled across her breasts. Certainly that was proof enough for her. But she waited, because she thought it would be a more beautiful gift if she were absolutely, positively sure.

Or she might have told him after she watched the home pregnancy test stick turn sugar-candy pink, but then she read the part of the instructions about false positives. Then, too, she might have told him as soon as she got the result of the real, official, scientifically controlled lab test. But even then she waited through two more days, searching for some perfect way to phrase it to him. Some way that would indicate she didn't expect anything. Though, of course, she did expect something, or at least sometimes she did, though a lot of the time she knew damn well that, spiritual love or not, this might turn out to be her problem and she might be in deep, deep trouble.

In the end he noticed something was up – he said she wasn't finishing any of her sentences. 'Why do you keep drifting off like that?' he asked her. He said he knew something was worrying her, and he wouldn't let up, kept trying to get her to talk about it till finally, when they'd just gotten back to his apartment after a movie, she started crying and just blurted it out, her head spinning like mad, so she could barely stand up. She fumbled her way over to the couch through a silence as harsh as ice water, but then he said, 'Hey, come here,' and pulled her on to his lap and kissed her face all over, little tender kisses that pulled at her heart and did, really, make her start to feel better.

He wanted to know how long she'd known and why she

31

hadn't told him and she ended up feeling just awful for having put it off the way she had, thinking he'd be angry, because, as he said, she knew he wanted a baby. 'This was where we were headed,' he reminded her. 'This is us.'

'See,' she said, 'the problem was, I knew you *said* you wanted a baby, but people say lots of things and then the reality hits and it's altogether different.'

'What I say is part of me, it is me, Sylvie. It doesn't change or fluctuate. I told you I want this baby, and I do. Did you think there was going to be some big change, that I'd want you to get an abortion or something?' She said she just didn't feel like it was that simple. He put his finger across her lips, shushing off her words.

'Listen,' he said, his voice gently leading in the way a storyteller's does. 'I've always believed that the best way to lead one's life was to accept the inevitable. And you know why?' She shook her head. 'Because the real pain in life almost always comes from trying to thrash out against what was meant to be anyway.'

But then something else occurred to her and she leaned back away so she could see his eyes, wanting him to focus on her, on this pregnancy, not on the whole world, the whole universe, and she said, 'What if I don't want a baby?' And then her view of him got all blurry from tears that flooded up into her lower lids, and she felt the air around their faces growing hot.

'Oh, Sylvie,' he said, his voice quiet, almost faltering. 'It's your decision. I only want you to know that it's fine with me.'

'You're sure?' For an answer, he kissed her mouth softly. 'Do you think it's right to do this even though I'm not even twenty-one yet?'

He pulled her close again, laughing, stroking her back. 'You'll be twenty-one by then; by the time the baby's born. You'll be a young, beautiful, vigorous mother.' She let her fingers creep into his hair.

'And you think it's all right even though we're not married?'

'That can be changed,' he said, his lips tracing a path just where her sweater scooped down toward her breasts. 'How long can getting married take? Ten minutes? Fifteen? Or let's be

32

conservative, we'll call it an hour because there must be papers to fill out, the license, that sort of thing.'

'Won't we need blood tests?'

He nodded, conceding. 'Okay, so we need to plan two, three days ahead, probably.'

'You want to get married?' she asked, and the question felt more strange, more embarrassing, than anything they'd ever spoken of before.

'If you do. If you think we should. I want to have the baby with you, that's the important part. If it becomes important to get married, then we'll get married.'

'And you're sure you want to have a baby with me? Really sure?' she asked him, her hand tightening around his as she spoke.

He kissed her, the little kisses that she loved. 'I want your baby, Sylvie, I've told you that a hundred times, at least. We both want it.' She lowered her head to his shoulder. He was right, it was what she wanted. She sniffled, for the tears had begun to fill her nose and throat. 'Now you'll move in, won't you?' he asked, for she'd resisted all his previous invitations to do so. 'We can get another stool for the counter, even, and we'll make the second bedroom into a nursery.' She'd been thinking of that empty room all done up for a baby, and of the two of them standing in the yellow radiance of a night-light, watching a baby sleeping in a crib.

'We'll get furniture for it?' she asked.

'Of course. Furniture, carpeting, wallpaper, curtains.'

'Something like yellow stripes with a border of teddy bears,' she said, pointing along the top edge of the walls of this room, the living room, so he could understand exactly what she meant. 'Or maybe something less cute,' she backpedaled, imagining her mother's reaction to baby patterns all over the walls. 'Maybe the border should be more sophisticated. A check or something like that.'

'And one of those old-fashioned wicker cradles for the living room,' he suggested. 'We'll go looking for it this afternoon.'

'It's too early for that,' she chided him, laughing, but hugging him, too, for wanting so exactly what she wanted.

'Too early for what? Too early to indulge this child?' His hand slid over her flat abdomen. 'Is it too early to indulge ourselves? This place belongs to all three of us now. I want this baby to feel part of it right away. So you'll have to humor me on this.'

'That's okay,' she said. 'I actually think it'll be fun, though the people in the store might laugh at us because I don't exactly *look* pregnant, you know.'

He sat up, crooked a finger under her chin. 'I don't care what other people think, you know that.' She nodded. 'I care about us. We're a family now, and we're all we need.'

'Do I look too much like a little girl to be a mother?' she asked him, leaning back so he could examine her. No waiter ever thought to take a drink order from her, she wasn't tall enough to reach top shelves without a chair, and she was always getting asked if her mother was home when she answered a ring at the door of her own apartment. She could still fit into a pre-teen size, too, which was nice because they were a lot cheaper than juniors.

'If you're pregnant, you're old enough to be a mother,' he advised. 'Personally, I like the idea of a child bride,' and he nestled his face against hers.

'Nothing's ever worked out for me before,' she said.

'This will,' he said, and she felt his eyes move over her, liking her.

'I think it *was* meant to be,' she whispered into his neck, and then they made love on the blue velvet couch and fell asleep in that narrow space, curled together under his shirt.

Hannah said, 'Fate, Sylvie? You're kidding about this, aren't you? I know you know how babies are born because I told you myself when you were – how old, Sylvie? How old were you when I told you how babies got made?'

'I don't know, Mother.'

'Well, I do. You were nine. You asked, and I told you. At nine you knew it had nothing to do with fate and fairies and magic. What happened in between then and now to make you think any different?'

Sylvie decided to stay quiet and tough it out. She'd driven

34

over on her lunch hour, thinking, If she's in her office, I'll tell her, if not, that's fate, too, and so be it, she'll just have to wait to find out. Truth was, she hadn't expected Hannah to be there, she so rarely was.

'What does he mean exactly by fate?' Hannah pursued.

'I don't know, but not magic and fairies.'

Her mother heaved out a wounded-sounding sigh, then leaned her desk chair back on two legs. 'Try to help me on this, Sylvie. I do want to understand.'

Sylvie looked at her straight on, trying to figure if her mother could really possibly want the answer or whether she was just looking for entertaining material to repeat to her faculty buddies over lunch. She wished she was more articulate. More organized in her thinking. She wished Peter was there to say it the way he'd explained it to her, with all that business about myth and patterns. Would her mother say myth was just magic and fairy tale? She took a deep breath – she wanted to get it said fast and smoothly, before Hannah could interrupt. 'I think he just means people are always trying to change what they are, to be something different and to fight what's meant to be. He says people shouldn't do that, that it's never worth it.'

Hannah shook her head. 'That's very cheap philosophy,' she commented. 'A rather inelegant version of "Who cares if the woman's the one who has to carry the baby?"'

'I *want* to have this baby,' Sylvie said as simply as possible.

'You think you do,' Hannah advised. 'Is he Catholic? Is that what he is, a raging anti-abortion maniac?'

'*No!*' Sylvie said, her voice rising against her mother in a wave of defense. Peter was a Mormon, but she didn't offer this information, for she wasn't at all sure what Mormons thought of abortion, though she was certain her mother would know.

'How old is this boy?'

'He's not a boy, Mother. He's thirty-three.' *Daddy's age when he died* she might have added, but didn't – her mother didn't like talking about the past.

'Married and divorced twice already, I suppose?'

'No. He's never been married.'

'In any case, Sylvie, you're only twenty. You're not married.

35

Having a baby is not an option for you.'

'Yes, it is.' She heard her voice rise sharply, felt the twist of a whine, the childishness of her tone. 'We're going to get married,' she said as levelly as she could. 'Lots of people have babies at twenty-one. You were only twenty-two.'

'And I was married and out of college.'

'I will be married and I don't care about college.'

'Sylvie, there's nothing wrong with an abortion, it's a very safe process. You can have anesthesia if you're afraid of the pain, but I can promise you childbirth is a hundredfold more painful than a simple D and C. It's just a scraping of the uterus. You don't even stay overnight in a hospital anymore.'

'I know what an abortion is, Mother, and that isn't what I want. I want to have the baby and I want to take care of it.'

'How? How will you take care of it? You stay at your jobs a couple of months and then quit. You have car accidents bi-monthly, and you don't finish anything you start, Sylvie. Believe me, a baby is not the sort of project you can just dump and walk away from. And I'll tell you something else right now. I will not be your baby-sitter,' Hannah said, shaking a slender finger at her daughter. Sylvie turned her eyes toward the window. She could see a few reddish buds on one of the trees in the art gallery courtyard. What in God's name had she thought she'd gain by this little conference? 'I will give you the money for an abortion,' her mother went on, 'but if you retain the pregnancy, you're on your own with this one.'

Sylvie turned toward her once more. 'I'm doing this with Peter, Mother, not you. I'm not asking you for help. I'm only here now because I thought it was the right thing to do, to tell you about it. I didn't expect that you'd be joyous.'

Hannah made a noise something like a tight laugh that had gotten caught up short somewhere in her nasal passages. 'Well, you've certainly guessed right on that one.' Hannah picked up an envelope from the desk, reached for the letter opener, and started to run it under the sealed flap. Sylvie stood up to go. She was familiar with the ways Hannah chose to end their encounters. 'Listen to me, Sylvie,' Hannah said, pushing the envelope and opener, surprisingly, aside. 'You can't do this.

You'll ruin your life. You said you were going to go back to school.'

'I said I'd think about going back to school, that's all. It was your idea to begin with.'

'They have this special guidance program now for people with attention disabilities. It's a free program and they offer one-on-one help getting you through the courses. It's emotional and academic help.'

Sylvie heard the heavy stress on *emotional*. 'To what end?' she asked her mother.

Hannah pushed her chair back and stood up. 'What do you mean, to what end? So you can pass the courses.'

'I know that, but why is that important?'

'So you can, in time, my dear, get a degree. So you can, in time, get a good job, something in a medical field, maybe, like you're doing now, but with more responsibility.'

Sylvie shifted her weight to her left hip. Her feet really wanted to be marching out the door already. 'Mother, I take patients from the waiting room to the examining room and tell them which way to put the opening on the gown. There's not much medical training necessary for that.'

'But that's my point – you can get the expertise for something much better. It's available to you now.'

'I don't like being indoors,' Sylvie said, knowing the comment was slightly off the wall and exactly the sort of thing that would enrage her mother.

'That's completely beside the point, Sylvie. Try concentrating on the subject at hand.'

'No, it isn't beside the point. I hate indoor work and—'

'Sylvie,' Hannah broke in. 'We *all* work indoors in the Northeast, and that's the reality of the situation.'

Sylvie started to say, 'Then I'll move,' but caught herself.

'What kind of man lets a woman get pregnant?' Hannah asked without transition.

'We got pregnant together, actually.'

'I hate that phrase "we got pregnant". It tries to mask the truth by wrapping it up in cute phraseology. Face it, Sylvie, the woman is the one who gets pregnant, has the morning sickness, the circulatory and respiratory problems, and the labor. Do you perhaps mean you both screwed up equally?'

'We both wanted it, I mean.'

'Oh, Sylvie.' Her words came out like a rumbled groan.

Sylvie took a deep breath before she continued. 'We think it's romantic.'

'Romantic isn't quite the word I'd have used. *Immature*, perhaps, or *stupid*, even. No educated person would confuse irresponsible behavior with romance.' Sylvie watched Hannah's hand tighten into a fist which she held close against her chest. The older woman took in a slow, deep breath. 'How long have you known him?'

Sylvie was suddenly aware that she'd twisted the fringes of her scarf so tightly round her finger that her pinky had turned cold and blue. Peter had told her not to come – why hadn't she listened to him? She unwound the strands of scarf from her finger and shook out her hand. 'We've known each other a couple of months,' Sylvie said, 'but we're together all the time. It's definitely long enough.' Sylvie looked at her watch. 'I've got to go. I've got work.' She waved one end of the scarf toward Hannah and as the soft chenille strands lifted and fell, she asked, 'Do you want to meet him?'

'Not yet, actually,' Hannah said. 'What I want is for you to think more about an abortion. This is not a light matter, Sylvie.'

'See you,' Sylvie said, and opened the door.

Chapter 6

For a while, Hannah didn't hear from Sylvie at all, though such silence was not terribly surprising. Sylvie had always been a stubborn creature, and a standoff was the common outcome of any confrontation – or even simple discussion, for that matter – between them. The way Hannah figured it, Sylvie would, in the end, have the abortion – she thought she'd made it clear enough how imperative that was. Once or twice she thought of calling and saying, 'You know, you really must get this taken care of within the first trimester' (or perhaps she would just say, *first three months*) because if you wait, it's a much more elaborate process, though it can still be done.'

But Hannah did not call. Not so much because she thought better of it, but because she lost track of it. Occasionally, when she had to be the unwilling audience to a harassed mother wailing threats at her toddler, she'd be reminded of the whole situation and think, I have to call her and make sure she has taken care of it. But given that she couldn't call from the supermarket (which was, invariably, where her responses got jogged into consciousness), and given that it wasn't something she was constantly thinking about otherwise, the weeks started to slip away. By the time Hannah did manage to call, she got a recorded message saying the number was no longer in working order. The tape offered no forwarding number, and no notice of a new address arrived in the mail. Even Directory Assistance had no record of her. Hannah suspected she might have moved in with the boy, but could not recall his name, nor whether she'd even been told it. Hannah tried to reach Sylvie at work, found she was no longer employed there, and the only number they had on record for her was the disconnected one. So,

Hannah thought, Sylvie had taken wing, and it was out of her hands – though she knew such respites were always short-term. Sylvie would be back. She only hoped it would be alone.

At the time, Hannah did not have much excess energy for such dead-end projects as chasing down somebody who clearly wished not to be found. Her attention was taken up in preparing for a promotion hearing at the university. Four years earlier, she'd been denied the rank of Associate Professor by a committee that found her publications on the hyper-realism of the eighties to be too frivolous. 'We are not into camp, popular culture, and kitsch,' one of them had informally summed up for her. She'd followed up the rejection with a three-day binge of first-run movies, Chinese dumplings, and brownie sundaes, then settled down to find a new subject. She discovered Deetha Morena, a relatively unknown American woman who painted from 1897 to 1909. Twenty-seven canvases and about fifty sketches, most of them studies for the paintings, were extant. Almost all the paintings were mother-and-child portraits, and sometimes the obviously aristocratic subjects were rather less than fully clothed. To her students, Hannah had recently noted that Morena's vision was an odd marriage of Mary Cassatt and Edvard Munch. Morena had been rejected by every academy in the United States and Europe, her letters to the great and not-so-great male artists went repeatedly unanswered, and in 1909 at the age of thirty, she committed suicide. Although Morena had left very little art, she did leave dozens of journals into which she neatly copied all the letters she sent out. These letters numbered in the thousands and were bursting with political observations about the art world, the relations of men and women, and ultimately the doomed nature of being a woman artist. Stylistically Morena was often dismissed as being derivative. 'Gauguin envy,' Hannah's chairman had once commented.

All previous biographical material on her pointed to her unmarried, childless status coupled with her obsession with the Madonna image as understandable and sufficient cause for her demise. Hannah believed that Morena had made an important statement about motherhood in the bored, shifting eyes of her women and the uncomfortable pose of her children, who often appeared to be resisting being held at all. Hannah's only disappointment in the artist was in her decision to opt out so early.

Hannah pursued Deetha with the zeal of a pirate in possession of a scribbled treasure map. Outside interest was piqued quickly – she began to be invited to speak at major scholarly art and women's studies associations, and she was asked to join a panel of guest curators for a show called *Behind the Mask* sub-titled *Through the Eyes of the Women* – a show that was to include a half-dozen of Morena's pieces along with other more mainstream artists.

When Sylvie finally called her, Hannah'd been so caught up in the details of her successful promotion bid, she couldn't at first pinpoint how much time had passed since their heated confrontation. It was Hannah's birthday, a fact Hannah had tried not so much to forget as to ignore. She was forty-three, did not, as yet, need to color her hair, and she still weighed what she had the day she married Eric. And if he were miraculously to reappear, she often thought upon eyeing her body in her mirror, he would not be disappointed. She kept in shape not through the compulsive jogging, lapping, or lifting that her colleagues were slave to, but by playing tennis whenever she could, choosing stairs over elevators, and walking, not driving, when possible. Of all the members of the art department over thirty-five, she was the only one who had no joint pain.

Hannah accepted Sylvie's invitation to lunch, though she warned her that they'd have to make it fairly brief – Hannah said she had enormous quantities of things to catch up on that she'd let slide during her preparations for her hearing. To that, Sylvie simply said, 'Okay, we'll say hello, eat, say goodbye, and that's it.' She did not ask, 'What hearing?' which in itself was enough to make Hannah want to say, 'Oh, no, I forgot that I actually have an appointment over the lunch hour and couldn't possibly meet you,' but by then Sylvie was suggesting restaurants and Hannah merely said, 'Whichever, Sylvie, you choose.' After all, Sylvie was the one who was supposed to pick up the check. Sylvie suggested Monti's, a small, quiet spot across from the campus that served, in Hannah's opinion, the best homemade pasta in town.

As usual, Sylvie was late. Part of Sylvie's problem was that she never could figure out how much time she needed to get from one place to another. Even if she knew it was a twenty-minute drive to town, she wouldn't think to add in the time necessary for finding a parking space and walking from the parking lot to the restaurant. It was very exasperating to deal with someone like that, especially when sitting alone at a table alternately rereading a rather short menu and staring into space.

When Sylvie did appear. Hannah was, quite simply, shocked. She'd assumed the pregnancy had been seen to, but she certainly wouldn't have imagined that had it been retained, it could possibly have been this far along. Sylvie looked even more like a child than ever – she was tiny to begin with, her face round as a six-year-old's, and today a pink velvet ribbon held her long white hair back from her face. The obvious swelling of her belly was utterly incongruous – she looked like a pregnant baby.

Hannah watched her walk the whole length of the restaurant toward her, and watched, too, as heads turned to follow Sylvie's progress. Hannah had stood to greet her, to see her more fully, and she saw not the slow trudge of late pregnancy, but the quickened, light step of a child. As though the pregnancy weren't there at all.

Sylvie reached the table, pulled out her chair, and took a seat. 'Happy birthday,' she said, and slipped a small package wrapped in paisley-print paper over to her mother.

'More to the point,' Hannah said, 'you obviously didn't get the abortion.'

Sylvie laughed. 'I would never have gotten an abortion. I'm in love with this baby,' she said with exuberance.

'And you're living where? I had the impression you'd disappeared off the face of the earth.'

'Oh,' Sylvie said, 'we have a wonderful, huge apartment on Livingston. The baby will have her own room, and we've already started decorating. Peter bought a beautiful wicker cradle for her. But we'll have a crib, too.'

42

'Are you and—' Hannah hesitated before pronouncing his name '—Peter – are you married?'

'We're getting married in two weeks.'

Hannah sat back in her chair. 'This is an awful lot to have to adjust to, Sylvie.'

'Well, really, Mother, you've known about it for months and months.'

Hannah shook her head. 'No,' she said. 'This is completely different from your telling me you're pregnant. Now you're talking about getting married, and clearly there's no room for any kind of discussion or negotiation. You have to get married, and the last time we spoke I honestly thought you'd have taken care of this, but look at you, you're big as a house now,' To illustrate, Hannah held her arms in a huge, open circle.

'I'm not big as a house, Mother. I'm not even big as a room,' Sylvie said, and gestured toward the outer dimensions of the dining area. 'Or big as a table. I'm just big as a pregnant woman.' With this, she pushed her abdomen even further out for Hannah's inspection. 'The midwife thinks I haven't gained enough weight – I've only gained fifteen pounds – so they're all trying to get me bigger. Peter's always making milk shakes for me.' Her hand moved in a slow circle over her abdomen. 'The baby moves all around now. I feel knobs, like her fist, maybe, or her heel, moving all across here.'

'*Her* heel?' Hannah repeated, surprised by her daughter's feminist-style reference.

'Yes. We know it's a girl.'

'Amniocentesis?'

'No, it's just that we both feel it's a girl, and it's such a strong feeling, it seems it has to be.'

Hannah indulged in her nasal almost-laugh. 'Well, I suppose you've got a fifty-fifty chance of being right on that one. Are you still working?'

'Oh, I've quit – it was a horrible job. But it's fine, Peter makes plenty of money for us.'

'Doing what, if I may ask?'

A waiter had come to stand at their side. 'Ready, ladies?' he asked, a pencil and pad in hand.

43

'Another minute,' Sylvie requested, though Hannah had had more than sufficient time for her choice. The waiter bowed his head slightly, smiled and moved off toward other diners. 'Where were we?' Hannah asked her daughter.

'You wanted to know about Peter. He designs security systems for stores and businesses. He's working on a really revolutionary one that has a voice response. If someone breaks in, an alarm just doesn't go off, a voice says, "Break-in at door six," or something like that. So the police can go right to the exact spot and they don't have to waste any time phoning in to the system or checking out a panel of lights when they get there.'

'Isn't that the way it's done already? Haven't computer-voice simulations been part of these high-tech systems for years?'

Sylvie flushed. Why did her mother always make her feel such an ass? 'I probably haven't explained it right,' she said. 'I know there's something about it that's dramatically new.'

'I see. And what company does he work for?'

'He's got his own business.' Sylvie smiled at her. 'He's just started it recently, since we've met, so it's all kind of new, and he's really swamped, but he's about to take on a partner, so things should get easier soon. Right now he travels a lot, which I hate. He's gone three, four days a week, but eventually that'll settle down, once he has this partner and a full set of clients and he doesn't have to go chasing for them all over the country.'

'It sounds very impressive,' Hannah said, though she was not actually impressed. It was what one said in conversation, however. Hannah motioned for the waiter to return to their table.

Once they had ordered, Sylvie suggested that Hannah open her present. The older woman peeled the paper off carefully, opened the white box, and lifted out a pair of gold-colored hoop earrings from which red stones were suspended. 'They may be too heavy for me.'

'No, no, you won't even feel them. They're the newest thing. Very, very current,' Sylvie said, and Hannah noted that her daughter's hand had moved to her own ear, and saw there an identical piece of jewelry, except that the hanging stone on hers was a deep purple. 'They're not heavy at all.'

'They're very nice,' Hannah said, putting them back in the box and folding the paper back around the gift. 'Thank you.' There was a silence then, which Hannah decided not to disturb. She would let Sylvie present her agenda – obviously there was one, why else call this meeting? Sylvie had begun to move the silverware into odd positions and combinations on the tabletop. Hannah leaned toward her. 'Sylvie, leave the forks and knives where they belong, will you please?'

Sylvie dropped her hands to her lap, then looked up at her mother. 'I'm very happy with my life right now,' she said. 'Happier than I've ever been, really.' Hannah nodded. 'I feel like I'm doing things right, for a change. I feel really good.' Captive audience to defensive blustering was not what Hannah would ideally have chosen for a birthday celebration. 'I'm really happy,' Sylvie repeated when Hannah did not respond.

Hannah took a deep breath, then said, 'I'm glad, Sylvie. And believe me, I'm very glad that you have Peter to help you through this, because it won't be easy.'

'Be glad about the baby, too,' Sylvie urged her.

'That, my dear, is a considerably more difficult task.'

The waiter placed their pasta before them and Sylvie eyed her luncheon platter with obvious pleasure. 'I'm always hungry, so incredibly hungry. I don't know why I don't gain,' Sylvie said, twirling too much spaghetti and bolognese sauce onto her fork.

'It'll just fall off if you overload it like that,' Hannah observed as she sliced off a corner of a ravioli stuffed with wild mushrooms, but Sylvie managed somehow, hefting it all successfully up to her mouth.

'When you want something badly enough, you can do it,' Sylvie observed of her gustatory performance.

'So it seems,' Hannah rejoined. 'Though not always with great delicacy.'

'Yes. Well,' Sylvie said, wiping her mouth with her napkin, 'I won't make any claims to delicacy just now.' She patted her large abdomen. 'Tell me,' Sylvie said when her hunger had been somewhat appeased, 'when you were pregnant did you feel like you were part of some huge plan, and like it made you

45

understand your place in the universe?'

Hannah laughed loudly, mouth open this time. 'I always thought people had their identity crises in adolescence.'

'No, it isn't that. I know who I am, I just didn't know how we all fit together before. I feel more important than I used to. Like I'm part of some grand scheme. Like I'm necessary for that scheme to come off.'

Hannah leaned toward her daughter. 'One baby more or less does not alter the course of the Milky Way, Sylvie.'

'Maybe not,' Sylvie sad, readying her fork for another liftoff. 'It's probably just all the hormones make me feel this way, but you know something? I *like* the way the hormones make me feel. I cry more, I laugh more, and I feel more part of the universe. I'd like to always feel this way. It suits me.'

'You know, the average woman is not quite so enthusiastic about pregnancy.'

'I know. My midwife said that, too, and she said it might be because I'm so young and don't feel the physical strains the same way. Like she said, plenty of women my age do intensive athletic training. This is just my version of track, or something, I guess. Whatever it is, pregnancy is right for me. And for Peter,' she added.

'Why shouldn't it be right for Peter? He's not going to be compromised by your physical condition.'

'Well, no, but the thing is, he wants to be part of it, he really tries to be involved, and not all men do that, do they?'

'I suppose not.'

'He keeps track of my vitamins and my appointments.' She paused and looked up at her mother. 'Not that I can't keep it straight – he just likes to be part of it, like I said.' Hannah nodded.

Then Sylvie was suddenly pushing her chair over toward Hannah, the sound of it scraping the floor, nearly silencing the whole establishment as heads turned their way. 'Quick,' Sylvie said, grabbing for her mother's hand. 'She's moving. Feel this,' and Sylvie placed Hannah's hand over her abdomen.

Hannah almost pulled her hand back, this was so strange, so very intimate, not at all the sort of thing people should be doing

46

in the middle of Monti's, but Sylvie held firm and then Hannah felt a series of tiny, quickened taps beneath her hand, and she lifted her eyes toward her daughter's. Sylvie was nodding, smiling at her. 'She's very lively,' she said to her mother, and then there was a much larger movement, as though the baby had decided to change position altogether and somersault through her daughter's abdomen. Hannah slid her hand over Sylvie's jumper, following the movement as it skimmed just below the taut surface. 'Her name's Cally, which is short for Calida.' Hannah moved her hand from one spot to another on Sylvie's abdomen, seeking more motion. 'She's quiet now,' Sylvie said after a few moments of search, and Hannah lifted her hand.

Sylvie steered her chair back toward the other side of the table. The busboy stood next to her, a pitcher of water at the ready. Hannah wondered how long he'd been standing off to the side, waiting till the exploration of Sylvie's belly had been completed.

'Calida,' Hannah said. 'Is it Spanish? Is Peter Hispanic?'

'No,' Sylvie said, smiling, almost laughing. 'He's got wonderful honey-colored hair.'

'It's a pretty name.'

'Thank you. We just chose it from a book because of that reason — because we thought it was pretty.' After a moment, she spoke again. 'Would you tell me about when you were pregnant, about your delivery?'

'It's really very long ago, Sylvie.' Hannah spooned some Parmesan over her remaining ravioli. 'You know nature has this way of making you forget it all, especially the pain. The details sink away.'

Sylvie changed positions in her chair, rising halfway up then reseating herself so the baby's weight sat differently on her. She extended her legs partway into the space between their table and the next one. 'I don't mean the pain — I suppose I'd just as soon not know about that — but things like complications, whether you went into labor early. Julia, my midwife, says some of those things run in families and you can be on the alert for them and plan for them.'

47

'There was nothing special,' Hannah said. And thought, Unless you counted all the terror and that sick, metallic taste of fear. Hannah had to put her fork down now, lean back, breathe slowly. What the hell was happening to her? She saw the bigness of Sylvie spread out across from her and her own, huge self, swaying, out in the middle of the movie theater parking lot, her legs trying to fold under her, and then the hot liquid rush all down her legs and Eric's voice saying, 'What is it, what's happening?' And now she was sweating, right here in the restaurant, and she remembered shouting at her husband, 'Call an ambulance, damn it,' and how even though she'd said that, issued it like a general's command, how terrified she'd been when he actually disappeared, sure she was going to die all alone there, shaking so badly, she could barely hold herself up against the car. And what could it have been, two minutes, maybe? Long enough for him to run back to the theater and tell them to dial the emergency number, then ease her back into the car where he stayed with her, holding her, telling her he loved her, till the ambulance came. Nothing unusual, they'd said. Just the membranes. Why hadn't anyone told her about that? They'd been so busy switching her from one doctor to the next, rotating her through a practice of seven doctors, each one of them assuming all the others must have told her the important stuff, only nobody had, nobody did. 'There really was nothing special,' she reiterated.

'What about my problem?' Sylvie asked.

'The learning disability?' Sylvie nodded. 'They never could say what it was from.'

'The doctor says lack of oxygen during delivery sometimes does it.'

'You were born screeching,' Hannah said.

'Was Daddy there?' she asked her mother.

'Yes.' There was a color photograph buried deep in some drawer or closet, a photograph one of the nurses had taken with Eric's camera. Eric, looking almost as swaddled as the baby, covered the way he was from head to toe in that mint-green hospital fabric, rocking the pink package that was their baby, talking to her, quoting Shakespeare and Emily Dickinson, so the nurse laughed and said, 'Whatever happened to Mother Goose?' It was Eric who rocked her into her first worldly sleep. It was Eric, always, so eager to hold and care for her. 'He loved you very much,' Hannah said, her voice sounding woefully maudlin to her own ears.

'I know. I remember the feel of his cheek against mine,' Sylvie said, laying her hand against her own cheek.

'You were seven.'

'Going on eight,' Sylvie said.

'He had just turned thirty-three, one week before.' Sylvie nodded. 'It happens. Sometimes people die younger than they should.'

'Had he been sick for a while?' Sylvie asked her. She heard the funny vibrato that sounded through the words – she wasn't used to speaking of him.

'No,' Hannah said. 'It was one of those things that couldn't have been known. An enlarged heart. He seemed healthy. The doctor called it a hidden time bomb.' She shrugged her shoulders. 'He went running, same as he always did, and he collapsed on the road. Do you remember?' she asked Sylvie.

Sylvie shook her head. 'All I remember is not having him there. That, and worrying if it was going to happen to you and to me. You told me those things don't happen twice.'

'They don't.'

The waiter had begun to clear their plates away, reciting the dessert menu as he did so. Sylvie said she wanted the tiramisu, but Hannah said dessert was out of the question for her. She looked at her watch. 'I've got to get back,' she said, so Sylvie was forced to cancel her order. The waiter brought the check and the women argued over it. 'Don't be ridiculous,' Hannah said. 'You gave me a gift, the earrings, so now I'm paying for lunch.'

As they were parting into the gray, snow-threatening winter day, Sylvie asked, 'Will you meet Peter now?' And Hannah said she would.

Chapter 7

Calida Weston was, at birth, a small but exquisitely formed baby with blue eyes and a soft, wispy crowning of pale hair. She put her mother through only two hours of hard labor and made her first appearance in the real world in her parents' bedroom. The midwife joked that she shouldn't have canceled her office appointments for this one because it could just as easily have been done by telephone.

A lot of people, Hannah mostly, had tried to dissuade Sylvie from a home delivery, but Peter and Sylvie together had decided right from the beginning this was their baby, and they were doing it their way. Doctors didn't like to hear about people wanting home deliveries but, as Peter said, there was a simple explanation for all that – they didn't want to lose your business. What the midwife told them was, if a pregnancy is uneventful and the baby is in the right position, home delivery is best. There are no unnecessary procedures, no exposure to infection, and no bureaucracy.

Sylvie'd spent four or five months working in an obstetrical office, so she was no stranger to the idea of the modern group practice where women are examined by each of many – in her office, seven – doctors. At delivery, it was anybody's guess which of them would walk through the door. You had a one in seven chance (or one in eight, depending on which group you chose) of getting the doctor you liked best, which, as Peter pointed out, were exactly the same odds for getting the doctor you liked least. Choose a midwife, though, and you saw her for all your appointments and you knew who was going to be by your side at the critical moment. And then in Julia's case – Julia was Sylvie's midwife – there was the added advantage

51

that she'd had two pregnancies herself. Talking to her was like talking to a friend about a shared experience. It had to do with sensations and feelings and worries, whereas talking with the doctors, she knew, was going to be measurements, statistics, and warnings. All Julia did in her practice was pre-natal care and deliveries – no surgery, no gynecological problems. She'd probably delivered more babies than most physicians ever do, and she still hadn't had a birth she couldn't handle. Maybe in the days before ultrasound there might have been the danger of unknown risks, but nowadays everything could be pretty well predicted in advance. And it wasn't like they lived out in the backwoods somewhere. If something had gone wrong, there'd have been an ambulance there in just a couple of minutes.

So there Cally was, breathing on her own, perfect and nursing like nobody's business, five minutes after she was born. No tension, no anxiety for any of them, just the most incredible feeling of amazement at how a couple of hours ago there hadn't been anybody named Cally, and now here she was, their baby, curled at Sylvie's breast. Julia said Cally didn't have any of the irritability or rigidity in her limbs that most babies have when they're born. That's what comes from having soft lighting and nice music and being in your own bed and having your own things around you. And, too, Julia said, of having it all happen so fast for Babe and Mom. Peter actually sat on the bed with Sylvie while Cally was born! And Sylvie felt great – she got up less than two hours later, didn't exactly spring around the block or anything, but she was fine. And the best part, she said, was she got to keep her socks on during the delivery, so her feet didn't freeze.

There was only one small marking on Cally's body – a blue, nearly perfect diamond shape on her right buttock. Peter fussed about it, asking the midwife and later the pediatrician, whether it was going to spread or whether more of them were likely to appear, and whether as she grew it would become more prominent; whether it was something that should be seen right away by a plastic surgeon, rather than letting it stretch into some kind of huge ugly splotch. Sylvie said it looked like an

52

elegant jewel-toned tattoo, and it wasn't like it was on her face. She was more concerned, she said, about how small Cally was – just over five pounds.

The pediatrician – he came to the house, too, for that first exam – told them not to worry on either account. Cally was small, yes, but so was her mama, and she had absolutely everything she needed. With such a lusty cry, there was no doubt she was completely vigorous, even though she had made her appearance on the early side. As for the mark, that was nothing to worry about. 'This is what we call a mongolian spot,' he said, 'and it's likely to fade over time, maybe even disappear entirely. It's not one of those port wine stains you sometimes see, and it certainly won't spread, if that's what you're worried about.' Still, Peter said wouldn't it be better to get rid of it now, before she was old enough to have trauma over it, adolescent body-image and all that? 'It'll be gone,' the doctor said, 'just give it time. Surgery will leave its own mark, and this probably will vanish without a trace, all on its own.' Sylvie was charmed by Peter's transformation into a concerned daddy.

Maybe it was because it all went so well – the fast, uncomplicated birth, the perfect baby – that Sylvie so immediately felt she was a born mother. 'I can do this,' she said to Peter, moments after Cally appeared and she held her new baby against her chest. And maybe it was partly because Julia kept telling her how well she was doing, how she was such a natural at it. The midwife made her feel nobody'd ever birthed a baby so well. And then Cally nursed, right away – something Julia told her almost never happened. Maybe that was because the labor was so short, or maybe Sylvie just was so relaxed, Julia said, but she didn't think she'd ever seen a newborn go for the breast so eagerly. 'I can do this,' Sylvie said aloud again. And to herself, she said, 'All right, finally. Something done right.' Peter had leaned over her, kissed her, told her the baby took his breath away.

The way Sylvie thought of it, Cally was like a missing piece of her. When she held her, there was the exact space for her in her arms. All she had to do was pick her up and Sylvie felt all different – mellow and easy. She liked carrying Cally around with her. She hated having to put her down, which drove Peter crazy, right from the start. 'She's going to get used to being rocked to sleep,' he cautioned. But Sylvie did it, anyway. When he was away she had Cally sleep with her in the bed. Sylvie would lie on her back and Cally would sleep on Sylvie's chest. Just like they were still one creature, physically bound together. Peter said Sylvie hovered too much. That she was spoiling Cally. That she wasn't letting their baby be independent. 'You shouldn't always be running to her the minute she squeaks. You know, I don't think I've ever really heard her cry,' he said.

'Why should she cry? Why is that important?'

'Because that at least would be something of her own, her voice, expressing something. All you do is quiet her. Don't you think she has a right to express her feelings, and isn't that what crying is for a baby? Babies should be picked up when they need care, not picked up for the parent's pleasure, which is what you do. And when you run to her the way you do, you're reinforcing negative behavior.'

But then he softened, just as he always eventually did, shifting his head sideways, looking at her that way like he had some special secret from way back to remind her about, and he touched her cheek. 'We shouldn't argue,' he said, not that he ever actually backed off on the words, but he'd just reach a point where he wanted to stop talking about it, and that was fine by her. She still loved him and all, and she knew people had trouble hanging together when there was a new baby. Once they could have sex again, she'd told him, it would be better. But what she wouldn't say to him was, now that there was Cally, she didn't think she loved him as much. It was like she'd had to take a piece of the love they'd had before and give it on over to the baby. Like she was allowed only the same total amount of love altogether. No, she'd never have the nerve to say that to him. Especially since she knew the bigger piece had gone over to Cally. 'Because she's just a baby,' Sylvie would tell herself. 'Later, it'll even out again.'

PART 2

Chapter 8

Hannah folded the clothing and put it back onto the shelves of the changing table: an orange-and-yellow-striped cotton romper, a blue-and-green-polka-dotted dress small enough to ball up in her fist. She thought of Cally's toenails, so paper-thin they were nearly invisible, and the tiny toes, which she'd taken between her lips to kiss yesterday (was it just yesterday?), to kiss, all five, at once. As she reached for a rumpled jumpsuit, a spider tumbled from the folds of the garment. Had the spiders already designated this realm deserted and up for grabs? Hannah pressed a tissue down, hard, onto the spider, then tossed the damp mess into a wastebasket. This is Cally's place, she silently advised the dead creature and all of his friends who might be lurking nearby. Hannah brushed her hands off, then returned to the task of folding shirts and dresses into neat, smooth squares, laying them one on top of the other in soft columns of pink, white, orange, and blue.

Neither she nor Sylvie even pretended that they might sleep that first night after the baby was taken. Earlier, right after the officers left, Hannah had tried to get Sylvie to lie down. 'For a few minutes,' she urged, but Sylvie refused. So Hannah simply tried to keep her occupied, but that, too, proved a difficult task. Just as Hannah thought she'd gotten her daughter calm by giving her some very specific task ('Why don't you flip through the channels and see if there are any decent old movies on?'), Sylvie would spring up, dropping whatever happened to be in her lap or hands, and rush from the room as though she'd just remembered where she'd left Cally. The suddenness of it, the sound of the remote control, or a magazine, or the plate of cheese and crackers hitting the floor in the otherwise still

57

room, startled Hannah quite badly each and every time. There was a wild desperation in the way Sylvie lunged through the room toward something Hannah couldn't identify. And she seemed wholly unaware of whatever had fallen at her feet, even if it was mixed shards of porcelain and crackers. Hannah found that the very act of trying to soothe Sylvie, of reaching for her and touching her, seemed to push her more doggedly away, to send her more deeply into wherever it was she'd begun to go. 'What time is it?' Sylvie frequently asked. And, 'How long till you think he'll call?' Sometimes Sylvie made sounds that were a little like humming and groaning mixed together, but mostly, there were long periods of silence. Hannah watched her as she sat on the edge of the couch, perched, really, not seated at all, rocking slowly, then stopping, her head cocked, as though she listened for a distant signal. 'What?' Hannah said to her one time, but Sylvie only began to rock again.

Hannah suggested a game of cards or Scrabble. 'I could read to you,' she proposed when she got no response to the other ideas. She repeated the offer – it didn't seem as though Sylvie had heard the first time, nor did it the second. By evening, Sylvie's breasts had swelled up so badly, they were leaking out across her shirt almost continuously. She cradled her breasts with her arms, lifting the weight of them off her small chest. Once or twice, when Hannah had looked over toward Sylvie, it'd seemed, for just a second, as though her daughter held a bundled-up baby in her arms.

'Maybe you should think about pumping your milk,' Hannah finally suggested. 'It'll ease the pain.' Sylvie didn't react. 'It keeps the milk from drying up, too, you know.' Sylvie turned toward her then, with a more focused glance, finally, and Hannah knew she was listening, considering. 'Do you have any bottles?' Hannah continued, eager to keep this concrete goal before her. 'You could put it in bottles and freeze it, couldn't you?'

'Yes,' Sylvie said, her voice alive with surprise. 'I have those plastic ones your friend gave me, remember?'

Hannah remembered. Plastic bottles painted with hearts and flowers in the usual pastel nursery colors. Not the sort of bottles that you should use for this purpose, probably. They'd need to be sterilized and then put in the freezer against the time Cally returned. The paint would surely peel off under such extremes of temperature, but what did it matter, really. Wasn't she just trying to get Sylvie to be doing something? Hannah went through the motions of heating the plastic bottles and nipples in boiling water (she had absolutely no idea how hot or how long the cooking was supposed to go on) while Sylvie went into the bathroom and closed the door so she could lean over the sink, as Hannah had suggested, and try to aim squirts of milk into the bottle opening. Through the closed door, Hannah could hear Sylvie crying. 'Do you want help?' Hannah asked.

'Leave me alone with it,' was Sylvie's negative, angry-sounding response, so Hannah returned to channel-switching in the front room. Ten minutes later, when Sylvie reappeared, Hannah looked up toward her daughter's exhausted face, her milk-soaked clothing. 'I sprayed the whole bathroom with milk and ended up with about an eighth of an inch in the bottle.'

'It's a start, Sylvie.'

'It's not a start, it's nothing. It's worthless.'

'Well, it's not important,' Hannah said, her mind casting about for some other diverting topic.

'It *is* important,' Sylvie said, shaking both her fists in front of her.

'Of course it is,' Hannah retreated. 'I didn't mean it that way, Sylvie. I meant we'll get it worked out soon enough. First thing in the morning we'll call the drugstore and get some kind of breast pump.'

'I need to have it work now,' Sylvie pleaded.

'No,' Hannah told her. 'Tomorrow is soon enough.'

'I'll have no milk by then,' Sylvie sobbed, letting both her arms fall, slapping down at her sides. 'It'll all be gone.'

Hannah put her arms around Sylvie and tried to draw her daughter's resisting body against her own. 'It won't be gone,' Hannah said, though she had no idea whether that was true or not.

Sylvie relaxed her head down against her mother's shoulder. 'Promise?' she whispered.

59

'I promise,' Hannah said, stroking her hand through Sylvie's hot hair.

After that, Sylvie was deadly quiet and Hannah talked into the silence about hope and faith, but the words, even when mixed with the metaphorical language of fluttering birds' wings – or perhaps because of that – sounded false to her. Then she tried to gather together all the tiny wisps of promises that she'd dragged out of Martinson: 'Most kidnappings are successfully solved, yes.' 'Most are misunderstandings, yes,' 'Most get resolved in forty-eight hours.' Hannah repeated the phrases, piling them up on top of themselves because she thought it might lend a volume and weight to the notion of Cally's redemption, though, in fact, such talk only seemed to make Sylvie more jumpy and to fill Hannah more thoroughly with despair. They both started checking their watches, subtracting the present time from ten a.m. when Cally had disappeared. They were watching the hours mount up toward forty-eight; they were seeing Cally begin to recede beyond being.

Forty-eight hours was also the time at which Martinson had told Hannah he intended to bring in the FBI. Did that mean he'd be giving up at that point? Kidnappings are usually solved in forty-eight hours, but if they're not, then what? Do the police just throw up their hands and admit defeat? Was that how it worked? She closed her eyes. *'Please, God,'* she said, speaking the words silently. No details or specifics, only those two words Please, God, as though that would cover it all.

Sometime in the very early morning hours, Hannah closed her eyes for just a moment and drifted into a sleep as uncomfortable as a turbulent plane ride. She woke with her arms outstretched, reaching to catch onto something solid in order to break her fall. She saw Sylvie pacing out circles and squares in front of her. Now Sylvie wanted to explain why she had thought it was all right to leave Cally. Sylvie's voice sounded oddly hoarse and Hannah suggested she should rest, lie down, save her voice, but Sylvie paid her no attention. She said, 'We didn't like to wake her. It's only in America they do that, waking them for feeds, making them fit into the adult patterns. In Europe and South America, they let the babies find their own pattern, and that's why they don't have all the hyperactive children we have in the States. They're much more mellow. You know, in Europe it's completely accepted that you can leave a baby in the house. Peter said people leave them in hotels when they go out to dinner, because they don't want to always be waking them. He never lets me wake Calida. It's something we agreed about because it's best for the child. People in America think they're so child-centered, but they're not, they're always trying to fit babies into their schedules, insisting they wake up at nine o'clock on weekends, which, of course, is ridiculous, don't you think? We leave her all the time and go out into the courtyard.'

'No one blames you, Sylvie.'

Sylvie knew she was repeating herself, or at least going over the same territory too much, but she had to keep talking, otherwise she got those pictures in her head of Cally; of people holding her wrong, or of her crying for hunger and needing to be fed, so she did talk more, she talked about how interesting it was that different cultures had different ideas about child-rearing and she knew people thought she and Peter were odd because they stopped them sometimes and said, 'Isn't that baby cold? Look how she's dressed,' but really, why should it be their business, some stranger on the street. 'In France,' she said, 'people don't ever wake babies, they don't fuss about whether they're hungry, or whether they're eating a balanced diet, they let the baby's body do the regulating. You'd be surprised, Peter says, how calm the babies are there from not being forced to this or that, from developing their own clocks and patterns, and some people might think all that was strange, but it was just different customs, that was all.' Hannah thought Sylvie sounded as though she were delivering a lecture on the comparative anthropology of infancy. 'No one blames you, Sylvie,' she repeated.

'I just want her back,' Sylvie said, her voice now so rasping, Hannah almost had to ask her to repeat what she'd said. 'Whatever I did wrong, I'm sorry. I'll never leave her again. Maybe I don't know how to dress a baby. Maybe I don't know anything. How would I know?' she asked into the open air. 'Maybe other people do know better, maybe they do.' She pressed her hands together just under her chin. 'I'll never leave her again, I swear it.'

'Hush,' Hannah said, and made Sylvie sit down next to her so she could rub her back for a while.

Days later, Sylvie could barely remember Peter's call, and not surprisingly – she hadn't been the one to talk to him. She'd gone as far as she could from the kitchen phone where Hannah spoke to him, on into the bedroom, where she'd lain down and pulled a pillow over her head so she wouldn't have to hear it, wouldn't know what Peter's reaction was. Hannah explained the news to Peter in broken sentences that piled up like rough-hewn, poorly fitted blocks, till finally the words described something like what had happened, and he understood that his child was gone.

He was shocked, Hannah said, but he definitely didn't say he was going to kill her. No, in fact, he asked if Sylvie was all right. Hannah thought maybe he was crying, it was hard to tell. 'He'll kill me,' Sylvie said, and Hannah told her no, it was over, he was coming home, it was okay now.

Peter didn't kill Sylvie, of course. He didn't raise a hand to her. Nor did he yell or accuse. He seemed weary, and he paced. He paced well off at a distance from her. And he shook his head, and he contemplated. She backed off further, watching only from the doorway. He breathed through his mouth, and she saw the ill-concealed hatred he bore for her seething just inside the barrier his teeth drew around it. And though he had traveled through the night to get there and not slept at all, he didn't protest at Martinson's suggestion that they get together immediately. The two of them spoke together behind the closed door of the small study.

Sylvie could hear the deep rumble of their voices, though not their words, and she received the vibrations against her heart and skull like the punishing blows he meant them to be.

When the policeman was gone, Peter came over to Sylvie, put his arms around her and said, 'Go ahead, cry, we'll both cry,' but the embrace quickly grew awkward, encumbered by mourning as heavy as a black lead cape spread out across their shoulders. She slid out from under the pressure of his arms so she could say, 'I'm sorry,' then repeated it so many times he asked her, please, to stop. She saw the blame, hot and unblinking, coming straight at her.

Chapter 9

The forty-eight-hour marker came and passed. Nobody mentioned it, but afterwards, there were FBI agents along with the police officers in the house. They were there twenty-four hours a day, waiting for the phone to ring; waiting for the kidnapper to call with demands. But there were no calls and no notes. Sylvie said to Peter, 'Of course they don't call. Why would they call with these agents all over the place? There are all these technological advances that allow the police to trace calls in a fraction of the time it used to take them. If I know about that, the kidnappers know about that. They won't call.'

Peter said, 'If they want a ransom, they'll call. They'll go into a phone booth and call. They'll travel to another state, if they think that'll help, but they'll call.' Then he held his arms out, reaching for her, but she felt so tense she didn't think she could mold into the curves of his arms and chest, and so she stayed where she was, one step off from him. He ran his hands up and down her nearly rigid arms.

'And if they don't want a ransom?' she asked, and she had to lift her arms, push off his hands, and cover her ears to block the sound of her own words and the terrible, reverberating implications of them.

The agents set up their phone equipment in the basement below the apartment, near the furnace, right in front of the storage area where all the tenants kept the overflow from their homes — fans, air conditioners, bicycles, exercise equipment, and cartons filled with letters, photographs, books, ashtrays, fondue pots, and figurines. The area had been closed off to other tenants now, so items could only be retrieved upon request. Sylvie rarely saw the agents, but she was never not aware of them. She could hear the sounds of the television they'd hooked up down there, the gurgle of their Mr Coffee machine, and she thought she could hear their footsteps, their laughter, their darts slipping into the target they'd set up on the wall, their cards slapping against one another as they shuffled and dealt, and sometimes, when the apartment was empty of visitors, she even thought she could hear their breathing. But then, she also, much too often, thought she could hear her Calida's breathing.

It was not exactly true that Sylvie never slept at all – she dozed in short fitful bursts and when she did, she almost always awoke to what she thought was Cally's cry, and then her breasts would let go their milk, streaming warm and wet over her shirtfront, ready for the baby. Everyone, seeing her huge, swollen breasts, advised her, or at least thought about how somebody else ought to advise her, to ask the doctor for medication to stop the milk.

Sylvie had no intention of taking medication to dry up her milk. She had learned to use the breast pump effectively, and so every day, every few hours, she attached the device to first one breast and then the other, and pumped milk into properly sterilized glass bottles. Dozens of these bottles, each bearing a sticker with a date, were lined up in the freezer where ice cream and pie-crusts and lamb chops and mixed vegetables had previously been stored. Peter had begun to protest, saying there was no point to this storing of milk; it only made both of them more depressed to see it accumulating, unused. 'When Cally comes back you can start nursing her. Right away. And then the stored milk will be superfluous anyway, won't it? Maybe,' he added slowly, 'it'd be better to let the milk go altogether. Really, Sylvie, it makes sense. That way you won't constantly be reminded of how she's not here.'

But she couldn't let the milk go. It was her connection to her child. It was the way she'd sustained Cally through their whole life together. To let it go now would be like cutting off the baby's life-line. She conceded on one point – storing the milk in bottles was probably wasted energy, but she still pumped. Now, though, she let the sweet-smelling, warm liquid run down into the bathroom sink drain.

'I want to be her mother again,' Sylvie said to Hannah.

'You are,' Hannah tried to comfort her.

'I don't know if I am,' Sylvie moaned. Sylvie could remember how she'd felt the first time she'd held Cally only seconds after she'd emerged from her body – she'd felt jolted in her heart by the familiarity of her baby. 'I know you,' she wanted to whisper in her ear, for it was as though they were being reunited, not introduced; as if they had always belonged together and had merely suffered a lovers' separation. Right from the beginning Sylvie had savored the fit of Cally in her arms and loved, too, the way that soft little mouth closed down with such violent determination onto her nipple. The baby's primitive noises and the silky feel of the bottoms of her feet made Sylvie light-headed with pleasure.

Cally's birth had wrought a metamorphosis whereby Sylvie had turned into some totally different creature. She'd left Stage One, Plain Ordinary Person, and jumped, two feet together, into Stage Two, Mother.

Now what was this she lived? Stage Three? Perhaps this was Stage Two with Variations, Mother Without a Child. It made her think of the prints of women holding children that hung all over the walls of Hannah's office – the women all had children on their laps, but it was the women's eyes you were really drawn to; that look of something fearful, some terrible secret whirling inside them. Was it that they knew it couldn't last, that they couldn't hold them like that for ever?

If that artist were to do her portrait, she would have to paint her arms shaped as though she held a baby – they would never comfortably fold any other way, and she would have to show her breasts heavy with milk. Sylvie was an ex-mother, a used-to-be mother, the mother of a missing child. And if Cally never came back, if she were with somebody else for ever and ever, Sylvie knew she wouldn't even exist in Cally's memory. Sylvie-as-mother would be wiped out completely for Cally. If no child called her Mother, was she no longer the mother of a child?

Sylvie was in a skewed state, drifted slightly off-course, and

she'd become something nobody, not even herself, understood.
There were no hormones that kicked in for this condition.
There were pills to take the edge off, as Hannah had suggested,
but nothing more. Forget the pills, Sylvie said, preferring to
keep the edge. How else could she watch, wait, and be constantly
on the ready? She still counted hours.

Sometimes she thought it was an illusion that she was in this
house talking to the concerned visitors who had begun to sit
upon her living-room couch and to assemble at her kitchen
counter. Her voice emerged sounding like a soprano's going
solo for the first time, searching for the pitch, feeling along the
line; almost in place, but then cutting out altogether. What? –
people's expressions in the audience asked. Has she forgotten
the words, the tune? Is she still singing? She could hear herself
speaking, but couldn't feel it as a physical act. She thought,
That's because I'm not here. I'm in an altogether different
place. I'm somewhere else, looking for Cally, constantly, totally.
Sometimes she spoke to them with a second voice that filled in
for her while her real self drifted, searching. People said to her:
'You're still in shock.'
    She knew they blamed her. Nobody is ever supposed to leave
a baby alone. She could see through the smiles and the soothing
voices. What she saw was that no one was going to forgive such
a fundamental lapse of judgment.

There were too many flowers. She hated the lilies most, the
way they leaned toward her, their white arms reaching for her,
spreading wide to advertise the purity of their own mourning.
And she hated the smells – the fresh earth in the potted plants,
the petals that no one had bothered to pull that had gone brown
and mushy, and the wet perfume of them, like sweetened
elderly aunts doing battle for her attention.
    There were too many visitors as well. She had trouble
thinking, and she complained: 'It's like they're pressing on me,
following me around, talking at me all the time.'
    'That's what they're here for,' Hannah said. 'To take your
mind off what's happened.'

Sylvie stared at her. 'You know that's not possible.'

Letters that came through the mail-slot now were heavy with rosaries, good-luck charms, inspirational poetry and essays, and even a brochure from an adoption agency that specialized in placing unwanted children.

There'd been the smallest of articles in the newspaper – 'Just enough to let them know we're on the case and not hiding that fact,' Martinson said. There was a number listed that people could call to report any leads. And people called it, Martinson revealed, but just as many, it seemed, or perhaps more, called her house ('Peter's in the book,' Martinson said, 'there's nothing we can do about it') and asked to speak to her. At best, they offered sympathy or spiritual guidance, but most simply fired questions at Sylvie: Where was the baby when she disappeared? Who was taking care of her? Had they heard from the kidnappers? Did she think she'd ever see her baby again? 'They want to hear us cry,' Peter said. 'They want to feel our pain and be glad it isn't theirs. We've got to put a stop to this, Sylvie. I'm going to have the number changed.'

'You can't change the number,' Sylvie protested. 'The kidnappers won't know where to call if you do that.'

When next the phone rang and she rushed toward it, he shouted after her, 'Don't answer that,' and he stepped between her and the kitchen wall phone, taking firm hold of her arm.

Sylvie began counting rings. 'Seven,' she announced, and his fingers sank more deeply into her muscle. 'I'll pick it up, but I'll get them off as fast as I can.' She was begging, and she knew it.

'I said don't answer it anymore.'

Sylvie's heart jumped, sure that this time it was the abductor and that he was ready to give them back their baby. Her pulse was pounding. 'What if it's them?'

He shook his head. He loosened his grip and rested his hand, gently, no longer controlling, on her shoulder. 'It's assholes, Sylvie, and we're not talking to assholes anymore.' Sylvie had counted ten rings.

She was startled by a sharp series of knocks at the back door, which then immediately opened to reveal the FBI agent from downstairs. 'One of you should get that,' he said, tilting his head toward the ringing instrument.

Sylvie grabbed at the receiver so quickly, it slipped through her hands and crashed against the floor. She retrieved it, and the coiled cord twisted like a vine around her arm. Her *'Hello?'* was breathless and overly sweet with hope.

'I'm just calling to say how sorry I am,' a woman's voice said. 'Is this Mrs Weston?'

'Yes,' Sylvie said, reaching with her free hand for a pad of paper and a pencil. 'Who's this?'

'Well, you don't know me,' the voice continued, 'but I feel like I know you, losing a baby like that. I had a friend once – but this goes back many, many years – she lost a baby, a beautiful tiny, tiny baby, not taken like yours was, but just dying from—'

Sylvie interrupted her. 'Do you know anything about *my* baby?'

'Well, just what it said in the paper, about her being six weeks old and being in her crib.' Sylvie started crying, so sudden and strong, she couldn't catch the sob from going into the phone, but then she quickly held it away from her ear and out toward Peter. At first he shook his head, but when she let the hand that held the phone hang loose at her side, he lifted the receiver from her.

'We have to keep this line open,' he said to the caller, his voice gruff and accusatory. He placed the receiver back into the cradle. Sylvie looked down at the pad – she'd written nothing. 'They're all crazy,' Peter said. 'I told you we shouldn't be answering.'

'We have to,' she said, pointing down toward the floor and the basement below where the FBI held sway. 'Besides, it might be them.'

'Fine. Then you answer it from now on, but you better learn how to terminate the calls.' He lifted the receiver. 'You don't cry for them. You put the phone down. Not like this,' he said, imitating her a few moments earlier when she'd let the receiver dangle from her hand, 'but this.' He slammed the phone back against the receiver. 'That's called hanging up.'

'Why are you so hostile?'

'Because it's all making me crazy. I can't stay here, Sylvie, with all those gossipy people in the front room, with the police downstairs, and with this goddamn phone going constantly. I just can't live like this.' He walked into the bedroom and came back out pulling on his denim field coat. 'I'll see you in a while,' he said, then stopped at the door. 'Unless you want to come, of course.'

She shook her head. The very suggestion made her feel like she was going to pass out. She couldn't leave. She had to be there in case. He left by the back door.

As though they'd agreed on the phrase together, nearly all Sylvie's visitors said to her, 'You're so brave.' And then, in a slightly louder voice, the sort that calls for confirmation from everyone else in the room, they proclaimed: 'Look how well she's holding up; how strong she is.'

To Sylvie, it felt nothing like calm. There was a swirling rush in her abdomen that never seemed to stop, and a heartbeat so quickened, so unremitting, the muscles of her chest would often ache from the exertion.

This was no ethereal serenity they saw, but a monumental form of distraction. She had a notebook now, small and compact, nearly identical in fact to Martinson's, in which she wrote down every question she had for him, and every detail of Cally's brief life. It was remarkable how many people had come in contact with the baby, she discovered, and remarkable, too, how many places they'd been together in just those few short weeks. She recorded her recollections of Cally's moods, her feeding and sleeping patterns, her developmental advances, the comments of the midwife and the pediatrician. She described the variations in her cries and noises, the way her hand wound about an extended adult finger, and the churning motion of her arms and legs as she lay upon the changing table. The way she had begun to lift her head and stare. The way her eyes followed a colorful object that Sylvie moved in front of her eager face. Sylvie filled the pages of her notebook and moved onto a second one, and then a third, recopying, reorganizing, making Cally more and more vivid.

Sylvie forced herself to put the notebook aside when she had

71

visitors, though that only increased the look of displacement, for her mind still raced on after Cally. And without paper and pencil, she felt compelled to repeat the words over and over in her head, protecting herself against the possibility of forgetting them before it was time to pick up her notebook once more.

Sometimes she got so focused on the morning of the kidnapping, she felt she really was back there again, hearing the same sounds, witnessing the same events, and she got to believing she could actually redo part of it, checking on the baby the very second she came through the door, for instance, instead of starting in on lunch, and have that make all the critical difference, just as the police had implied it would have. She spoke aloud of it to Peter, saying, 'It makes me think of those wood puzzles that you can't take apart no matter how you push and pull on the individual pieces, but if you know which piece is the key, and which way to turn it, it slides right out and the whole thing slips apart. That's how it feels, like if I can go over the whole thing in just the right order, with just the right emphasis, something's going to click back into the right shape.'

'And then there wouldn't have been a kidnapping?'

'Well, not exactly that.'

'What, then?'

'I don't know. That I'll understand it, I guess.'

'Sylvie, you can't change the past by thinking about it differently.' He shook his head. 'This is irrational stuff you're saying.'

'I know that, I didn't mean I really thought it. I just wished it,' she assured him, though some part of her thought or at least hoped he might be wrong because it seemed so close, sometimes, to not having been a kidnapping. So close.

'You have to stop saying, "If only I hadn't." What happened, happened. When you keep asking, "What if?" and "Why?" all you're doing is making yourself crazier. You're making us both crazy.'

'I know,' she said, and her face colored with the stupidity of it. Was she so foolish that she actually thought she could turn back time? That life was simple? That her daughter could be

72

saved? That words in a notebook were flesh and blood?

Whenever she looked at him, he turned his face away. When she thought about holding out her hand toward him, her fingers grew achy, then turned numb, as though she'd thrust them into a winter ocean. When she tried to close down the space between them, to walk toward him, her feet grew fuzzy beneath her, and she fumbled and shuffled stupidly in place. It got so all she had to do was lean in his direction, and she could see him flinch. He still spoke to her, but his voice was now crisp and polished, entirely given over to information transfer. 'Martinson called and said he'd be here at ten-fifteen,' he'd inform her.

'Thank you,' she'd hear herself say. And still, and yet again, she said, 'I'm sorry.'

One time he turned from staring out the window, and she wasn't sure, she thought he was looking at her, seeing her finally, and she said, 'I would never have done it if you hadn't said babies *should* be left alone.'

'Don't push it off on me, Sylvie. I never said it was all right to leave the baby completely alone. I never, never said that.'

'But you talked about all the people who did – how I was too protective,' she said.

'I was trying to make a point about cultural differences, Sylvie. I never said this baby should be left alone *here*, in this city.'

'You and I took those walks through the courtyard, out onto Livingston. I didn't feel comfortable doing that, but you said I was being silly. I did it, though. Now, tell me what's different about that?'

'We didn't go into stores, that's what's different. I never lost sight of the entryway.'

'But you kept saying I was too protective.'

'Yes, but I meant I didn't like you hovering over that crib. But that's a lot different from leaving her alone. I never said that you should leave Cally alone and I think it'd be better if we just drop this. You need to accept that there was a misunderstanding, and forget it.'

'I can't forget it,' Sylvie said. 'I can't forget any of it. I can't chalk it up to a little misunderstanding.' She flung her hand toward him. 'I close my eyes and I see myself walking out that door.' She was rising from her chair. 'Like it's somebody else, and I want to grab me, pull me back.' She knelt then, next to his chair. 'But I can't, I can't stop it, and it's the most excruciating sort of pain. Peter, I never saw her again after that moment.'

'Sylvie, please, this only makes it worse.' He rubbed a hand across his eyes.

'I'm sorry,' she said, unable to go on, her chest already burning with pain. But no weeping, no frenzy: this was too important. 'Peter, explain to me what you did mean. Maybe if I understand, it'll help.'

'Don't be ridiculous,' he admonished. 'Why do you want to keep punishing yourself?'

She saw the pain in his eyes, the tense, drawn lines of his forehead, but still, she pushed him: 'Tell me what you meant.'

'Fine,' he said, drawing a deep breath before beginning. 'I was talking about leaving a child in a place where it's common practice to do so, where you alert the others around you to what you're doing. You go to the next apartment – where you know the people well – and then they listen while you're out. But I'm talking about places where child-rearing has a true communal aspect to it. Where children are protected by everyone, where everyone cares about his neighbor. Close-knit cultures like Native Americans, Mormons, and Shakers, or – I don't know – Mennonites. This is New Haven, Sylvie, did you think somebody here cared like that? We're all on our own here, we don't even know our neighbors. In American cities, people break in, take and steal whatever they can, flesh or not.'

She covered her ears. No, of course this didn't help her. How could she have misunderstood so miserably? Had he said Mennonites? Who the hell were the Mennonites? Had it been so absurdly obvious? She saw that he had closed his eyes and was shaking his head. Everything she ever did she screwed up because she couldn't remember how to get from A to B, what anything was called, or what anything meant. She was always misunderstanding everything people said. She was just a stupid, stupid person. She deserved no forgiveness, no respite from pain, it was true.

In the night, if she moaned or cried and he was there with her in the bed, he didn't reach for her and she didn't dare wake him – if he found some peace in sleep, let him have it, she thought. She curled tighter toward her own center, and pushed the comforter against her mouth to muffle her complaints.

Then she realized, most nights he was wide-awake and only feigning sleep. She couldn't hear that quiet, well-spaced creaking, that hint of a snore, somewhere back behind his throat, that she'd grown accustomed to when he slept. In fact, she could barely make out his breathing at all. Yet when she whispered his name, he didn't answer. So she lay awake beside him, making her own breaths fastidiously silent as well, till he slept, which he always finally did, and then at least the even sound of that rhythmic quasi-snore soothed her and made her believe something had withstood transformation.

One night she dreamed she found Cally in a shoe box, her body twisted and bloody, and she woke with the sharp edge of a scream lodged sideways in her throat and reached across over his body, clutching at arm, shoulder, even the buttons on his pajamas. She felt him start. 'I'm sleeping,' he said. She pulled back, well over onto her side of the bed, her hands cradling the weight of her breasts.

When she did sleep, the dreams were always ugly, and she woke from them as quickly as she could. Those times, she often found his side of the bed empty.

He said to her, 'It would be better if I got back to work.'

Hannah, too, had started talking about desertion, about class times, about picking up the pieces, as she put it. 'I'll lose my students if I'm not available for conferences,' she explained. 'But really, I think it's better this way.'

'Better for who?' Sylvie asked them.

'It'll be better for everybody,' Peter said. 'It doesn't do any of us any good to have me pacing back and forth, wearing ruts into the flooring. And we certainly won't be any better off if we have no money.'

'You can't give up,' she said to him.

'It isn't giving up,' he said. 'It's trying to get some balance back into our lives. I can't think rationally anymore. I'll think better about the situation if I get some small aspect of my life back to normal.'

'You won't think about her when you're working.' Sylvie's words had the cool, polished surface of statement. She imagined all their thoughts as the spiritual umbilicus that kept Cally alive. If they deserted her in their thoughts, the connection would wither, and Cally would be doomed. 'You can't give up,' she pleaded with Peter.

'Sylvie,' he said, speaking more gently than he had of late, 'we can't let this kill us.'

Chapter 10

Martinson was there, with his notebook and his Styrofoam coffee cup, two, three times a day. She listened for the creak of the back steps – no one else came in that way. She was waiting for his news, his new ideas. Or maybe even The Answer. He was better than any of the other investigating officers. They only wanted everything reduced to figures, or at the very least, to some extremely small number of words that they could fit into the spaces on their forms. Forget emotions, their bored looks said to her. They wanted to know, Yes or no? In or out? Two o'clock or two-ten?

Maybe she simply preferred him because he called Cally by name, didn't speak of her as The Child, as did the FBI agent, whose name, in neat reciprocity, she'd managed to forget.

Martinson always asked to see what *she* had that was new. He actually took time to go over the notes she made, asking for more detail than she'd included. 'This woman,' he said to her, 'the one with the shopping cart and dog. Did you interact with her at all?'

'Yes,' Sylvie said. 'She was always asking to see the baby's face.'

Martinson nodded. He was biting his lower lip.

'She has these ugly thick plastic flowers all entwined around the handle of the cart,' Sylvie told him. 'And she ties the dog up outside stores so it yelps – a high-pitched, whiny bark. The dog's a real odd color of yellow,' she added, trying to remember everything. As Martinson was always saying to her, anything could be important.

'Can you remember what she asked, what the conversation was like?'

77

Sylvie nodded. 'She always said, "Can I see her little face?" and then, "How old is she?" "What's her name?" "Is she a good baby?" That sort of stuff.'

'Was it the same each time?'

Sylvie nodded. 'That was what was creepy about it. And that she always asked to see her *face* – that's a weird way to put it. It really bothered me that she couldn't remember anything from one day to the next. I started avoiding her, crossing the street, that kind of thing, because I didn't want to hear it all again,' Sylvie said, and then she had to stop talking, had to close down the picture that had started to come into her head of Cally tucked away inside the green plastic trash bag that lined the old woman's cart.

'Did she ever touch Cally?'

'No.'

'Try to?'

'No, but I got nervous just having her near the carriage. After the first few times anyway. She was loony.' She could hear a strained sort of pleading in her own voice. 'I had to be on the alert.'

'For what?'

'I don't know. The way she kept moving closer, maybe, sidling up. I didn't like the smell of her breath, I didn't want it floating down all over Cally.'

'We'll check it out. Do you have a name or address for her?'

'No,' she said, though she was barely able to get the word out and realized then how fast she was breathing, like she'd been running, chasing this woman down Orange Street, seen her in the distance running down Linden, or was it Lawrence?

'We'll find her,' he said, though he knew he shouldn't promise like that. It was the way she was shaking that was getting to him. He remembered that part. How he couldn't really control his limbs once he'd actually seen his son on the hospital gurney. He remembered, too, how afterwards his brain would not give him peace; how it insisted he watch the spectacle of every moment of his son's life in steady flashback. He used to see his child everywhere, his countenance shining out at him like a ghost projection on walls. He saw him in full color, smiling, laughing. He'd had to endure repeatedly his child's first step, his first ice cream, his first Christmas, his second Christmas, his third, his first time at bat. He had to listen to the charming way Evan, at two, had said, 'knifes, folks, and fooms.' Why wouldn't it all go away?

And he had known the ache of coveting other people's children. How many of them had he actually followed through stores, children Evan's height and coloring, who couldn't be Evan, couldn't possibly be, but still, he had to make sure. His heart ached again in his chest just remembering those days of chasing his almost-Evans.

With a new baby, though, after less than six weeks together, he wondered, could it be so bad? Without the years of history together, wouldn't it be easier for her to move on?

'I'll check out the stores where you've seen her,' he said. 'Somebody'll know her. She's probably lived in the same building and shopped in the same stores for thirty years.'

'Try the Grove Market, Detective,' Sylvie said. She saw that her hands were shaking. If this woman was crazy, really crazy, she could have done something terrible – not fed Cally, let the dog at her, forgotten she even had her. If she was deaf, if that was why she asked the same questions, never having heard the answers, she wouldn't hear Cally's cries.

She saw that Martinson was turning to a new page in his notebook. 'Were there any people who touched Cally, maybe reached into the carriage, people who weren't really friends, but broke past the accepted stranger etiquette barrier?'

It was difficult for Sylvie to refocus; to move off the old woman, to put aside Cally's unheard cries. 'I don't know.'

'If something comes to you,' he started to say, and then she remembered, remembered how she'd felt like grabbing the stock boy's hand, pushing it hard, away. She could see the flash of his hand – the blue stains on it – and how she'd wanted to shove the carriage beyond his reach, but some constraint, some need to avoid creating a scene (for what was it over? the admiring of a baby?) kept her there in place, watching the discolored fingers wave and wiggle in front of Cally's face. She told Martinson about him. 'He works at the market. He bags, sweeps, puts out stock, that sort of thing.'

'Anybody else?' he asked, and she said she couldn't think of anybody just that minute and he said, 'Call me of you do,' and she felt excited, close to something, getting there. She wanted to grab hold of Martinson's arm, to say, 'How long will it take? Twenty minutes? Thirty? Isn't one of them sure to have her?'

'What do you think?' was what she actually said to him.

'I think we check out each of them, one at a time. There will be lots of leads.'

'But one'll be it,' she insisted. It was past the forty-eight hours, she wanted to remind him. Way past.

'One'll be it,' he said as he stood up to leave. 'Though not necessarily one of the ones we went over today.' And then they were standing right there at the door, and she had to open it for him and let him go.

Everything took so much longer than she'd have thought. Martinson just disappeared on her for half the day, didn't even call her to let her know what he'd found. She told Hannah about the crazy woman, and going over it again, she cried because this really, finally, looked like they had something. But still, Martinson didn't show. Hannah stopped by to make sure Sylvie had lunch, setting out deli meats and cheeses and flaky croissants that she swore were the best in town. Sylvie made a sandwich, lifting a slice of meat, then one of cheese onto the pastry. She carried it with her, untasted, while she paced. Hannah saw the puffy layers compress into a thin, flat casing while her daughter moved back and forth through the kitchen, the sandwich clutched ever more tightly in her hand.

It was already dark by the time Martinson actually rapped out his four knocks on her door, and she was asking the question before the door was fully open, before she was even certain it was he standing on the other side of the threshold. 'The old woman with the dog and the shopping cart, Detective,' she said, so eager, she couldn't remember how to phrase a proper question, couldn't wait even for him to sit down.

'There's nothing there,' he said, and she heard the sound of her own moaning sigh.

'It isn't her?'

He shook his head. 'She's a befuddled old woman, plain and simple. She probably remembers the baby, or at least *a* baby, or thinks she should remember a baby, though she can't remember when she saw it last, can't describe Cally or you, and certainly has no idea who you are or where you live. She just barely remembers how to navigate from her third-floor rooms, down the street to the store and back. And when she gets there, they tell me she has trouble remembering what she came in for. And it's not thirty years, but more like fifty that she's lived there, people think, though nobody I spoke to goes back anywhere near that far themselves. I suspect the dog is the main brainpower there. He's the one probably remembers where the house is and what floor they live on.'

'But she could be involved. She could be lying about describing us, couldn't she?'

'I don't think so,' he said, shaking his head and moving on to explain, next, why the stock boy, 'a kid who's somewhat too anxious to show his stuff, but harmless,' was no longer being scrutinized either.

'You're sure? You could tell that fast?'

'Nothing's closed and put aside,' he said, 'but yes, I'm sure for now. He's somebody who takes on roles. He was just being the adoring baby-watcher that day. Today he played model witness for me.'

'Did you search her house?'

'Sylvie, she's a loon.'

'But don't loons kidnap? Isn't that precisely who *does* kidnap, Detective? A normal person doesn't take somebody else's child; somebody with a loose screw does, somebody who doesn't remember the rules. This woman doesn't remember anything!'

'Well, yes, that's true, but this particular woman is too far gone, Sylvie. She wouldn't be able to figure out where you lived, get herself over there, through the door, find Cally, and get her back home. She doesn't even have the physical capacity to go the extra four blocks that would be necessary.'

'But suppose she did,' Sylvie insisted. 'Suppose she lived for something like this, finding herself this "good baby."' Sylvie

81

had half-risen from the stool and now leaned toward him. 'Suppose she asked at the Grove where I lived – they have my name on the charge sheet – and then she got this incredible surge of adrenaline and went for her. That means Cally could be in there starving.'

'She can't move that fast, Sylvie. She supports herself on that cart. She couldn't do the distance in the time you were gone.'

'With adrenaline . . .'

'Hey,' he said, holding up his hand as a signal for her to halt. 'Cally's not in there, Sylvie. The apartment is small – a living room, bedroom, bath, and kitchen. We could see into all the rooms. Cally's not there.'

'Did you look in drawers and closets, under the bed?'

'No,' he said with an exaggerated show of patience. 'I need a search warrant for that. And I need probable cause to get one. It's simply not justified in this case, Sylvie. Look, she's got grandchildren and even a great-grandchild, an infant, who come to visit. She's got photographs of them in magnetic frames on the refrigerator. She's got the dog, too. She doesn't fit the need profile.'

Sylvie was having some difficulty breathing – the air felt as stuffy as on a blazing-hot summer day. She slumped back in her chair. 'Last night when I first thought about it, and this morning when we talked about it, especially this morning when you were asking me all those details, it seemed so logical to me. I believed it. I thought you believed it, too.'

'I'm sorry if you thought that,' he said. 'I have an interest in every piece of information, and I therefore explore every piece of information as best I can, but this woman seemed no more likely than the dozens of people we've talked to so far. You believed it because you made up a story that went with it, that's all. It did have possibilities, but they led nowhere. We check everything, but when there's nothing there, we have to be able to go ahead and put the energy and manpower into the next idea. Like now,' he said. Then, after a pause, 'I need some personal information from you.' He stopped, waiting, she knew, for her signal that she would allow him to venture further.

82

'Ask,' she urged, impatient herself for some new line to explore, now that the old woman and the market boy had almost certainly been taken from her.

'You and Peter aren't married, are you?' Sylvie shook her head. He knew this, so this was a kind of review, some form of soft entry into what he really wanted to know. 'Okay,' he said, 'you need to tell me why you're not married.'

'Only because we're not married *yet*. We're planning to be married,' she said.

'So then it's not like you've taken a firm personal stand against the institution of marriage?'

Sylvie assured him that wasn't the reason. 'But why would that be important?'

'I don't know that it is. It's something to know about you and Peter and Cally. Maybe it means something to someone else.'

'Like what?'

'Well, I'm not sure. I'm still exploring, collecting data. Tomorrow or the next day, I'll see the connections – if there are any.'

'Do you mean maybe there's someone who thinks unmarried people shouldn't have children?'

'That's what you said, Sylvie, not me.'

'But were you thinking it?'

'No. I told you, I'm still at the collecting stage. Can we just go on?' She nodded grudgingly. 'Okay. Now forgive me this one, but do you have a date set?'

'For a wedding, you mean?' He nodded. 'No. We've had some complications.'

'Such as?'

'Such as the baby being born early.'

Martinson nodded. 'How early?'

'Three weeks. She took us by surprise.'

'But you'd put off getting married through the whole pregnancy?'

'It wasn't that we were putting it off, really.'

'What, then?'

'There were a lot of reasons we needed to wait.' She shifted in her chair.

'Such as?' he asked, one hand open, extended toward her, ready, it seemed, to receive her answer.

'Peter travels a lot, and he has to be available to do that traveling on a last-minute basis, so it's hard to plan very long-range. Also, I'd promised I'd take a Mormon training program and convert because he said it was really important to him that we get married in his church. I hadn't quite gotten around to all that. Everything gets difficult when you're eight or nine months pregnant or you've just given birth, or you're trying to care for a newborn, you know.'

'Yes,' he said. 'I remember that from when my son was born.'

'And it wasn't that important to either of us. We're not opposed to marriage, like you said, but neither of us cares that much one way or the other. We were going to do it.'

'And you've known him how long?'

'About a year and a half,' she said, stretching it to avoid that knowing look, the one that said, 'Hey, I know how to add and subtract. You barely knew the guy, did you, when you were making that baby?'

'Can you tell me the date you two met?' Martinson asked quickly, not taking the time, she realized, to count weeks and months.

'I don't remember.'

'I know it's hard. Approximately.'

'Winter, I guess. It was snowing.' This was vague enough, she figured. Maybe he'd think it was actually the winter before last. Maybe it wouldn't occur to him it could have been so recent as last year. But of course Peter would remember, and tell it off, maybe already had told it, neat as could be. 'February twenty-second,' she said. 'One year ago plus a few weeks.'

'Good,' he said. Why did it make her feel so much better to have him say that one word, *good*?

'So,' Martinson said, lingering on the word, gathering up all the little unfinished sentences that now hovered round them, but which would have to be stowed away for another day. 'We may move in small steps, but we'll get there.'

'Will we, Detective?' she asked him. He would leave now, she knew, for she'd learned the rhythms and gestures of his closing.

84

His flat hand had already slapped down gently on the counter, the stool had been pushed back, and he'd issued the soothing but empty assurances. She wanted him to stay.

'We're doing very well. I'll give you a call later if I have anything new.' He found his way, unaided, so quickly through the door that by the time she reached the threshold he was gone from view.

Chapter 11

Like a doctor arriving at the examining room, Martinson knocked, then opened the door without pause and caught Sylvie crying. She started down the hallway toward the bedroom.

'What's going on?' he asked, following rather closely behind. It was the morning of the tenth day. Cally had been missing more than 225 hours. Fifty, maybe as many as sixty feeds had passed. What if they were feeding her sugar water? What if they were feeding her formula and she became allergic to it?

Sylvie glanced over her shoulder at him. 'Don't follow me, Detective.' He stopped at her command. 'And don't you ever knock before you barge into somebody's house?' She stood at the doorway to the bedroom.

'I did.'

'Then you didn't knock hard enough,' she said, fumbling ineffectually with the doorknob to her bedroom. It wasn't even turning under her hand. Why couldn't she do the simplest things anymore?

'Why don't you just stop the crying now?' he suggested as he started down the hall toward her.

She turned to face him. 'You stay right there,' she said, pointing at the end of the hallway. 'And next time, and all the times after that, could you please wait for me to open the door, or at least wait till I say you can come in?'

'I *am* sorry.'

'And why can't I have some privacy?' she continued in her harangue. 'Why can't I just go into my bedroom without you shadowing me?' She raised her hands, palms out, fingers spread, pointed upward, shaking.

'I'll come back later,' he said.

87

She let her arms fall to her sides. 'No,' she said, and her sigh went on longer than either of them thought possible. 'What difference does it make whether it's now or later? I'm always crying, I'm always upset. Later isn't going to help that.'

'Fine. Time to settle down, then. Unless you'd rather I talk to Peter first?'

She started back down the hall toward him. 'He's already gone. He's off to Chicago for three days.'

'Chicago?'

'Yes. He said you gave him permission to start traveling again.'

'Yes, we did do that. He left an address and number, I suppose?'

She walked past him, on into the kitchen. A white porcelain goose magnet held a scrap of paper against the refrigerator. She slipped the paper out and handed it to Martinson. The tiny blue ribbon round the goose's neck had come undone and she busied herself with trying to retie the short length of satin. 'Of course he didn't ask *my* permission.' She tugged at the ribbon and it came away completely from the little drop of glue that had held it to the bird.

'These things can take their toll on a relationship.'

'Don't say *these things*,' Sylvie snapped, and twirled round to face him. 'Cally is not a thing, we are not a thing.' She tossed the ribbon in his direction.

'I know,' he said, 'I'm sorry. It's just a phrase.' He bent and retrieved the satin strand from the floor. 'It's a way people use language. A shorthand, I suppose.'

'I don't want to be put into shorthand,' she complained.

'I understand that. It's just that it's hard to talk directly about the personal issues in other people's lives.' He held the ribbon toward her, but she turned from him.

'I thought you were such an expert at cutting through the crap, getting to the heart of things. What happened?'

He shrugged his shoulders, put the blue satin on the counter. 'I'm a detective, not a social worker.'

'But you understood that old woman. Two seconds with her and you knew she didn't take the baby, right?'

'Not two seconds . . .' he protested.

'Five minutes, then.'

He raised his eyebrows, considered for a moment. 'I spent enough time with her so that I thought I understood whether she was capable of the crime.'

'So why can't you find the right person?'

'I'm trying.'

Why was she doing this to him? And goddamn it, why had Peter left for three whole days? 'Look, this isn't getting us anywhere, I know that. Take out the notebook,' she said. 'Ask me something. Ask me the right question, the one that does it.'

'I'll try,' he said, slipping the notebook from his jacket pocket, then leafing through the pages.

She saw his Styrofoam cup on the counter. 'And you should drink your coffee,' she said, her voice gone, perhaps, a shade softer. 'I'm sorry for the fuss, for the delay.'

He pulled the stool out from the counter, sat down, pried the plastic lid off his coffee, and breathed in the fragrant steam for a few moments, then sipped the dark liquid. 'Do you have anything new?'

'No,' she said, though she'd had a dream, a dream in which she'd heard Cally's cry coming out of an enormous loaf of black bread. She'd started breaking off the crust, little pieces of it, and dusting the crumbs away with her fingertips, opening the bread up slowly and carefully the way an archaeologist works at a dig, moving toward the underlying precious content, but ever wary of protecting it. And then she'd looked around and realized how much discarded bread was piling up, so she'd started eating the pieces as they came off in her hands, as though it were important to get rid of the evidence. Even now, as Martinson spoke to her, she could remember the feel of those wads of fragrant fresh bread under her fingers. She could still hear the muffled crying, and she still had that feeling in her fingers of needing to grab more, to work faster. She'd wakened before she'd cleared away enough of the dark stuff to reveal Cally's pale skin.

Sylvie walked over to the counter and sat down. Martinson sipped at his coffee. 'Nothing?' he asked into her silence.

89

'Nothing real.'

'Well, that's a perfect entrance line for me to ask you about psychics.'

'Psychics?' she repeated. 'Are you bringing a psychic in to find Cally?'

'I wasn't thinking along those lines. I was thinking about the fortune-teller you visited in Toronto.' He held the notepad at such a low angle, she could see his pencil markings. Though his scribbly handwriting seemed wholly unreadable, she thought she could make out the capitals letters, *F* and *T*, rising above the rest of the scrawls. He closed his hand down over the notebook, it was that small.

'How do you know about Toronto, Detective?' she asked him, taking a seat on the remaining stool.

'A couple of people at the bank where you used to work mentioned you'd gone on vacation there and that you'd consulted a fortune-teller right before you quit.'

She wrinkled her nose at him. 'Sasha told you, right?'

Martinson looked down at his notes. 'Yes, Sasha was one who mentioned it. And Brian, too.'

Sylvie shook her head. 'She wasn't a fortune-teller. Did they tell you she was a gypsy with a crystal ball?' The detective shook his head. Sylvie let out a loud breath. 'Listen, Sasha hated me, I don't know why, well yes, I do. She hated me because I was always asking her to help me do stuff, like how to do a cashier's check or what the codes were for transactions. Every time I asked, she'd seem really put out and she'd say, "How many times does it take you to get this stuff?" But she probably told you all that, didn't she?'

'Not exactly, but I didn't get the feeling you were close friends.'

Sylvie rolled her eyes at the idea. 'Brian and I got along, I suppose, but he's a lunatic. It gives me the creeps that you're using him to get information about me.'

'Look,' Martinson said, 'this information was coincidental to finding out who your co-workers were and if they could give us any information about Cally. I'm talking to everybody who knows you. That's how we do this.'

'I know,' she said. 'You've said that a million times.'

'Right. So you're starting to understand it, I hope.'

She sat up straight. 'Look, don't put me down like that, Detective,' she warned him.

'That wasn't my intent.'

'And I hate all those legal-sounding words like *intent*. Words like that just allow you to sleaze out of things. You *sounded* like you were putting me down and I don't happen to care what your intent was.'

'I'm sorry.'

'Good,' she said, surprised by the harsh tone of her own voice around the word. 'And what about my co-workers? Did you get anything on Cally?'

'No. They were all at work that day. Absolutely accounted for.'

'The last thing any of them would want is a baby anyway,' Sylvie mused. 'It'd muck up their lives.'

'That was my impression, too. Can we talk about this fortune-teller?'

'Why?' she asked him, not entirely sure why she was giving him so much trouble.

'Because you've had contact with her during the last year—'

'It's more than a year,' she interrupted him.

'Not a lot more,' he said, and she allowed the observation to stand. 'You don't have to tell me anything, but I thought there might be something to it.'

'It was before Cally was born. Before I even knew Peter.'

'True,' he admitted. 'Humor me again. It may lead somewhere else. If she's not a fortune-teller, what is she?'

'Her name is Mrs Yun and she doesn't have a crystal ball and there aren't any palm readings or séances or any of that garbage. My friend Tisha brought me over there and the woman talked to me, asked me some questions, and gave me some advice. She's into the healing arts, herbs and energy and balancing forces, and massages. You know, all the stuff about getting your life in harmony.' Sylvie made a circle of her hands, fingertips just barely touching, exactly as Mrs Yun had done. 'If you saw her, you'd know she had nothing to do with Cally.

91

She's a tiny little woman – she couldn't weigh more than eighty pounds. Besides, she's in Toronto and she didn't know about Cally. You should be looking here, in this neighborhood. It's got to be somebody who sees her every day.'

'I'm not saying Mrs Yun had anything to do with it, but you saw this woman and talked with her and you undoubtedly gave her some information about yourself, which, if she was unscrupulous, which I'm not saying she is, she could have used at some later date. We follow up on anything that looks possible till we see it isn't possible.'

Sylvie's pulse had started beating faster, thumping deep and hard in her abdomen, and her armpits had gone suddenly wet. What if Tisha had mentioned to Mrs Yun that she'd had a baby, and the woman had connections to a baby black market ring or something? What if she passed information on to a gang member, a brother, say, without realizing she was even doing it?

'Why don't we start with you telling me how you met Mrs Yun?'

'My friend took me there,' Sylvie said, her voice whispery, hard to catch, she could tell, from the way Martinson leaned toward her.

'Tell me about your friend.' He had his yellow wood pencil out, the notebook still open to the FT is for Fortune-teller page. He turned that page over, got ready to start a new one. His pencil was worn down very low, the eraser nearly flat against the top of the metal tube.

'Not much eraser left on that pencil,' she observed aloud.

He tilted the top toward himself and checked it out. 'True.'

'You want a pen, Detective?' she asked, and reached her hand toward a nearby empty marmalade jar filled with writing utensils, scissors, and ruler.

'No, this is fine. I like the feel of pencil better,' he said. 'I don't need to erase.'

Sylvie wanted to add more, to turn the words into conversation, not interrogation, but Martinson wanted to get back to it, to know about Mrs Yun. Sylvie wanted to know: If Mrs Yun stole babies, what did she do with them? That was *her*

92

only question. She stared at Martinson for a moment and decided not to ask, not to know for now.

'Your friend's name?'

'Tisha. Patricia Perry,' she clarified, and she watched his pencil point plunge into motion across the notebook paper. Then Sylvie had another question for herself: If Mrs Yun stole babies, did Tisha have any inkling? 'I was visiting her in Toronto,' she said to Martinson, returning to his question, trying not to hear her own, and again the pencil moved down, below a line, then above it. It did look like the word *Toronto* to her, but then, it did not look like any word at all, but only a sweeping flourish of gray. 'Tisha wanted to treat me to a foot massage and advice. We're always giving each other crazy birthday presents.'

'How do you know Tisha?'

What was this about? Tisha or Mrs Yun? 'She was a friend from high school.' There wasn't any possible motive for Tisha to be involved.

'What's she doing in Canada?'

Could Tisha have unknowingly revealed things? Sylvie would call her, sound her out. 'She lives there.'

'I meant, why does she live there?'

'She went to college there, was at the University of York for a while, then she stayed on. But it isn't Tisha.'

'She's American?'

'Yes.'

'That's unusual, isn't it, an American going to school in Canada?'

'I guess so. But Tisha does things like that. She likes to be deliberately different.' Sylvie almost told him how during their last visit together Tisha had said she was thinking about going to Bangladesh, but there seemed no point in supplying this information. At the time Tisha'd said it, she was stretched out on the couch with an almost-drained glass of port wine in her hand, and it'd seemed more joke than itinerary.

Martinson asked for Tisha's address, which Sylvie gave him. 'Are you going up there to talk to her?'

'I doubt it. This is for just in case. Like you said, it seems far-fetched that anybody in Toronto would have a connection, but why don't you just tell me a little about her,' he urged.

'Tell you what?'

'Start anywhere. How about a physical description?'

'You think it's her?'

'No.'

'Then what?' she asked, her hand coming down so hard on the counter, Martinson's coffee cup bounced side to side.

'It's a process of elimination, that's all. We say, okay, these people didn't do it, let's look at somebody else.'

'But it's got to be somebody here, not somebody in Canada. This is wasted energy, and meanwhile, Cally's in danger.'

'Yes,' he said, then paused. 'So we should get through this as quickly as possible, dispose of it, and move on. Are you concerned that there's some secret that you'd be giving away in telling me about your friend?' She said nothing for a moment, then shook her head. 'It's a kind of favor I'm asking you, really, letting me take this shortcut instead of flying up there and staring foolishly at her for five minutes while she gives me the same information.' Martinson tapped his pencil in a rhythmic tattoo against his notebook.

Sylvie waited a few long beats before she began. 'She's tall, around five-ten, my age, skinny almost, but not bony. She's got long black hair. Very beautiful hair with a silky texture.' Sylvie paused, letting her hand slide down her own much more rough-textured mane. 'Is that enough, Detective?'

He looked up from his scrawlings and smiled. 'It's a start. Where does she work?' he continued without pause.

Sylvie had to think for a minute. 'She works for a corporation and she buys their art for them; she also makes sure their gardens are cared for.'

'What's the name of the corporation?'

Sylvie shrugged. 'I think it's a computer company, but I'm not sure. All I know is they employ lots of programmers.'

'A lot of places employ lots of programmers. Insurance companies, for instance.' She decided his comment didn't require a response. 'Do you remember the name of her company?'

'No.' Her breasts were getting full again, threatening to

94

overflow down her shirtfront. She was relieved – this was the first time she'd felt any pressure of milk since the evening before. The worst of the engorgement, the painful, hot, swollen breasts of the first few days, had subsided so dramatically, she'd become worried that the flow was going to stop altogether. When Cally nursed, she drained Sylvie's breasts down to empty every single time. A mechanical pump simply couldn't compete with that level of efficiency. 'The body knows,' she'd said to Hannah. 'It knows she's gone. It knows it doesn't need to keep up the milk.' Now she felt the prickling of the milk as it let down, and she folded her arms across her chest, then closed her eyes for a moment, remembering Cally's face, that wide-eyed eager stare she gave before plunging toward a nipple.

'Why are you resisting me so fiercely today? We've been working together so well up till now.'

'I don't know.' The pressure of her arms had blocked the flow of milk, for now. 'I told you this seems stupid to me. And on top of that, Tisha's a friend. I don't want to be mistrusting her.'

'I'm not asking you to. I'm asking for a picture of where you've been and with whom.'

'But that's Tisha, in this instance.' She'd gotten up and gone to the refrigerator for her Pepsi. She'd started drinking it in a mug lately. It had a more comfortable feel that way, almost like she was immersing herself in it, not just sipping it.

'It's all right,' he said, closing the notebook. 'Some things bother some people more than others. I'll send somebody up there and that'll remove you from the process, get rid of your guilt.' He stood up and Sylvie felt nervous – he looked like he was getting ready to leave.

'That's it? You don't have anything else?'

'No, but don't worry, we're doing fine.'

'Wait a minute,' she said, standing, too.

'You remembered something?'

'I guess it doesn't make much difference whether I tell you about it or she does,' she capitulated.

'Actually I think it'll be easier on her. Most people don't enjoy finding a police officer on their doorstep.'

'And like you said, it's not as though there are deep secrets that I'm going to reveal about her.'

'No.'

She asked him to sit down again.

She couldn't remember the name of the company Tisha worked for, but she answered his questions about how often they wrote and spoke on the phone, and about Tisha's most recent visit to Sylvie, too.

'And the mystic stuff, the predictions?' Martinson asked, pushing things along.

'Like I told you, there was all this stuff about balancing forces, and how some of my life was empty, some full.'

He laughed softly. 'In other words, no content, just a lot of yin and yang.'

'Yin and yang and balancing things canceling each other out.'

'Nothing concrete, no specific warnings?'

'Not really. A lot of circles and palms pressing close by each other,' she said, her hands crisscrossing each other, a movement Martinson recognized from Tai Chi.

'And that,' he said, moving his hands similarly, one over the other, 'made you change jobs?'

She let her hands flop down across her lap. 'I really hate this.'

'What do you hate?'

'You knowing my whole life but acting all innocent like you don't know a thing.'

'I don't.'

'Oh, come on. If you know I changed jobs, you must certainly know why.'

'I know what Brian said.'

'Screw Brian.' She drummed her fingers against the table, then asked, 'What did he say?'

'He said,' Martinson began, turning back through his notebook, '"This fortune-teller told her her job was destroying her life and she better get out fucking quick."'

Neither of them spoke for a few moments and then Sylvie smiled at him. 'Mrs Yun would never use the F-word,' she said. 'And Brian is the kind of guy who's always trying to get the female bank tellers into narrow spaces with him.'

'But the content was approximately the same?'

'Yes and no. See, it's more like I asked her, really.'

'Meaning what?'

'Meaning I said, "Is it my job?" and she started nodding big nods and said, "Hate job, right? Hate writing in boxes, right?" Which scared me a little because in a bank you're constantly double-checking everything onto these forms. If you pay out cash, like twenty-seven dollars, say, you have to count it twice, then put the bills into the adding machine as two ten-dollar bills plus one five-dollar bill plus two one-dollar bills and enter each figure onto your chart. Now, that is sick. All that does is take up time. And then the end of the day is a special nightmare with the close-out sheets and all the things you have to count and recount and enter into tiny boxes. Some days I'd be there for hours past closing, I just couldn't get it right. Sasha would tell me I was a jerk and she'd breeze out of there while I was practically in tears. One time my supervisor grabbed the sheets from me and sent me home because she was tired of hanging around while I finished up. That was during the week before I went to Toronto. We called that whole end-of-the-day business "boxing out," so when Mrs Yun said that thing about writing in boxes, it gave me the shivers.'

'Like she really could see into your life.'

'Right. Though Brian said to me – and he probably said it to you – she could say the same thing to almost anybody and there'd be something about their job that was like that. Everybody's got some kind of boring, repetitious thing in their job they hate.'

'And so you quit your job and gave notice to your landlord the day you got back from Toronto?'

'You tell me, Detective.'

'Brian helped you find a new place.'

'Not really. He went with me. I went through the classifieds, made the calls. He was along for the ride and the free dinner I promised him. But you know, I don't like this, because it feels like we're talking about me, not Mrs Yun.'

'Yes and no. We're talking about her influence on you, which, you'll have to admit, was dramatic.' She shrugged. He raised his eyebrows.

'I wasn't exactly in love with my job, you know. I was probably about to get fired. And there was also that stuff about Tisha's uncle.'

'What stuff?'

'Brian didn't tell you?'

'I don't think so.'

'When it was Tisha's turn, Mrs Yun told her there was trouble in her life, that there was a man who had pain in his shoulder and had to go to the hospital.' She stopped and looked at Martinson. 'We didn't take it very seriously.'

'Why not?'

'Because it was fortune-telling, like you said. And because there were no men in Tisha's life just then, at least the way we figured it. Mrs Yun seemed sort of upset, but that just seemed part of the entertainment aspect.'

'What made you take it seriously?'

'We went out for breakfast the next morning, and when we got back, there was a message on Tisha's machine from her mother. It turned out her uncle, this one she was really close to when she was a kid, had died during the night of a heart attack. She asked her mother, "Did he have warning pain?" and her mother said yes, he'd had pain in his upper arm, on and off, for two days. He'd thought it was from carrying boxes down out of the attic.'

'So you decided Mrs Yun really must know what she was talking about and you'd better get out of those boxes as fast as you could.'

'Right.' She looked directly at him. 'You don't have to tell me you think it sounds stupid. Everybody thought it sounded stupid, and everybody told me that. My mother said I should be committed. But it's not like it screwed up my whole life or anything. Good things happened to me – I got a better job, a better apartment, I met Peter. It was like my life was turning around and everything was better. Till Cally was taken, of course.'

'One more thing,' he said, and she could feel the change,

something about the way he shifted so far to one side on the stool.

'About what?'

'About you and Peter.' She waited. 'Did you two both want this baby?'

'Yes,' she said, her voice a whisper, her throat suddenly sore and coarse.

'So soon after you met?'

'Yes.'

'Did he ever leave or threaten to leave before the baby disappeared?' She shook her head. 'Your mother says he was devoted to Cally.'

'She said that?'

'Why are you surprised?'

'She's not very quiet about her dislike of him. She says he's too old, too judgmental, too taken with himself. She really gets off on detailing his faults to me. And they avoid each other as much as possible – barely talk when they have to actually share the same room. He can't stand having her hang around me, she can't stand having him here, but they both tolerate it, because of Cally.' Her jaw ached with the pain of tears she didn't want to let loose. 'He's starting to hate me,' she said, and bit down hard on her lip.

'There's definitely tension in the air when you're both here,' he observed.

'That's a nice way to put it.' She almost laughed, then asked, 'Can you call it "tension" when two people don't talk except for major public announcements like, "I'm flying to Chicago for three days"?'

'Anytime a child is involved in an accident or a crime – as a victim – it seems to divide the parents, just when you think they would draw together.'

'It's the blame.'

'Yes. Someone wasn't watching. Wasn't being careful. It's irrational. Both parents can actually have been there, both can be completely exonerated by a court, but somehow it's something the other one did that was the critical mistake.'

'This time, though, it's me. He's right about this one.'

'Some people might say, if Peter weren't away so much . . .'

'No. This time it's clear to everybody, including me. This is my mistake.' She breathed in deeply, fighting tears.

'You're the one who said you're not a thing, not a situation or a case. Not a kidnapping scene. You're three very real, very different people who aren't just another example of some pattern. You're you,' he said, but she'd begun to cry and the milk had come, forming the hot dark circles across her chest. She didn't try to hide either form of grief. 'Hey,' he said, laying one hand lightly on her arm, 'don't be so hard on yourself.'

'I should be dead,' she said through her sobs, and he tightened his hold.

'Put blame aside, already. You should be trying to help each other, believe me.' There was a long silence in the room, and then he began again. 'I had this same thing happen to me.'

'Had what happen?' Sylvie asked him when he said nothing more.

'Well,' he said, then stopped, shrugged his shoulders. 'I mean about the two of you falling apart.' He wiped one hand across his mouth. 'I mean I had a child who died, and then my wife and I didn't speak another civil word to each other from that moment. Even in the hospital, right after he died, we cried, but in opposite corners of the room. We didn't even hold each other.' He shrugged once more, then said, 'Right when we should have been there for each other, we weren't. We killed the marriage, as though it had no meaning without him. But it had meaning before,' he said quietly, and she saw his throat move in a hard swallow, saw, too, how his eyes sought the upper reaches of the high ceiling. 'Look, I'm sorry, I really shouldn't be talking about my own stuff. It was all a very long time ago.'

'Are you over it, then?'

'Oh, no.' There was a trace of a laugh to his words. 'That doesn't happen. You learn to live with it, but it never goes away. He still comes to me in dreams. Sometimes he's bruised and bleeding, the way he was in the hospital, but sometimes he's perfect, brought back to life, older, sometimes, younger, others. But he always warns me, "Daddy, I'm going to die," he says,' and Martinson's voice crumbled into the words. He closed his eyes.

'I'm sorry.'

He nodded. 'Try to help each other. You can save each other.'

'You mean, if we can't save Cally?'

He hesitated a moment, then said, 'Yes, I suppose I do mean that. Don't lose it all,' he advised.

Chapter 12

Sylvie had taken pains to compose her ideal kidnapper. She was a young woman – younger even than herself – a girl, really, but a very healthy girl whose own baby had died, completely unexpectedly, at birth. She was an otherwise perfectly rational human being who'd unfortunately gone a little mad with the loss. She'd waited so long for her baby that it suddenly seemed any baby might do, and poor Cally had just been in the wrong place at the wrong time by being visible in the neighborhood to this girl. But having gotten this baby, that is, Cally, this girl became balanced again and took wonderful care of her, and loved her, too, and even breast-fed her. And given how devoted she was, Sylvie figured she'd eventually start thinking of how to return Cally to her real mother.

This line of thinking had gotten Sylvie into a tight place: If this girl was so devoted to the baby, as was required for her to be if the fantasy were to reassure, why would she then give her up? If she'd experienced a full-term pregnancy, who'd ever guess this wasn't the baby that'd been in her womb? Then, fortunately, it occurred to Sylvie that once the birth hormones had leveled off, maybe the girl would be rational again. Remorseful even. So it was just a matter of time, then, till the girl called the police.

Another notion that made Sylvie feel better was thinking about how Cally was six weeks old when she was taken, certainly much more robust than any newborn (though she was very small), so people would notice the difference. People around this girl would suspect and come forward to report the kidnapping. Clearly there couldn't be a husband, because he'd have to know the baby had died. But there might be somebody

103

like an aunt who came by once a week or so. And of course it would all be so obvious to her – the girl comes home from the hospital with no baby, says it died, or maybe says it was too sick to bring home just yet, but then suddenly a couple of days later has a fine, healthy baby in her arms. The aunt wouldn't go along with that. She'd put two and two together. Maybe she'd seen the piece in the paper about Cally disappearing. She'd go right to the police, wouldn't even mention it to her niece first.

Then Sylvie thought, no, no one's gone to the police because this girl lives alone. There is no aunt, no sister, no mother, no grandmother, or friend. Which would account, partly, for why she'd gone mad to begin with. And if there were no concerned principals, who would speak up? How was she going to get her baby back?

And try as she would, Sylvie couldn't manage to compose a kidnapper who was any bit better than this girl. What other choices were there? A Canadian black-market baby ring of some sort? A mad person who liked to kill or torture helpless creatures? A lunatic woman who wanted a baby but couldn't figure out how to care for her? Somebody who wanted ransom money but had gotten scared and run off and left the baby in a phone booth or deserted warehouse? Where was her comfort? How could Cally possibly be saved if those were the choices?

That was when Sylvie started to venture out of the house, stapling notices with Cally's description onto trees, telephone poles, and bulletin boards in store entryways. She took to stopping people with babies – they were bound to be the most sympathetic, right? – and asking if they'd seen any baby Cally's age in a strange place or with a strange person. She walked along the streets and through the stores looking for her, feeling rather mad herself at moments, when she realized she was almost always looking also for the girl, a person who existed only in her imagination. Maybe she'll see me, she sometimes thought. Maybe this girl, or damn it, whoever it was, would see her, would feel her grief and say 'Here, take her back, I love her, but she's yours.' It wasn't likely to happen, Sylvie knew, but she had to do something, didn't she? If she waited for the powers-that-be, the sleek, hotshot FBI agents and the grumbling, procedure-bound police, she might wait forever.

Regardless of what Sylvie thought of the effectiveness of the FBI, they were relentlessly thorough when they questioned her. After enduring yet another hour-long interrogation session, she told her mother: 'I'm not talking to that Agent Dillon or Dolan or whatever his name is anymore. Next time he calls, I'm going to be out or say I have an appointment, something like that.'

'Don't waste your energy trying to avoid him,' Hannah advised. 'He's not going to disappear because you say you're going to the dentist, you know. Just deal with him and get it over with.'

'He's a sadist,' Sylvie complained. 'He doesn't have any real interest in Cally.'

'He has an interest in finding her, surely?'

'No, he doesn't. He's interested in making me squirm, and that's it.'

'Well, I'm not crazy about the way he does his interrogations, I have to admit. He's got those clipped sentences that come at you like automatic-weapon fire. But you have to try to ignore that. He's a typical tight-assed authoritarian who wants to impress you with his efficiency.'

'It's not just the way he talks. He's a mean, mean bastard. He says horrible things. My jaw and cheekbones ache from trying to hold back tears.'

'So don't hold the tears back.'

Sylvie shook her head. 'If I cry, he'll say it has significance.'

'What kind of significance?'

'I don't know. I don't know what he wants, but he scares me. He's so different from Martinson. He lets these long, long silences drag on while he just stares at me and then finally he does this wicked smile where he opens his mouth a little and lifts one corner of his upper lip.' She poked her own lip upward by way of illustration. 'And he says things like "I'm just curious as to your opinion," when I know he isn't. I feel like how I move,

105

how I breathe, matters. It all gets picked over and examined.'

'To what end?'

'I have no idea, I just know I hate it.'

'Stop trying to second-guess him. If it turns out he's analyzing everything you say and do, it doesn't matter one bit whether you cry or not, because he'll have some analysis either way. If you don't cry, he'll say you're cold. You don't win with FBI agents, you merely survive.'

'Given the choice, if he's going to make something out of whatever I do, I'd rather not cry in front of him because I really think he'd get off on that.'

'Try to think of him as a cipher.'

'What's that?'

'A cipher? A zero. A nothing. A place-holder. A body that has to be here because there was a kidnapping. Or think of him as a vessel you need to fill with information.'

'A sadistic vessel.'

'A vessel can't be sadistic or sympathetic, Sylvie, it has no emotion. It's clay or metal or glass. To think of him otherwise is to let him have the upper hand and, ultimately, to get to you.'

'But the man is torturing me,' Sylvie said, raising her voice. 'He says things like "Locating infants is much more tedious than locating older children." What does he expect me to do, say, "Oh, I'm so sorry, I didn't realize that, but I see now how inconsiderate I've been. I definitely ought to have had an older child kidnapped, and of course in the future, I will"?'

Hannah lifted Sylvie's hand and held it between her own. 'He's trying to impress you with how hard he works. But you're right, he is a bastard.'

Sylvie lowered her head and spoke quietly. 'I can't bear to hear anything more about how difficult this is, how bad the odds are.' She looked up at her mother. 'I want them to lie to me. I want them to say, "Cheer up, we'll get her back in no time."' Sylvie tilted her head back and let the hot tears flow over her aching face. 'I can't bear it anymore.' Hannah's hand tightened round her daughter's. 'He said most babies have straight blonde hair. Most babies have blue eyes. He even produced the statistics for me. So I'm supposed to understand that it isn't his fault he can't identify her from all the other babies in the world. She looks like everybody else's baby. She has no dental records, no documented speech defects, no X rays of broken bones.'

'*You* could identify her.'

'Yes, but I'm not out there, investigating.'

'And there's the birthmark.'

Sylvie nodded. 'A fading birthmark. "Like an ice cube on the beach," he said. There's nothing, Mother, that can be used to identify her.'

'Blood type?' Hannah asked, racking her brain for some possibility.

Sylvie shook her head. 'She wasn't blood-typed because she was born at home. There's no real reason to blood-type a baby just for the hell of it. And there are no fingerprints, either, with a home birth. I didn't even know they footprinted babies.' Hannah nodded. 'He says baby eye and hair color change through the first six months to a year. He says she could have black curls and be brown-eyed by now. Maybe he's right, maybe even I wouldn't be able to recognize her.'

'He says that?'

'Yes.'

'No,' Hannah said. 'I don't believe that.' She spoke softly. 'Martinson hasn't made it sound so ominous.'

'No,' Sylvie admitted.

'It does sound deliberately cruel. Talk to Martinson about it, get his reaction. Maybe he can do something about it.'

Sylvie nodded. 'We're at their mercy,' she said. 'It shouldn't have to be this way.'

Chapter 13

Hannah was surprised to find Agent Dolan at her door quite so early. She was still in her robe, her hair still stuck up from where it'd gotten crushed into that position by the pillow. He was in his dark suit, polished shoes, and red foulard tie.

'Just give me a minute to change,' she said. She'd cracked the door only just enough to see who it was and to deliver this message.

'It'll just be a few questions, please, Mrs Pierson,' he said, the flat of his hand against the door, not pushing exactly, but counterbalancing, at least, her hand upon the other side. 'I have very little time.' And so she'd opened the door wider, though she knew she still wasn't opening it really wide enough. He almost had to turn sideways to edge his body through.

She didn't know whether to ask him to sit down. She certainly didn't want to – making him more comfortable would only prolong his visit. And she knew she didn't want to sit down herself because she'd have to keep fussing with her robe, pulling it together over her pale legs that were needful of a shave, trying not to reveal, too, that she wasn't wearing any underwear. So, let him stand, she thought, he's the one who's in a hurry.

'It's come to our attention,' he said when he was barely in the door, 'that you counseled your daughter to abort her pregnancy and that you opposed that pregnancy openly and vigorously.'

'You could probably put it that way.' Hannah had no need to ask where he had gotten the information – she'd ranted rather fiercely on the subject in a faculty meeting, saying. 'I don't want this baby,' causing her colleagues to roar with laughter. 'Did it occur to you, Hannah, that you're not the one who's

109

pregnant, that this isn't your baby?' any number of them had pointed out.

'Explain your opposition.'

Oh God, that's what she hated about him. That imperative, militaristic style. It made her want to shout '*No!*' every time he issued one of his commands. Instead, she gave him an answer, though she did give her words an unusually sharp stress that she thought adequately parodied his. 'She was unmarried, very young, and she had attention deficit disorder.' He, too, like Martinson, carried a notebook, though his was in marked contrast to the police officer's spiral-sided version. The agent's leather-bound notebook was, like his silk tie, of obvious quality. She was pleased to see he found it somewhat awkward to have to hold it in his open hand and write while he stood up.

'Attention deficit disorder,' he repeated, not even looking up from what he had written.

'Yes. It's a learning disability. It means she had trouble in school with staying focused and interested, and that, in turn, interfered with learning.' She realized that while she'd been doing her defining and explaining, she'd been stroking at one of the wayward clumps of hair sticking up off her head, and she realized, too, that Dolan's eyes were following every movement of her hand. She stopped – only a shampoo was going to get her hair to lie flat anyway.

'And?' he asked, raising his eyebrows, expectant.

'And that's all. Those are the reasons I had a problem with it.'

The agent shook his head. 'There's something I'm missing here. What does this disability have to do with a baby? Are you saying she didn't have the basic intelligence to care for a child?'

'It isn't a question of intelligence,' Hannah said. 'It's a question of interest. Of carrying through on a project. Sylvie gets excited about things, like a new job, say, then in no time she's suddenly bored with it, or overwhelmed by the demands of it. So she quits, sometimes with no explanation, and she just doesn't show up the next day. That's usually when I hear from her, when she's got no job and she's ruined her chances at decent references, that sort of thing. She would always show up when she wanted somebody to make it all better, but by then, of course, it was always too late.'

'Six jobs in two years.'

'That sounds about right.'

'So you thought she might just drop the baby off at your house and disappear?'

'I didn't say that,' Hannah insisted, though, in fact, that had been precisely her thought at the time.

'I see. What are your feelings about the baby now?'

'I love her.' Hannah took a deep breath, got the tears to back off. 'Look, when Sylvie first told me she was pregnant, it just seemed like another problem she'd decided to drag home. Once Cally was born, once she was real, that completely changed.'

'Changed how?'

'I already told you,' she said, furious with herself for becoming rattled in front of him. 'I didn't feel what I felt before, I didn't feel so angry because I started thinking of Cally as a child, not some concept, not an issue between us. It wasn't a fight with my daughter anymore, it was this new, beautiful human being. And I felt different about Sylvie, too. Like we had a new connection.'

'Explain that.'

'What, the connection?'

'Yes, ma'am.'

She sighed. 'This is rather more than a few questions,' she protested.

'We're about done. The connection,' he reminded her.

'Connections are spiritual. You can't outline and rank-order epiphanies.'

'An epiphany?'

'A revolution,' she explained.

'Yes, I do know the definition of the word. I'd just like to hear some more detail about this epiphany. You don't have to actually outline it if that bothers you.'

'It wasn't an epiphany,' she said, tired of this, not wanting to have to put into words what she had seen in her daughter's eyes right after Cally's birth. That look that grabbed onto her, that said, 'I understand now,' that made her almost shudder, because she too, understood now, that they were connected by this secret of how mothers turned their bodies nearly inside out to have their babies, then handed over their minds and their souls, to keep the connection going. 'There were no drum rolls, no trumpet calls. It was more like a whisper. A shared secret,' she mused aloud, still working it out for herself. She looked up at him, at the tight way his lips pressed upon each other, and knew she was being foolish to speak of mystical connections to this man who bore such smoothly forged features they looked as if they'd been ordered from a plastic surgeon's catalog. 'Don't you have any noses with less obvious nostrils?' she imagined him requesting. She saw how he was waiting again, saw how those perfectly shaped lips opened slightly, then closed, as if suggesting, silently, that she should speak. But she had nothing else to say. She'd already exposed more of herself and Sylvie than she was comfortable with. He had no right to her thoughts.

'But the point is, your daughter has this history of lack of commitment, so you thought she might have trouble staying interested in caring for a baby.'

Hannah didn't like the way he picked out those words *caring for a baby*, saying them so slowly he set them off as though they'd been printed in six-inch-high red letters on her living-room wall. 'That's what I had thought,' she said quickly, though the sound, even the look, of those letters had faded only the slightest bit. 'I stopped thinking that as soon as I saw her with the baby.'

'Now, why is that?'

'I saw that Sylvie loved her. That this was not a job, not another project. It was a commitment that was intense, and I had no need to worry at all.'

'But you said, Mrs Pierson, that she started lots of things with great enthusiasm and then dropped them, didn't you?'

Sylvie was right – the man had a real nasty, mean streak. 'I said this wasn't the same.'

'But how could you know that?' She hated the way he smiled at her as he spoke his barbed words.

'I did know. I do know. This was a child. This was not a job in a bank. This was very, very different.' She readjusted the overlap of her robe, tightening it across her neck, pulling harder, too, upon the tie at her waist.

'Was it?' he asked, his lips pressed slightly forward, his eyes wide in what Hannah supposed was meant to look like an expression of disbelief.

She dialed her daughter's number the moment Agent Dolan left. 'Sylvie,' she said, then stopped. What could she say? Every one of her daughter's calls was monitored.

'Yes?' Sylvie asked.

She couldn't say, 'Don't talk to FBI agents anymore.' She couldn't say, 'Be circumspect,' or 'Don't let anyone in the house,' could she? 'I'll be over as soon as I'm dressed,' was what she told her daughter.

Hannah's arrival at Sylvie's apartment was slowed down by haste. First, the collar of her robe got caught on a brass hook when she bent over to pick up the tube of toothpaste that had slipped out of her hand. Had she not been in such a rush, she might have thought to slide out of her robe, and thereby escape. But instead, she fought against the hook, tugging away from it, growling, 'Let go, goddamn it,' as though it were a person holding her against the wall, till finally the terry cloth separated and tore, and she was free. Then, once she was dressed, she couldn't find her keys and wasted time searching under and over everything in the house until she thought to scrounge through the hamper for the black slacks she'd been wearing the day before and found the keys in that pocket. And then she got caught behind a school bus.

What she tried to tell herself was that there was no reason to assume that Dolan would head right back toward Sylvie's house. He could have gone any number of places after he left her. And she had plenty of time to think about this while she sat behind the bus watching mothers walk their kids up to the bus door, chat with the driver, then wave. Couldn't they see there was a line of cars behind, couldn't they cut the crap, already? And then she thought, even if Dolan did go right to Sylvie's house, he might not have had that much time with her.

Maybe he got held up, too, behind a school bus. Though, of course, he'd have known exactly where *his* keys were.

When she finally got to Sylvie's, Dolan's black car with its government plates was parked in an Emergency Vehicles Only space right in front of the apartment building. Hannah had to drive another three blocks north to find a parking place, then take the distance back on the run.

She rang the bell, but no one answered. She knocked, pounded really, but still no one appeared. She knew why. It was because they were holed up in that tiny little back room where he liked to run his inquisition. Sylvie called that room, which had probably once served as a servant's bedroom, her study. Someday, she'd told Hannah, she was going to put a desk in there so she could write children's books. Now the only furniture it held was two folding chairs and a card table she'd dragged down from Hannah's attic. Each of them, Sylvie, Peter, and herself, had passed, singly, into that room any number of times, to be grilled, very privately, by Dolan. And now Hannah was certain that even though there was no one else in the house to overhear or interfere, Dolan had taken Sylvie in there and closed the door. He had his way of pressing down on those he interrogated, of conducting his interviews in tight, narrow ranges of time and space. Maybe Dolan thought anxiety, no matter what the source, worked in his favor. Hannah let herself in with her own key.

'Sylvie!' she shouted as soon as she was in the door, and she heard the stony echo her voice produced in that huge, nearly empty space of the apartment. She tried to keep herself from walking toward the little room, so as not to let on that she knew exactly where her daughter was, exactly what was happening, but when no answer came, she headed directly to it. 'Sylvie,' she said sharply against the shut door.

Dolan opened it. 'We've almost done,' he said to her. Sylvie, seated on a folding chair, had turned to look at her mother. Hannah expected to see weeping and panic on her daughter's face, but there was none of that. 'Just a few more minutes,' Dolan said. He held a coffee cup, one she recognized from Sylvie's kitchen, and he took a sip from it now, though he kept his eyes on Hannah's as he did so, peering over the edge at her. Damn him, she thought, what right had he to take coffee from Sylvie, then lock her up in there for one of his attacks? With his free hand, Dolan closed the door.

It was not long, it was true, till the two of them emerged from the study. Hannah had gone to the kitchen and put up a kettle of water for herself, and it had only just come to a boil when she heard the door open. 'Goodbye, ladies,' Dolan said as he came through the kitchen. Sylvie did not accompany him to the front door. The two women stood facing one another in silence till they heard the front door close. When Sylvie started to speak, Hannah gestured with a finger to her lips that she stay silent. Hannah went out into the living room and looked around, then went to the bedrooms and checked both of them.

'He's gone,' she said to Sylvie, who had followed behind her on her rounds.

'There's something wrong,' Sylvie said.

'I know. You can't talk to him anymore without a lawyer.' Hannah was holding her breath, waiting for Sylvie's reply.

'He thinks I did something,' Sylvie said, her voice softened, her look nearly dazed.

'Did he tell you what he thinks?'

Sylvie shook her head. 'No, but he's going over odd things, like he's putting the pieces together to say that I had some kind of fit and that I took her.'

'But that's absurd! Why would you do such a thing?' Sylvie didn't answer. 'What was he asking?'

'He asked me if I was saying, "He'll kill me," you know, right afterwards, before you even got here.'

'What did you tell him?'

'I told him I was.'

'Oh, Sylvie,' Hannah said, shaking her head vigorously. 'You have to stop talking to him. All along you've been telling these idiots way too much.'

Sylvie looked at her mother. 'The thing is I did say that, and those two cops heard me, and they wrote it down. What the hell good does it do to pretend I didn't say it when he knows I did?'

115

'Well, it's meaningless anyway.'

'Not to him. He wanted to know why I said it, why I felt I needed to be punished.'

'And what did you say?'

'I said I felt I'd failed, that it was all my fault because I'd left the baby. I was imagining Peter's pain, what he'd say, what he'd do, how he'd cry and scream, and hate me, and I just wanted to die. I didn't want to face him.' Sylvie's voice was remarkably steady. Hannah had the urge to shake her, to put her hand over her mouth, anything to stop the unmonitored flow of confessional outpourings.

'You said too much, then. Much too much. Why didn't you just say, "I didn't think I needed to be punished"?'

Sylvie shrugged. 'Because I wanted to be punished.' She held her hands stretched out open before her, as though to emphasize the obviousness of her statement. 'I was definitely hoping I'd die before he got here so I wouldn't ever have to face him. Or maybe I was hoping he'd put me out of my misery when he did get here.' Sylvie lowered her face to her hands.

Hannah groaned. 'You said all that to him?'

Sylvie looked up. 'I don't know. I started crying when I was telling him. I don't think I said that bit about wishing he'd kill me. I don't think I exactly ever even thought that before this minute.'

'Sylvie,' Hannah said, her voice pleading. 'Dolan isn't a therapist or a priest or a lawyer. I know he makes it seem like he's there to help you, that if you just tell him all your innermost thoughts, everything'll be fine again, but it just isn't true. He doesn't care about you. He'll use every bit of this against you. Now, the next time he comes by, you've got to tell him you've thought about it, that you really think you just said those things because you were upset and that people always say crazy things like that when they're upset. And then you've got to be careful – very careful – of what you tell him from now on. No more analyzing your psyche. When he asks about times and places and clothing, fine, tell him, but when he asks about you, what you are thinking or feeling, you don't have to tell him. You mustn't tell him.' She realized she had taken Sylvie's

116

hand in hers and she was squeezing it hard, emphasizing her words.

'Then he asked me did I maybe leave her somewhere that I had forgotten to tell him about,' Sylvie said.

'Meaning what?'

Sylvie ran her hand absently over her lips, then spoke. 'I don't know. At first I thought he meant was it the first time I'd ever done something like that, gone out of the house without her, but when I looked at him, and the way he opens his eyes too wide, I could tell that wasn't what he meant. I didn't say anything, so he said I should try to remember. Did I ever walk away from her, maybe, in a store, forget she was with me? Did I ever want to just walk away? he asked me. He said he knew I had trouble sticking with things, that he knew things were tough. I shouldn't be ashamed to admit it, that under pressure, it was no wonder I might want somebody else to take care of her.' She stopped for a moment and smiled. 'It was almost funny, that I would want to give her up. I said that to him, but you know him, he doesn't even blink.' She turned away, walked over to the window. Hannah followed her. 'Something's wrong,' Sylvie said, and then, 'Peter called while he was here, and they're meeting downtown.'

'Can we reach Peter?' Hannah asked. 'We should call him back, tell him what's happening, warn him.'

Sylvie shook her head. 'He called from the airport, he's on his way. He's going directly to their meeting.'

'I'd like to kill that bastard Dolan,' Hannah said, her hand pulled up hard into a fist.

Chapter 14

'They suspect me,' she told Peter, her voice so wobbly, he had to ask her to repeat what she'd said.

'Wait a minute. Give me two seconds' breathing time, I just walked in the door.' He took off his field jacket and hung it in the front hall closet, then picked up his suitcase and made for the bedroom. 'Who suspects you?' he asked as he swung his suitcase onto the bed.

'The FBI, the police, they were questioning me, asking me did I leave her, did I want to leave her.' She leaned into the bed right near him, her fingers grabbing at the white tufts of the bedspread, then letting them go. 'I wanted to tell you,' she said, 'to warn you, but there was no way to reach you.' She hadn't looked at him, not straight on, really, since he'd come in the door. She hadn't wanted to see how he would look at her, but now when she tried, his eyes were on his luggage, helping his fingers find the zipper tab. 'Did he ask you about me, about me leaving her?' Peter was unzipping the suitcase, raising the lid. She thought of pushing it back down so he'd at least look at her. 'Did he ask you about me?' she repeated, her voice a brittle whine.

'Dolan, you mean?'

She couldn't sit still any longer, she was moving back and forth through the room, taking the corners of the bed nearly at a run. 'Yes, Dolan. Did he ask about me?'

'Sylvie, slow down,' he said, grabbing for her as she tried to pass behind him. 'Sit down.'

She tried to do what he said, but the best she could manage was to sort of hover over the double bed, rather than actually light upon it. 'Did he ask about me?'

'Yes, of course he did.' Peter lifted a shirt from the case, unfolded it, then put it down on the bed. 'He always asks about you and I'm sure he asks you about me, doesn't he?' She said yes, but that she thought it was completely different this time. 'It doesn't mean anything,' he said. 'Don't get so worked up over it.'

'Peter,' she said, squirming over to his side of the bed, pulling at the fabric of his shirt sleeve. 'I'm not making this up.' She'd caught his eyes, finally. 'He thinks I did something with Cally. What if he wants to arrest me – what are we going to do?'

'Arrest you?' She felt his body straighten back, away from her.

She nodded. 'We have to get a lawyer. My mother says we can't talk to him anymore without one.'

'Sylvie, a lawyer is not what we need here. All a lawyer will do is tell you not to answer questions. And all that will do is make Dolan more hot on the idea that you have something to hide, and believe me, that's not what you need just now because he's damn hot enough as it is.'

'What do you mean?' she asked, and she felt like she couldn't breathe, like the air had been completely sucked out of the room. She gripped his arm.

'I mean, if you want to know the truth, I *was* concerned about that session he had with me. Halfway through, I thought, Where the hell is he going with this? What's all this stuff about Sylvie's life doing here? But I thought maybe I was acting crazy – paranoid, you know? I thought, I'm not even going to mention this to Sylvie, but if you had the same reaction, hell, I don't know, there must be something to it.' He took her hand between his own while she moaned softly. She was choking, dying, maybe. She told herself to breathe slowly, that there must be air in the room, Peter was breathing perfectly well, and then, just when she thought she was going to pass out, she felt her lungs capitulate and open, but it hurt, it hurt to breathe.

Peter sat down next to her. 'We'll handle it, just don't panic, because you'll never get through this if you're running around being hysterical. Breathe,' he said softly, his hand pressing down gently on her shoulder. She *was* breathing now, but slowly, and each breath jarred her heart into a wickedly fast response. 'We're not rushing into anything. We'll think it through very, very carefully. I'll help you,' he promised. 'I'll coach you.'

'A lawyer,' she said, then nearly choked with the effort of turning breath into speech.

He nodded. 'I know what your mother thinks, but I just don't happen to agree. Your mother is a classic academic – whenever there's trouble, she thinks the answer is to bring in another academic with a higher degree than herself. She never uses plain old common sense. Common sense is downright scary to her. Don't forget she's the one who ranted on about how babies had to be born in hospitals, how you wouldn't survive, how the baby wouldn't survive, if you were so foolish as to use a midwife and have a home birth. Would you go back and do your delivery over without Julia, would you rather have had one of those doctors who couldn't remember who you were, and who would have had you on a stainless-steel table with your legs up in stirrups?' Sylvie shook her head. 'Right. Your mother probably still thinks we did it wrong. But we didn't. And we'll do this right, too, because we're intelligent, and we want to be in control of our own fates, right?' Sylvie nodded.

'Your mother doesn't think you can do anything on your own, and she's been telling you that your whole life. And Syl,' he said, lifting her chin so their eyes met, 'she's wrong. I'll tell her any day of the week. She is dead wrong about you.' He moved closer, brought his lips to hers, and kissed her. 'Your mother knows all kinds of stuff about early twentieth-century portraiture, but she doesn't know shit about anything outside that narrow little scope of hers. You need to keep her out of your life, because she's got lousy instincts on this one.' Sylvie nodded. 'Now, let's start really dealing with it, okay?'

'Yes.'

'Here's the thing: Dolan's decided you're telling inconsistent stories – which in police terms means your lying, making it up as you go along, or trying to figure what they want to hear at any given moment and giving it to them. He says you've got six different versions of how long you were at the store. You changed your mind three times about whether the French doors were locked, closed, wide-open, whatever.'

'I was upset. Nobody pays attention to that kind of stuff when it's happening.'

'Right. But it doesn't add up for them. You're calm on the 911 tape, but you tear the house apart.'

'So?'

'I'm just telling you what he's looking at.'

'He said that – that I'm inconsistent?'

'Yes.'

'Let them have an emergency, let's see how they behave!'

Peter shook his head. 'Don't get off the track here, Sylvie,' he warned her. 'This isn't about them. It's about you figuring out how to talk to them. You have to think first, you have to understand the implications of every single word you say.'

'I do,' she protested, flinging one hand wide.

'You don't. You haven't. For instance,' he said, and leaned toward her, 'why'd you tell him we were fighting?'

Sylvie felt her face color, her cheeks flare with heat. 'I don't think I said we were fighting.'

'No? He seems to think you did.'

'I might have said things were tense, something like that.'

Peter laughed. 'That's polite company phrasing for "We are fighting." Did you think for one tiny second about what he might do with that kind of information?'

She closed her eyes. 'What?' Her voice was a husky whisper.

'Sylvie, when parents aren't getting along, the child is often the one who takes the brunt of it.'

'But I meant *now*, because of the kidnapping – not before it. I can explain that to him. I'll call him, tell him.' She started to rise from the bed, but Peter held to her, kept her there.

'No. Don't give him yet another story. What I'm trying to tell you is you have to weigh every single word you speak. If you say we're fighting, or not getting along, or however you put it, little child-abuse bells go off in his head. Once you've said it, though, it's done. It's in his head. Any clarifying you try to do after that's said is simply going to make you seem defensive or scared, but worse, it'll just remind him of his original reaction: child abuse.'

'He asked me, Peter, he said, "How are you two getting along?"' Her voice was as thin as a child's. 'I couldn't lie to an FBI agent, could I?'

'Did he hold a gun to your head?'

'No, but it's like court, isn't it – don't you have to tell the truth?'

'You can leave things out, can't you?'

'What am I supposed to say – "It's none of your business"?'

'Is it his business what goes on between us in the privacy of our home?'

'No, but . . .'

'No, it isn't. You say we're getting along fine – that's enough. Fine is a wonderful word when you're being questioned. It keeps you out of trouble. More than that will do nothing toward bringing your baby back.' His voice was hard-edged, definite. He lifted a shirt from the travel bag, then turned to the closet and slipped it onto a hanger. He settled his black shoes in their regular place on the closet floor.

She lay back on the bed, next to the valise, her breathing achy in her chest. She hated Dolan tripping her up, catching at her with his lasso of words, laughing now, probably, at how easy she'd been.

Chapter 15

Peter would talk to Dolan. He could explain the inconsistencies without being too obvious. He'd catch up the loose ends. Fix it. Then they'd get off her back. And get working on the real problem, finding Cally. Hannah said, 'Chances are he doesn't really think you left her somewhere, he's just trying to impress his boss with how thorough he's being. And how utterly lacking in emotions he is, too.' Dolan's hair had a swath of white that cut through the darkness, right over his forehead; an unusual pattern, especially on one as young as he appeared to be. Hannah said it was an example of the chilling effect of his brain upon his surroundings. 'He could probably get a promotion just based on the slowness of his pulse rate,' Hannah observed.

'I doubt it,' Sylvie said. 'I think it turns him on to see me squirm.'

Sylvie waited for Peter, pacing out the whole living room and much of the rest of the apartment while he met Dolan for coffee downtown. She was at the door as soon as she heard his key in the lock. 'How'd it go?' she asked him before he'd even stepped inside.

'It was okay. I brought you back some muffins.' She didn't reach for the box he held out to her, didn't even look at it. 'I bought them when he was there, watching, because I thought it'd look good, you know, like I was thinking of you, like we were tight.'

'Good,' she commented. He put the box down on the floor, took off his field coat, then handed it to her, perhaps because he expected her to hang it up, but she dropped it down onto the same spot where the muffin box had ended up. 'How'd it go?'

she asked again. He'd moved to the couch, but she knew she couldn't keep still long enough to sit, so she stood in front of him, shifting from one foot to the other, trying not to actually begin pacing again.

'I guess it was something of a two steps forward, one step back routine, I'd clear up one thing and he'd immediately hit me with something else.'

'Like what?'

'I don't know. Like what your post-partum depression was like.'

'What'd you tell him?'

'I said you didn't have any.' She nodded. 'But then he said he thought that was very unusual, none at all – wasn't post-partum depression caused by hormones, and weren't you therefore certain to have had one? Or maybe you didn't have any hormones, he said. You know how he is. There was this implication that I was trying to put too good a face on it.'

'And?'

'And nothing. I wasn't going to backtrack and say, "Well, maybe she had a little depression."'

'I didn't anyway.'

'And then there was stuff he just implied, but didn't actually say outright.'

'Like?'

'Like you deliberately messed up the apartment to make it look ransacked, so it'd look like there'd been a break-in.'

'What'd you say to that?'

'I said that wasn't true. That you had done it out of confusion and grief.'

'I told him I was looking for the baby.'

'Well, I think he accepted the idea of confusion, whatever.'

'Good.' She was nodding, small little non-stop movements of her head.

'I said I *think* he accepted it, Sylvie. I can't read his mind, you know.'

'Well, of course I know that, but you do think he accepted it, it seemed like he did, right?' She bent now, bringing her face level with his, but he turned away.

'Maybe this wasn't such a fabulous idea, backtracking with him this way, I just don't know.'

She sat down abruptly on the couch. 'Peter, you're the one who suggested it. Why'd you do it if you didn't think it was going to work?'

'Jesus, Sylvie, I am not a miracle worker, understand? You want to give it a try?'

'You told me that would be a disaster. You were the one who nixed that.'

'And I still say no. But it doesn't mean I'm going to get every detail right, okay?'

'Okay, okay.' She took in a deep breath through opened lips, shuddered, then let it go. 'Peter,' she said, her voice nearly strangled by the terror that rose in her throat, 'Cally could be dying somewhere while they waste time going over and over this stuff about me.'

'I know, but this isn't an exact science we're dealing with. We're just going to have to do what we can; operate on instinct and then be satisfied with the results.'

'What else did he ask?' Peter took a deep breath, didn't speak for what seemed like the longest time. 'What, Peter?' she asked him.

'He keeps going back to this business about how calm you were on the 911 tape.'

'I needed to get the police here. I *needed* to be calm.' Her hand was curled into a tight fist.

'Yes, I told him that.' He looked up at her. 'But Sylvie, he doesn't believe it.'

She stared at him. 'What does he think, then?'

'He thinks you were calm because you had it all worked out, like a script with a step-by-step procedure all written out. That the hysteria was put on once the police were here to see it.'

Sylvie rocked back and forth. 'They should be looking for her, Peter, this is horrible.'

'He thinks the police may have gotten here faster than you thought they would. That something was missing, that you took off for the Grove to get that something, then either couldn't find it or realized you didn't have enough time.'

127

'It was the baby I couldn't find, Peter.'

'Sylvie,' he said, his voice a muted, hesitant appeal. 'They think you can help them.'

Sylvie stopped rocking and stared at him. 'What does that mean?'

'It means,' he said, pausing, gathering his voice, 'they think you know where she is, and Dolan asked me . . .' He stopped speaking.

'Asked you what?' She saw his chest rise and rise, like he was taking in all the air in the room. 'What?' she shrilled at him.

'He wanted me to ask you if you know where she is.'

She stood up, clutched at the fabric of her turtleneck, it was so tight, so suffocating. 'I don't know where she is, Peter,' she said, her voice surging through the sentence so that the sound of his name filled the room. He looked away. And then she felt so dizzy, she had to sit back down, lower her head to her hands.

'It needed asking,' he said, and she thought to herself, I will never look up at him, I will never speak to him again, I will wait here, head down, till he leaves. And she waited through the stuffy silence till she felt him rise off the couch, heard his footsteps go to the other side of the room. He wanted her to speak, she could feel it in the tight sounds of his labored breathing, then the throat-clearing, the short, shuffled steps first to one side then the other, all these sounds coming into the air and dissipating. And still she waited. Her back had begun to ache from being bent over. And of course he wasn't going to go away.

She lifted her head and sat back up. 'Do you think I took her somewhere, Peter? Do you think I gave my daughter away?' He had his back to her, his hands raised high on the window frame, looking out. 'How can you think such a thing?' she asked him without waiting for his answer.

He turned to face her. 'I don't know. It's these questions, all these questions; he makes it seem so logical, I guess. He lays it out, boom, boom, boom,' he said, striking the side of his hand against his other open palm with each repetition, 'and it starts to sound so seamless.'

'Tell me, then, tell me what he lays out,' she said, walking toward him, repeating his hand-striking gesture, 'and let me be the judge of exactly how seamless it is.'

'There's nothing, really,' he said, gesturing as though to push a tangible mass away from his face. 'Let's forget it.'

'No,' she said, grabbing for his arm. 'Tell me, what do you say to all this? Do you say, "Oh, yeah, that must be it"?'

She could hear traffic going by outside, and a bus pulling to a stop, brakes squeaking, gears grinding, and then the low rumble of the wheels as they found the center of the road once more. She heard a car horn. A siren, too, though that was far distant. 'You were supposed to be steering him away from me, Peter.'

'I know that,' he said. 'I'm just telling you he's a very devious guy. He turns things inside out. Maybe you're right, neither of us should be talking to him.'

Sylvie felt the sudden sting of milk pierce through her nipples. She pulled her arms up tight against her breasts to stop the flow. 'What about my milk?' she said to him.

'What about it?'

'Why would I keep it? I wouldn't be expressing my milk if I thought she was never coming back, would I?' He had turned back to the window again, given her more silence, more time to identify two dogs barking at one another, a garbage truck beginning its compacting operation.

'It can be explained. There's a different way to look at everything.'

'Explain it to me, then.'

He shrugged. 'Could be a way of making people *think* you expect her back.' She shook her head. 'Or maybe,' he said, one finger pointed toward her, 'at first you were so distraught by whatever it was that you'd done, you convinced yourself she was coming back. You really believed the story you made up.' She shook her head again. 'Maybe you thought if you had the milk that you were still her mother, and that it could somehow erase what you'd done to her.'

'What are you saying, what do you mean, *what I did to her*?'

'I'm sorry,' he said, his voice dismissive, and he'd begun to walk away from her.

'What?' she shouted after him. 'What do you think I did?' He'd turned into the hallway. She was following right behind. 'What is it you think I did? Do you think I killed her?'

He stopped, turned toward her. 'I don't think you meant to,' he said.

'You think I could do such a thing, kill my baby?'

'I said, I don't think it was deliberate. Something happened, I don't know what, maybe it was some kind of accident. With a baby,' he said, looking into his uplifted, open palm as though Cally lay right there, 'they're so tiny, it doesn't take much.'

Sylvie's milk was flowing now, hot like tears down her chest, along her belly. 'I never hurt her, Peter.'

'I believe you never meant to hurt her. I believe that. But I also believe that now you need help in coming to terms with this. With remembering clearly what you really did.'

Sylvie's legs were giving way – she could barely stand. She nearly fell against the wall, leaning into its support. 'I have no trouble remembering,' she insisted, her words tight.

He hadn't moved. It was as though he were a giant statue guarding an entryway, she thought. 'I've heard of things like this,' he said, his voice soft, as though he reminisced of times past. 'The baby cries, the mother shakes it or squeezes it.' She watched his hand rise in a tight fist, watched the sudden jerk of his wrist and had to turn away. 'And then it's done,' he continued. 'It's one of those bad things that can happen to good people. It takes just a second. Then the mother, her brain won't accept that. Won't believe it, and she goes into some override condition to block it out. Her mind would want to pretend it happened some other way. You'd look for explanations everywhere, so as to make it be something other than you having done it.'

'She was asleep,' Sylvie said quietly.

'And?' Peter asked.

'And then she was gone.'

'Yes,' he said. 'Exactly.' He took a step toward her, but she slid back away along the wall.

'Did you tell him, Dolan, did you say you thought I did something to her?'

He shook his head. 'I only answered his questions.' He stared at her. 'I don't think anything's going to happen to you, Sylvie. Not if they don't find the body.'

'Stop,' she shouted at him.

'I'm just saying it's unlikely it'll come to a trial.'

She'd put her hands over her ears before he even began his sentence. She turned her eyes toward the ceiling, remembering the little face, the soft round cheeks, the white hair, the tiny red mouth. She dropped her hands to her shoulders.

'Perhaps this is the point at which you should get a lawyer,' he said slowly, his eyes opening wide, looking to catch hers, and for a moment, she let him hold her there, visually, her body swaying as though she tottered on a rock in a stream, trapped by the swiftly moving water, yet searching, still, for the next foothold.

'She was here,' Sylvie said, and a shiver went up her back. 'She was here,' she repeated, this time moving toward the bedroom, pointing, thinking he would follow and she would show him, as she'd shown Martinson, exactly where Cally had lain, head here, up against the end, feet curled under her, but he wasn't following; in fact, he'd gone into the other bedroom. 'I did go out,' she said as she passed into the room. 'I know I shouldn't have, I'm sorry, but that's what I did. I went out. But someone, not me, took her, Peter, I swear to God, I swear it to you,' she said, coming back to where he stood and dropping to her knees in front of him. 'I swear I didn't hurt her.'

'I think,' he said, one hand coming down to light on her head, 'that I need to leave for a while. I need the space. I'm going out to visit my brother for a while, two weeks maybe, I'm not sure. I can work from out there as easily as from here. And then when I come back, I'm going to move out. I've found a small place for myself. I'm hoping I can sign the lease this afternoon. It'll be better. Maybe things will start to sift down properly; maybe you'll start to remember some more things, especially if you don't have to put up such a front for me.' She had her arms around his knees and she could feel the resistance, the stiff fierceness of him. He pushed against her hold, one knee leading toward a stride. She held tighter, he pushed harder. 'Sylvie, I don't want to hurt you,' he said, his voice thick with disgust. She let him go.

'I'm going to pack,' he told her.

Chapter 16

That afternoon, perhaps only an hour or two after Peter had left the house, one of the agents who manned the phones in the basement knocked on Sylvie's door. 'I just wanted to let you know we're all finished down there,' he said.

'Finished with what?' she asked him, confused for a moment into thinking this had something to do with the coffee cake Hannah had brought down to them a few days earlier. Was this a coy request for new refreshments?

'Didn't Agent Dolan tell you we'd be terminating our station?' She shook her head. 'Oh, well, then I'll be the one to give you the good news. We're taking out the phone.'

'Good news?' she asked. Her heart was pounding. 'Have they found her?'

'No, not that good, I'm afraid,' he said, holding up his hand so as to halt that line of thinking. 'It's just the FBI's off the case now, so, of course, he's taken our tracers off, too.'

'Off the case? Why?'

'Actually, I don't know that myself. He'll fill you in. You've got his number, don't you?' She said she did.

When he had gone, she felt dizzy; exhilarated, too, like she'd just finished a long, hard run. '*All* right,' she said aloud, raising a fist aloft. 'That bastard's finally off my back.'

She was asleep on the couch, deeply asleep, probably for the first time since Cally had disappeared, when Martinson came round later. When she finally floated up into consciousness, it was to the realization that he'd been knocking for a long time – she'd heard it in her dream as a brightly colored red and yellow woodpecker perched on a tree in the courtyard. She stumbled toward the door, not really even fully awake, and let him in.

'There's been a change,' he said. She combed her fingers back through her hair. She knew she probably looked like a rag. 'The FBI's dropping the case.'

'I know,' she said. 'They've taken out the phone line.' He nodded.

'Do you want some coffee?' she asked him. She'd noticed that he hadn't brought his own this time. Didn't he always?

'Not for me,' he said. But she wanted her stuff. She pulled the plastic bottle of Pepsi from the fridge and poured herself a full mug. 'How can you drink so much of that?' Martinson asked. 'And I never see you eat anything. Do you take all your nourishment out of that junk?'

'It's no worse than your coffee, is it? And I never see you eat.' Something was definitely bugging him. He was picking up her loose change from the counter, spinning the quarters. 'Where's your fix today?'

'I didn't have time to pick any up. I had some things I needed to tell you about.'

'What?' she asked, and that cold feeling flowed through her swift as a river. She closed her eyes – better they should never find Cally, she thought, than find her dead. 'Is it something bad about Cally?' she managed to ask, putting the words together slowly as though they had to be snapped and connected one to the other like cars in a child's pull train.

'No, we've nothing new. I came to tell you the FBI is leaving the case because it's no longer part of their jurisdiction.'

'Good.'

He shook his head. Where was the laughter? 'It may not be that good.'

'Why not?'

'They're leaving because they don't think there was a kidnapping.'

'What do you mean?' she said, but she knew. It had to do with her.

'They've turned it back to us. It's a local issue now.'

She was shaking again. Shivering too. 'Are you here to

134

arrest me?' He shook his head. She turned from him so he couldn't see the tears. 'I didn't hurt my baby.' The words were soft, delicate as gauze.

'Do you know where she is?'

She lowered her head and whispered her response. 'No. Do you think I did something to her?'

'No. But you should understand that that's a clear minority opinion. You *are* a suspect, Sylvie, and I'd be doing you an injustice to hide that truth from you.' His voice was solemn and measured. Like a terrible, quiet warning, she thought. 'See,' he continued, 'there's not a lot here that points elsewhere. There's no evidence of a break-in, for one thing. And you and Peter aren't high-visibility people with tons of money who'd be obvious targets for a big ransom.'

'But a crazy person,' she broke in. 'A crazy person who just wants a baby?'

'Dolan believes there isn't any indication of the presence of anyone else. He puts together a good story, I'm afraid. My boss, Brown, he likes Dolan, too. The department, they like his story, too. See, Dolan's got all these diagrams and charts that he loves to draw.' Martinson's raised hand moved phantom chalk in scribbles across an imaginary blackboard. 'He gets the details to add up. He's thorough as hell. And so damn sure, too, and you never feel anything tentative in his voice. He says, Sylvie Pierson can't finish a project. She lets fortune-tellers direct her life. Her boyfriend won't marry her. She's quit a dozen jobs in frustration. And, of course, he gets a real charge out of feeding things into computers and flashing print-outs around. And he talks about "preponderance."' Martinson crisped the word up exactly as Dolan might have. 'Like, "a preponderance of impulsive behaviors," that kind of thing. Me, I see there's careful, attentive behaviors, too, but he doesn't want to put that on his charts, it mucks them up too much. He wants patterns, and he wants them clean and easy to read. I don't think people are simple like that. But I get a feel for them, just the same.' He stopped, looked at her, then quickly added, as though perhaps he'd said too much a moment before, 'How you do things in this world isn't by columns and numbers. All that gets you is the bottom line on your taxes. Take weather reporting,' he said. 'You know how many people have tried outsmarting the weather? You know all those fancy multicolor maps you see on the tube? That radar stuff where they put the clouds in motion across the Northeast?' He moved an open palm in slow arcs in front of himself. 'Sometimes it's right, sometimes it's wrong. Those people who dedicate their lives to figuring it out can't say for sure whether those clouds won't blow off in some other direction before they get to you. I saw a show once, one of those what's-new-in-science ones, and they said the world's fastest and biggest computer still can't do any better than the average person's best guess when it comes to predicting weather. I tell tomorrow's weather by smelling the air and listening to the wind. And I'm right as often as the computers are.'

He was talking so fast, so long, like he was trying to divert her attention or something. She didn't care about science programs or the weather. What was wrong with him that he couldn't see that? 'What about the dogs? He sent dogs around, sniffing the neighborhood. They didn't find anything, what about that?' she said, returning him, she hoped, to the subject.

'He doesn't try to explain that, except to say dogs don't always pick up a trail. He finds his evidence still outweighs their failure.'

'Peter thinks I did something to her.' Her voice had gone whispery on her.

'You have to remember that Agent Dolan is awfully convincing,' Martinson observed. 'I'm not surprised Peter's taken up his point of view. People want answers, and when they're hurting, they're willing to believe anything. Almost any solution will do if it reads smoothly enough.'

'Seamlessly, you mean? That's what Peter said. Dolan made it sound so seamless, he said.'

'That's Dolan's special skill, yes.'

'Oh God,' she moaned, 'why does this man hate me so much?'

'I'm sure he doesn't hate you. You don't feel things like love and hate toward a puzzle piece, which is what you are to him. He's a law enforcement officer. And any such officer knows, much too well, that you never get all the information. There's always blocks of time, for instance, that can't be explained. What he does – what we all do – is line up the pieces he does have, in their proper order, then he proposes possibilities for what happened in the spaces that fall between. Not randomly, you understand, but thoughtfully, projecting missing pieces from what he does have.'

'But these are the wrong pieces! I'm not like that.'

'Yes, but they're also the pieces that fit his end result, the result he wants. He comes up with his hunch, then he puts the data in to explain that conclusion, and suddenly he's got a story with no obvious holes in it.'

'But it's the wrong story. It's a story that's going to put me in jail. Why is he doing this when he knows it isn't true?'

'He doesn't know it isn't true. I promise you, he believes it. Because the pieces make sense to him now. They make sense to other officers and to Peter. And they'll make sense to his superiors, and to a jury – if it comes to that.'

'He *must* hate me.'

'It's his job, that's all.'

'Well, I hate him.'

'Of course you would.' He stepped off a pace from her, his lips parted, hovering over words that fluttered, briefly, unspoken, between them.

'What?' she asked, her voice plaintive, needing to know.

'I've asked Brown to drop our case here. To close the local investigation as well.'

She started shaking her head, like she could shake off what he'd said that way. He'd turned his eyes toward the door. 'Wait a minute,' she said. 'What are you saying? Are you trying to get them to stop looking for Cally?'

'Yes, but only because if the Department stays in this, they'll go for you now, Sylvie, and just you. They'll find more and more little pieces about you that'll bridge the gaps in Dolan's story. They'll find something in every word you've said, in everything you've done. They won't be looking for Cally at all.'

She lowered her head. 'They'll arrest me,' she said, and she felt the hairs rise up along her arms.

'Not if I get it dropped, and that's what I'm working on, bit by bit. I'm pushing the idea of insufficient evidence on them, and I'm talking them all toward thinking inactive on this.' She was shaking her head, not seeing him anymore. 'Sylvie,' he said, and he waited till she looked toward him, till he knew she'd hear what came next. 'I've got to slow them down. If there's no pressure to solve this, they're very unlikely to come looking for you. They'll start concentrating their energy on other cases.'

'And what's going to happen to my baby?' she asked, her hand clutching at her own throat.

'You need to find Cally.'

'Of course I need to find Cally,' she said, her voice wobbly, trying to be shrill, but collapsing into soft puddled words. 'Hasn't that been true all along? Isn't that what you're supposed to be doing, what Dolan and Brown and all of you are supposed to be doing, finding her?'

'Yes and no,' Martinson said, then looked toward the window.

'What do you mean?' she demanded of him.

'Explaining,' he said slowly, 'is what Dolan's after. What we're all after, I suppose. Making sense of a strange, unpredictable world.'

'Then what good are you, Detective?' She spun round, away from him. 'I want my baby – I don't give a good goddamn about how the universe is organized.'

'I'll try to help you,' he said, his hand coming up unseen, behind her, then falling into place on her shoulder. She started at the touch of his fingers on her neck. 'I mean to help,' he said, and after a few moments, because he was the only help she had now, she nodded.

Chapter 17

There was a limit to the outside world's tolerance and understanding, Hannah was learning. Bills still had to be paid, deadlines had to be met, classes had to be taught. People expressed concern, of course. Gregory, Hannah's chairman, for instance, said he knew just how much pressure she was under, how difficult – tragic, he said – it all was, but she did need to get her students back on a regular class schedule. 'If you need help with preparation or grading,' he offered, 'don't hesitate to call on me. But don't, please, stop giving assignments altogether.'

She appreciated his patience, she told him. She had it under control. It would all get done, never fear. And he needn't worry, she would reschedule the classes that she'd missed and it would all be made up with the students. Things had settled down, she told him, which perhaps was true, perhaps not, but did it matter exactly how she phrased it to Gregory? What was true was that her life had been altered, and that it was, clearly, not a temporary change. This is how life is going to be from now on, she told herself. This is my new real world, and it's time to find some way to function in it.

And this she was trying to do. She was showing up three times a week at nine-thirty for her lecture class and finding her way also to her two afternoons of seminars. It was the concentration she still couldn't muster. She'd sit down to prepare a class and realize an hour, perhaps more, had passed in which she hadn't written a single word on her legal pad and class was only fifteen or twenty minutes in the future. She'd taught for enough years to be able to wing her way through most of it, coming up with tidbits about the artist and the period as she stood at the lectern. When things got bad enough, she'd ask students to fill in with information they were supposed to have gleaned from the reading assignments.

'Here,' she said, clicking a slide up on the screen in the darkened Morris Hall, 'is Renoir's *Le Bal à Bougival*, an utterly charming rendition of a couple dancing at a café. What could be simpler than this elemental meeting? She wears white, he wears blue so dark it might as well be black. But note,' she said in that full-bodied lecture voice she'd learned to cultivate, 'how they lean toward one another and yet away, all at the same time. What tension!' she gushed, and then stopped. She was definitely overdoing the enthusiastic art scholar business, but just now, unfortunately, it was necessary. If she didn't pump up the language that way, she'd be thinking about Cally or Sylvie and she'd be staring into space. The florid verbiage worked to drag her physically into contact with her students. 'Can't you feel the heat of that energy wherever their bodies touch? His black knee crosses her white dress, her white hand crosses his black jacket, making the viewer's eye spiral up and down along their bodies, virtually turning them into a whirlwind of black and white. At the height of this cyclonic whirl, we have a wonderful splash of color – the woman's orange bonnet and the man's yellow hat, touching, overlapping, an intense flash of heat that draws us to their faces, and to the possibility of a kiss, or, perhaps, more. Such marvelous, palpable anticipation. We're caught right up in their longing. Look, too, at the motion in the flounces of that lovely white dress, how the upturn of the skirt gives us the revelation of the lacy petticoat beneath. Remember,' she asked them rhetorically, 'how we talked about Renoir's polished paint tones, the jewel-like colors he uses against the simple backgrounds? These are reminders of his youthful work as a painter of porcelains, of how his brush must have put down hundreds of thousands of dots of paint that were to become petals of flowers on fine white china. See this fine edging of orange along her dress?' Hannah asked, moving the pointer, following the path of color as it traveled toward the woman's face. 'Doesn't it remind you of a border on a dinner plate? Of course it draws our attention not to food, but rather to the dancer's lips.

'Now,' she continued, 'we've talked about Renoir's love of high contrast. We've seen over and over how he plays complementary colors against one another, how he contrasts textures, as well as lights and darks. Here we see, too, how he plays with contrasting subject matter. Just look at the frankness of this young woman's face, how she's turned nearly full face toward us, at how,' she said, pausing dramatically, 'she's fully revealed to us. Yet he, this huge presence, is almost as effectively hidden from us as if he were behind a wall. His clothes are dark and loose-fitting, showing us nothing of his body's form. His hat covers his eyes and half his face, and his beard and mustache cover half of what remains. He is nothing, an unknown. So we have the delicate female, the ponderous man.'

She let the pointer fall on one figure, then the other. She preferred the old-fashioned pointer to the small projected arrow the rest of the department used, for she liked the sound of the stick as it hit the screen, thought it probably helped keep awake those who tended to drift toward sleep in the dark. 'The candid woman, the secretive, absent man,' and again the pointer dropped down upon them in turn. 'But what is romance,' she asked them, 'if not some fine amalgamation of beauty and mystery like this?'

Here she stopped, as she always did, to glance at the painting one last time, so as to catch something new, along with her students, and to give them a few moments, too, to ask questions. When she turned toward the huge screen, she was struck by how vulnerable the woman appeared – perhaps it was the fullness of the face, the forever-baby quality of those pudgy cheeks – a bit like Sylvie there, she thought. She straightened up, though, and drew her thoughts back to Renoir.

'In this master we have contrast and duality,' she intoned slowly. 'Look again: Is the motion *toward* this would-be lover or *away*?' she asked, and she heard a murmur of conflicting answers from her audience. 'We cannot know. Just as we cannot, as Renoir hints, know the true nature of courtship or of loving. But you might ask, under the circumstances . . .' she said, turning back toward the painting, forgetting her hanging sentence, seeing, yes, something else now – that thrust of his

141

jaw. Didn't that jutting chin twist his features into something very like a snarl? She could almost hear the whispered threats. That heavily veiled condescension. What was it Sylvie had reported he'd said? 'I don't think you meant to hurt her.' Yes, that was it. 'This happens,' Martinson had said. 'People lose faith in each other when they're deep in despair. They turn against one another.'

She heard a confusion of restless whispers from behind her. 'Yes,' she said, standing straight again. 'Perhaps there are some questions here we haven't considered before. For instance, do we want him to kiss her? Does she want that kiss?' Then she stared again at the painting, her back to her audience. Hannah had the urge to reach toward the enormous screen and draw them apart, to unhinge the helix of their bodies. 'Look,' she said to her students, out there, somewhere in the dark, 'how she turns away from him. Look at all the questions Renoir poses to us: Who is this man? Why are his eyes completely obscured by that hat? He's not charming at all, really, is he? Brutish, perhaps clumsy, too, in those dark, ill-fitting clothes.' She stopped. The man was an oaf, his leg pushing relentlessly toward his partner, spoiling the delicate white fabric, and he was too heavy, too unkempt under that stupid straw bowler. 'I see polite fear written all over that poor girl's face,' she said, then immediately called for the lights. The moment they were on, she gathered up her papers. 'Thank you,' she said, 'we'll finish next time,' and she headed fast for the exit.

She ran to her office. Took the stairs two at a time, fumbled badly with the key in the lock, then grabbed at the phone from the near side of her desk and punched at the buttons, her fingers awkward and stupid at the task. 'Sylvie,' she said, her voice broken from her run. 'I've got this very weird feeling about Peter. I can't really explain it – it might be nothing. It's just a funny feeling.'

'It's real,' Sylvie said, her voice cutting sharply into Hannah's vague phrases. 'He's taken every penny out of the bank account.'

Chapter 18

'You have to remember,' Martinson lectured her, 'there isn't anything illegal in a person withdrawing funds that are in his name. No second signature is required on a withdrawal slip for a joint account.'

'But it isn't the right thing to do, the fair thing,' Sylvie said, and Hannah thought Martinson almost laughed. Certainly he took in that long breath before he responded. Suppressed the laugh, maybe.

'All I'm saying is, fair is different from legal. We're not talking about a crime here. I can't put out a bulletin on him. I couldn't arrest him if he were standing right here. Even if he were still in the state and it *were* a crime, personally I wouldn't be so quick to press charges against him because all it'll do is get his back up. It isn't going to make him behave more fairly toward you.'

'I have no money,' Sylvie pointed out, the belligerence directed full-frontal at the detective.

'Chances are you'll hear from him in a day or two. He'll have thought it over, and he'll arrange to get the money back to you. I'm willing to bet he'll tell you he was all screwed up, that it was a terrible mistake.'

'But he's also accused me of murdering our child. He hasn't taken that back.'

'I know. He's looking for an easy explanation, and so are you. And I'm personally not buying either version. I'm seeing the usual blame-placing stuff, is all. Let's talk about what needs to be done. Maybe you can make some headway with the bank, tell them they should have consulted you before the withdrawal. They weren't required to, but maybe they'll give you some kind of loan for the interim. If that doesn't work, you could try telling them you're in discussion with your lawyer about why they allowed the withdrawal. Maybe that'd make them a little nervous, make them a little more helpful.'

'But there's nothing you can do as a police officer?'

He shook his head. 'If you want, when he comes back, I'll talk to him about the stress – non-cop stuff – see where I can get with him, but right now there's nothing I can do.'

'It's not a therapist we need,' Sylvie said.

'This is what I can give you. I'm sorry if it's not enough.' He started for the door and Sylvie followed him. 'I see this all the time,' he told her. 'Emptying a bank account is pretty standard, angry stuff. At least he's not destroying your property. I've seen that, too.'

So, she thought after Martinson and Hannah had left, if the police were backing out, she'd track Peter down herself. She'd figure out what the hell he was up to. She'd call his brother. Call his mother, too, or whatever it took to put some pressure on him. To make him shape up. And she'd get some money out of him, too, while she was at it.

She dialed Salt Lake City directory assistance and asked for the number of William Weston. 'I have no one listed under that name,' the cool voice of the operator came back at her.

'How about Bill or Will or just the initial *W* or *B*?' she suggested.

'Nothing under those, either.'

'Do you have a Peter?' she asked. Maybe Bill had never changed the phone out of his brother's name.

'Nothing.'

'Maybe I have the wrong first name. Maybe that's his middle name, or his nickname. Could you tell me what names you do have listed for Weston?'

'Ingrid,' the operator told her.

Sylvie waited in silence for the woman to continue her list. 'Ingrid?' Sylvie said, thinking the repetition might encourage her to continue.

'Yes.'

'And that's it? That's the only Weston in Salt Lake City?'

144

'Yes.' Sylvie asked for the number, waited for the orderly computer voice to dictate it to her, then dialed.

Ingrid Weston's voice sounded thin but expectant. Sylvie apologized for disturbing her. 'I'm looking for Bill or Peter Weston,' she explained.

'There's just me here now, no other Westons anymore,' the woman said. 'My husband died eighteen years ago, and my daughter lives in Seattle now. But of course she's not a Weston anymore, anyway. She married David Sloane, so she's a Sloane now.'

'And you don't know any Bill or Peter Weston in Salt Lake?'

'No, I can't say I do, but it is a big city.'

'They're Mormons,' Sylvie said.

The woman laughed. 'Every other one of us is, dear.'

'Their parents are out there, too,' Sylvie said, suddenly remembering that connection. 'Rose, I think is the mother's name. I think the father's name might be William, too, but I'm not sure.'

'Could they live out in South Salt Lake, or Murray, one of the towns?'

'Oh, right,' Sylvie said. 'He said Salt Lake, but it could be anywhere out there, really, couldn't it?'

'Midvale, or Sandy City or Draper.'

'Do you know Westons out there?'

'No, dear, I don't really know anyone out there. I just meant you could try those towns.' Sylvie wrote down the names she'd mentioned, then asked for more. When Mrs Weston couldn't come up with any more names, Sylvie thanked her and apologized again.

'No bother at all,' Mrs Weston said. 'I'm glad to help. Call again.'

She found nine more Westons, but no William, Peter, or Rose. She dialed each of them anyway, asked questions to those who answered, left messages on machines for those who didn't. She expanded her search further, asking each voice she reached for the names of other Westons, or simply, other towns. Occasionally she'd stop for a while, convinced that he

145

must have been trying to call her while she tied up the phone. But then she'd start calling again. Doing something, even something that by the minute was becoming more and more obviously fruitless, seemed better than just empty waiting.

Just after one o'clock Hannah came by again. 'I've been trying you for two hours,' she said as she slipped off her coat. 'Who've you been talking to?'

'Everybody in Salt Lake City who's named Weston.'

'And?'

She shook her head. 'Nobody. At least, so far.'

Sylvie took her into the kitchen and showed her the list of numbers that she'd made. Hannah took a deep breath. 'Could it be unlisted?' she asked.

'I suppose it might be. But if it is, he knows it's unlisted and he knows I won't be able to find him. He's hiding, plain and simple.'

'Maybe you could call that place at the mall where he used to work.'

'For what?'

'They have to have some kind of records on him – a telephone number for a previous employer, say. You call there and get his number where he used to live. Isn't that supposedly where he is now, back at his brother's place?'

Sylvie had already gone for the phone book. 'Now we're hot,' she said with a smile. But Shawn Decker, the personnel manager at Best Security, said he couldn't give out such information. 'I'm his wife,' she lied to him.

'You two got married?'

'Yeah, last month.' She held her breath, waiting for him to claim he'd just spoken to Peter and how he'd mentioned he was still single.

'Then how come you don't already have that information?'

'Because he never told me,' she said, and felt herself break out into a full body sweat. 'It isn't something married people talk about, you know, telephone numbers of employers they had before they even met each other.'

'But can't he give it to you now?'

'No,' she said, and the blood was surging through her head so vigorously she could hardly think of what to say next. 'He's gone out there on business and he forgot to leave me his number. He's got an unlisted number and the phone company refuses to give it to me. I thought if I could get his old work telephone number I'd call there and they'd get in touch with him for me. It's an emergency. Something's come up and I have to reach him.' She could hear her own rapid breathing against the receiver.

'I want to help,' he assured her.

'Then what's the problem?' she demanded of him.

'How do I know you're you? You could be anybody. You could be one of those tabloids, wanting to do something on the kidnapping. I can't just give out information on the phone. It's not right.'

'If I came in?' she asked. Her mother stood next to her now, leaning toward the receiver, trying to pick up his voice.

'I suppose I could give it to you then.'

'I'll be right there,' she told him.

They welcomed her as though she were a Hollywood starlet returning home. Shawn Decker and his crew of security personnel were lined up at their computer consoles, gaping at her as she came through the door. So this is celebrity, she thought as Decker rolled a chair over to her side and asked her how she took her coffee, and whether they couldn't perhaps get her something to eat.

But she knew they only wanted to hear about it; to plumb for the juicy details that the papers had failed to provide. She was likely to be better fun than the tabloids Decker had claimed so to fear. She started to refuse the offer of refreshments, then thought better of it – perhaps they had things to tell her, too. About Peter. Perhaps they even knew where he was.

She sat with them: Damien, who she remembered as the one Peter had had difficulty with, April, a co-worker whose high cheekbones blazed with blusher, and Cadge, Peter's very young replacement.

They showed her how it all worked, what Peter had done when he had, once upon a time, sat in the same chair Cadge now sat in, how he, too, had checked through a bank of twenty-four screens, each focused down on a spot in the mall below, each capable of zooming in on an individual or an act of crime.

'God, how do you keep up with it?' she asked. 'All those stores, all those screens?' Two sips into her coffee she'd decided to ask as many questions as she could so there wouldn't be any empty spaces for them to poke questions at her about Cally.

'It actually gets pretty boring,' Damien told her. 'It's not like much happens. You watch people go into a store, you watch them touch a few things or move some pieces of clothing along a rack, and then they leave. You log in the time you checked the store, and then you move on to the next monitor.'

'Some days the biggest challenge is trying to stay awake,' April said. At the moment, Cadge was the only one of them checking screens.

'But of course if it wasn't boring, you and Peter would never have met,' Decker said, and the others laughed.

'And I'll tell you one thing, though, he didn't follow you very long before he went down to the floor,' Damien reported.

'What do you mean?' she asked, and the three of them grew silent, though Damien's eyes opened wide toward April, and Sylvie saw April do the same in return.

'Didn't he tell you he'd seen you on the screen first?' she asked Sylvie. Sylvie shook her head. April was letting her desk chair, anchored by her feet, swing from side to side. Sylvie watched her knees, narrow and white below her leather miniskirt, dance left, then right. 'Well, that's all, he saw you on the screen. Then he went down to the floor.'

'Why was he watching me?' She gripped the edge of her chair.

'Hey,' Damien said, with a dismissive shake of his hand. 'It was no big deal, just forget it.'

'See,' April said, stopping her chair suddenly so that her knees pointed straight at Sylvie, 'he started this thing, this game, where we watched people to break up the monotony. We were fooling around, you know? We'd find somebody on the screen – anybody – and then we'd follow them around, trying not to lose them, like we do for a real suspect. It was to have something to do, that's all. What we're supposed to be doing here is trying to catch people who are shoplifting. But we're here eight hours a day, not counting lunch, and in that eight hours we get maybe, at most, a half dozen possible suspicious types, right?' she asked, turning raised eyebrows to each of the men in turn.

'Right,' Damien confirmed. 'And most of those just turn out to be your plain old weirdos, no felonious intent, if you know what I mean.'

'Peter was the one said if we were following somebody all the time, the whole job would be easier to take. So he started following people, just anybody, they didn't have to be suspicious. He'd follow a mother, say, and her two kids, watch where they went, what kind of things they did, or he'd check out an old couple, try to guess which food place they were headed for. It's a whole lot more fun than logging from camera A to B to C to D, in the same old order, hour after hour, every day.'

'And that was allowed?' she asked, looking toward Decker.

'Hey, as long as the logs get done right, that's all that matters. It's not one of my personal life goals to be Mr Mean Machine here, you know.'

'It's a kind of spying, though, isn't it?'

Shawn Decker laughed. 'You don't think all of this isn't spying anyway?' he asked, his hand sweeping past the three walls of screens. 'Every time you're down there, we're watching what you're doing. We're watching you in the dressing room, too, you know, some of the stores anyway.' He walked over to the console where April was seated and told Sylvie to look at a screen toward the middle of the bank. First she saw a table piled with sweaters, then that image disappeared and she was looking at a woman in a dressing room pulling a sweater on over her head. He pressed a button, and there was another woman, entering a dressing room, another button, and another dressing room, this one empty; another button, and a woman was undoing her skirt. Sylvie recognized the decor of the dressing room – she'd changed in there herself.

'But I'm the only one who does the women's fitting rooms,' April clarified. 'And I switch them off if one of the guys is

149

standing by me.' The camera zoomed in on a profile of the woman's face. Sylvie turned away from the screen.

'Dressing rooms is where we catch the most people. Dropping things into their shopping bags, or so-called forgetting to take a shirt off. If people didn't steal, we wouldn't have to watch, of course,' Decker continued.

Sylvie looked toward another bank of screens, saw people sitting on benches eating, walking through stores, laughing together, sorting through bins of CDs. 'This is really weird,' she said. 'After he went down there, did you all sit up here watching?' None of them answered. 'I mean, did you watch him pick me up?' She was thinking about all that stuff he said about how fate had brought them together. Her face flushed with the memory of her mother's laugh-swollen words, 'Fate, Sylvie?' And the whole goddamn thing was staged for his stupid co-workers. She must have looked like a real jerk to them, practically passing out while she watched him come toward her. Great. He was doing it to break up the monotony. 'Well, thanks a ton,' Sylvie said, getting up from her chair. 'Anytime you need a victim, just let me know, all right?'

'It was just a game, Syl, no harm intended,' Damien instructed her. She hated that he'd shortened her name, acting like he was some close friend of hers or something.

'Really, it was just a game,' April confirmed.

'I'm sure it was just a game, but you know you didn't bother to ask me if I wanted to play.'

'But we didn't do anything to you. And it was sort of romantic, the way he picked you out, the way he really seemed to like you. And it wasn't like we watched everything you did, if that's what you're worried about.'

Sylvie didn't like the knowing smile that April had put on. So they had watched his hand reach for her across the table. They'd seen their hands entwine. They'd seen his fingers push the hair back from her forehead, seen, too, that she'd turned her lips up toward his while they waited for their ice cream cones, and how he hadn't kissed her right away, how they'd just stared at each other, at each other's lips, waiting, anticipating. Had these people laughed? Had they cheered? Had they watched

150

when she traced one finger over his lips? 'Did this game have points, or something?' she asked. 'I mean, did he get extra points for the kiss?' Sylvie stood up and turned toward Decker. 'I need that phone number now.'

'Right,' he said.

April followed her to the door. 'You're making it sound a whole lot worse than it was. He really liked you, and isn't that the important thing?' Sylvie shrugged, looked away. 'I mean, he picked up other people – we all did, that was how we played the game – but he didn't pick anybody up after you. It was like he was looking for you all along.'

'Uh-huh,' Sylvie said.

'I mean, what difference does it make how you met, if you stayed together?' Sylvie nodded and took the paper that Decker held out toward her.

Damien had walked over. 'I swear to God, it was like he was looking for you right from the beginning. He was always following blondes with long hair. They were all slender, pretty, and young. It was like they were all different versions of you, but none of them exactly right. It'd turn out one was too young, or too bitchy, and that'd be the end of it; he never even sat down over a cup of coffee with one of them. Then you came along, and all the pieces fit. It makes me think of those old fairy tales, you know? Where the prince roams the whole earth to find the perfect girl. Only this is the modern world, so he gets to roam it through the screens.' Damien swept his hand back toward the monitor wall. 'And then he asks the three riddles or something – you were the only one answered them right, is all. But you shouldn't think badly of it. It came out all right, didn't it?'

Again she nodded. 'Thank you for your help.'

'We got you upset, didn't we?' April asked.

'It's just that I don't like thinking I was being watched. Looked at. Looked into.'

'Oh,' April said, 'it wasn't like that. Really.'

'I don't know,' she said. 'I feel like it was.'

The numbers from Peter's file led, as she suspected, nowhere.

She noted that there was no previous home telephone number given, only his Livingston Street number. Her number. West Security Plus, Peter's employer before Best Security, had the standard recording that said the number was no longer in service. No new, forwarding number was given on the tape. And Salt Lake City information had no listing whatsoever for a company by that name. She called the Chamber of Commerce, the Better Business Bureau, the Small Business Association. No such company.

'Maybe they folded,' Hannah suggested.

'Maybe,' Sylvie said, tapping her pencil against the counter. 'But it wasn't that long ago. Somebody should have them in their records.'

'Didn't this Mr Decker contact them for a reference?' Hannah asked.

Sylvie called Decker back, asked him if he'd actually called Peter's former employer. Yes, he said, he'd spoken to the owner of the company and the man had given Peter an excellent recommendation.

'Okay, so where the hell is that man now?' Sylvie asked Hannah when she'd hung up.

'I don't know, Sylvie, but where is this going? You're trying to chase down some guy who ran what was probably a two-bit security operation that probably doesn't exist anymore.'

'I know that's what I'm doing,' Sylvie retorted, her voice quivering with anger. 'It's what I have to do.'

'Right now you need to calm down, Sylvie. All I'm saying is you shouldn't be wasting energy on this. What you need to do is think about the broader picture, not this single elusive telephone number.'

'Then you tell me exactly what you think the broader picture is, so I'll know.'

'I guess I don't know, either,' Hannah said, and Sylvie heard the catch of breath, the fear, hot between them. 'Let's sit down, please, Sylvie,' she begged, and the younger woman allowed herself to be drawn toward the couch.

They sat in silence for a time, and the only sounds were the hum of the refrigerator motor and the drip of water into the pan beneath. 'Maybe I need to think about what I do know,' Sylvie said after a while.

'Yes,' Hannah said.

'Like for instance,' Sylvie said, taking her time through the words, 'I know he's hiding.'

'And he's got everything about himself covered over.'

Sylvie nodded. 'He's somewhere now, but not where he said he was going to be.' She stared straight into her mother's eyes. 'He lied to me about how our meeting was pure chance. So we know he lies, we know that. The next question has to be what else did he lie about? Probably where he was born,' she said, beginning to tick the list along her fingers, 'how old he was, that he had a brother, that he'd never been married, that he loved me, that he . . . I don't know, everything, probably – right?'

'Yes,' Hannah said, the simple word ringing its harsh bell tone through the empty room.

Sylvie was scanning the living room from where she sat. 'Look at this place – almost no furniture, except what we needed for Cally. No curtains, because we had to wait till we knew exactly what we wanted. No pictures on the walls, because we had to wait till we knew exactly what we wanted. So what have we got? Some white dishes, a couple of mugs, junk stainless-steel cutlery that I have to straighten the tines out of every time I set the table. Enough pots to cook a meal. I kept thinking we were saving for something, but maybe we weren't. Maybe he was never planning to stay.' She looked at her mother again. 'Maybe he wasn't planning to get married, either.'

'You don't know, Sylvie, you're just guessing at things.'

No, Sylvie thought, I'm listening to the wind is what I'm doing. 'Remember that stuff I told you about with his security business that you said didn't sound like a breakthrough?'

'No, I don't think I do.'

'I told you about it – he said he was doing this stuff with voice reports when there was a break-in and you said, "Hasn't that been done before"?'

'And?' Hannah asked when Sylvie didn't continue.

'I don't know. Maybe he made that up, too, made up that he even had a business. How would I know if it was some kind of dramatic breakthrough or not? I'm just some stupid girl with attention deficit disorder. I'd never remember it anyway, right?'

'You remembered,' Hannah said.

Sylvie nodded. She'd gotten up from the couch and walked over to the French doors. 'Maybe he didn't even like courtyards, or birds, or whatever those kinds of moldings were, or any of it. How much of it do you suppose was lies?' she asked Hannah, who only shook her head in response. 'He was probably just glad when Cally was taken. I mean, how would I know? Maybe he never wanted a baby at all. Maybe he was relieved, maybe it gave him a perfect chance to cut out. He could just walk through his beloved French doors and disappear.' She bit down hard on her thumbnail. 'Maybe—' she said, then stopped.

'What?' Hannah asked.

'I've got to talk to Martinson,' she said, and headed for the kitchen phone. Her fingers weren't behaving, weren't steady enough to strike down at the proper buttons. 'I need Martinson,' she said, and finally her fingers tapped out in slow, steady motion the code that would connect her to the detective.

Chapter 19

Martinson said all that she was discovering was that Peter didn't want to be found. 'There's still nothing that would constitute a charge,' he told her.

'But look at all the things he's lied about,' Sylvie said, pointing to the paper on which she'd penciled her list.

'Lying is not a criminal act,' he advised.

'But you have to look at the lies,' she said, shaking the sheet in her outstretched hand. He didn't take it from her.

He pulled one of the stools out from the kitchen counter and took a seat on it. 'Sit down,' he said, pushing the other one toward her, but she couldn't sit still. She was walking out small circles near where he sat, holding her mug of Pepsi in both hands. He began to peel the thin plastic cap off his oversize Styrofoam cup. She watched him raise it, then, eyes closed, breathe in the aroma. She was not so delicate with her soda. Her mug was half-empty in the time it took him to get ready to drink. 'Where's your mom?' he asked.

'She had to go. She had a class.'

'But she was here? She knows about this new business?'

'Yes.'

He sipped the steaming beverage. She knew that later, when the cup was nearly empty, he'd let his teeth sink into the rim. It was part of his coffee ritual, his way of marking out his territory, though oddly, he did it just before casting it from him into the garbage. 'I think you two hype each other up too much.'

She wanted to knock his coffee right over. Bite into it herself. Squeeze hard against the sides of the cup till it split and those little cells of Styrofoam tore back from each other with a snap

155

and lurch. 'Oh, terrific,' she said, kicking instead at the leg of the other stool. 'Now you're really into low blows, Detective.'

'At least I'm not kicking things.' He put his coffee down and leaned toward her, resting his forearms on his thighs. 'I just don't know what I can do for you anymore.'

'What you need to do for me hasn't changed from the minute you first walked in here. You need to find Cally.'

'I want to, Sylvie, you know that. All I've got right now is cold leads and—'

She broke into his sentence: 'You have Peter, Detective.'

'Come on, Sylvie,' he said, reaching for her arm, though she stepped quickly back, beyond his touch. He stared at her. 'What are you saying, that Peter took Cally?'

'Yes.'

He stared at her for a second and then his gaze was gone, beyond her, sweeping the room as though searching the corners and cracks for something she couldn't even see. She waited out the time till he was looking at her again. 'He wasn't here,' he said, but she heard something fuzzy around the edges of his words.

'That's too simple an answer,' she said, and she knew he felt this now as surely as she did. 'He *said* he wasn't here.'

'He was in Florida, Sylvie,' he said, and she heard the firmness again. 'We checked the airline, the hotel. He went down there.'

'He never took me up into that place he worked; never introduced me to anyone there.' She pointed a finger at him as she spoke, as though she hoped to push the words into that sliver of a crack that she'd seen open in this thinking.

'People do that. They separate their work and play.'

'He said he never picked up anyone before. They said he'd picked up lots of girls.'

Martinson took a deep breath. 'I can't arrest a man for knowing how to charm a woman. What was he going to say to you – "I do this every day, you're one of forty-five women I've pulled this on"?'

'They said all the girls were alike. He was looking for something really specific. It gave me the chills when they said it, how he always went for girls with long blonde hair, all young, all thin. Why?'

'Guys get fixated on types, that's probably what that was. Maybe his mother looked like that. Or his last girl, you don't know.'

She shook her head. 'Damien said this thing about the fairy tale, too.' She looked at Martinson and he nodded to indicate he remembered that part of her narrative. 'He said it was like how the prince went around asking questions – "riddles" was what he said. Like he was testing each of the girls, and I passed. Like he was trying us out for something. Interviewing us.'

Martinson clasped his hands behind his neck and tilted his head back, contemplating what she'd said before he spoke again. Then, 'What you're talking about is a courtship dance: Two people feeling each other out about a possible relationship. He'd be asking them – you – "How old are you? What kind of work do you do? Are you engaged?" That kind of thing.'

'With these other girls, it happened very fast, Damien said. A couple of questions, and he dropped them. They didn't even get a cup of coffee out of it.'

'He doesn't like to waste time, that's all. These girls weren't right, you were.'

'Exactly. Look at the questions he asked: Was I dating anyone, who'd I live with, did I get along with my parents, who'd I hang out with?'

'What else do people say when they first meet? He wanted to know of he was going to have privacy in your apartment.'

'No.' She pointed at him again. 'He had this whole huge place all to himself. Our pick of private bedrooms. And how did I get along with my *parents*? Who asks questions like that? Why would he care?'

She saw his hand tighten around the white cup, saw the dark liquid shiver and slide. 'What I'm telling you is people who have just met don't necessarily care what the questions and answers are, they just need to have talk going. So he was stretching it a little. Maybe you're just saying he wasn't very good at this flirtation business.'

'Oh, but he was. Soon as he got the list out of the way, he was very romantic, seductive.' She felt her face flare with heat.

'The others just weren't his type.'

She shook her head. 'We were all his type. We all looked alike. It was because he got right down to business, asked his questions, one, two, three, and when the answers were wrong, he forgot about those girls.' She picked up the mug again, drained off the last of the beverage, then fingered a rough spot where the glaze was chipped away.

'I'll bet anything that close up they were ugly, had bad skin or stiff hair. The sort of thing he couldn't see on the screen. So he backed off, soon as he got close enough to really see.'

Sylvie shook her head. 'They've got a zoom. It shows everything, believe me.'

'Bad breath doesn't show on a screen. Neither does a screechy voice.'

'They didn't all have bad breath or screechy voices.'

She pulled the stool out finally, sat next to him. 'Could you just pretend for one minute that I'm right, that he was looking for something very, very specific?'

Martinson put up his hands in a gesture of surrender. 'Okay,' he said, ' you can even have a full five minutes.' He checked his watch. 'Ten minutes.'

'I think the key question was that one about my parents.'

'Why?'

'I told him I didn't exactly have parents.' Martinson narrowed his eyes at her. 'Well, I didn't, just then. I told him my father had been dead for twelve years, and my mother and I basically weren't talking.'

'You and Hannah?'

She nodded. 'We used to have constant battles. We'd been staying as far apart as we could.'

'I wouldn't have guessed that. You seem so close.'

'It's recent. It didn't happen till after I got pregnant – very pregnant, actually. Babies do that to people, I guess. Before that I'd really been putting effort into staying angry with her for ever, but then, I don't know, I just ended up wanting her to be with me. Wanting to know all this stuff about when she was a new mother.' Sylvie shrugged, smiling. 'Only thing is, now

158

she's right about Peter.' She shook her head slowly, her eyes following the intricate patterns of grain in the wooden kitchen floor. 'I spent my whole life fighting her, having her always say I was wrong, trying to prove I could be right. I really don't want her to be right about this. I really don't.'

'What is it, exactly, that she's right about?'

She shrugged, then reached for the plastic Pepsi container and poured herself a refill. 'I don't know. I guess she never liked him. But I thought she wouldn't like anyone I went out with. She never has. I figured it was because she was the mother, I was the daughter. But here's the thing,' she said, catching his eye. 'He didn't want me patching it up with her. He gave me all these passionate warnings about how she was going to ruin what we had between us if we started letting her into our lives. He didn't want me to tell her anything. He said she was the cause of all my problems – from the way she labeled me, the way she was always saying I couldn't do things, couldn't remember things.' He nodded. 'I think Peter's right about that part, so the rest of it kind of fell into place, too, and made sense. He wanted me to keep my life – our life – secret from her, so she couldn't control me anymore. He didn't even want me to tell her about the baby because she was only going to object to everything, he said, like the home birth, what we wanted to name her, how we'd dress her – everything and anything, according to him – and I figured he was right because she'd always loved hating what I did. So I listened – obeyed – for a long time, then finally it was like I had to see her anyway. I had to have her see me full with that baby. And then after we smoothed things over, my mother and me, he said she had an ulterior motive, that it was only a matter of time till she turned on me again.'

'Right. But that's just a classic reaction to the mother-in-law. Protecting his turf, demanding loyalty and all that stuff, now that he was the master.'

'Maybe. But he kept bringing it up. He'd tell me, "You said you didn't get along with her, so why are you doing this to me?" To *me*, he said, like it didn't matter if things had changed between us, all that mattered was that I'd violated an agreement

I had with him, or something.' She stopped, fingered a cash register receipt that lay on the counter. 'We never had an agreement. though. I probably said I didn't care if I ever saw her again. I know I never promised anything.'

'Okay. So he wanted a woman who didn't bring a mother with her. Where does that get us?'

She sat up taller, pulled her shoulders back. 'He wanted an unattached girl who lived alone, had very few friends, and didn't have anything to do with her parents.'

'Why?'

'Because he was up to something, Detective, and he wanted somebody who wouldn't have a whole lot of help when it happened.'

'Are you saying he set you up to kidnap a baby that hadn't been born? Hadn't been conceived?'

She hesitated for a moment. 'I think so.'

'Forget it.' He started to get up.

'Wait,' she begged him, catching at his arm. He sat again. 'He wanted a baby. He talked about it after I hardly knew him. He made it sound romantic, exciting. I never met a guy who wanted a baby before. Do you know a lot of them?'

Martinson sat down again and said he had to admit that he didn't.

'Peter really wanted a baby. And I'll tell you something else,' she said, taking a breath, feeling her cheeks flare hot again. 'We hardly made love once I told him I was pregnant. Hardly ever,' she said, breaking the words into discrete, emphatic syllables.

'That's probably not uncommon. I've heard men say they're afraid of hurting the baby. Or their wife.'

'Right. He said things just like that. And when I talked to the midwife and she said it was perfectly fine, he still wouldn't.'

'It's a psychological thing. You can't reason with people once they get fixed ideas like that.'

'And after Cally was born?'

'She's not very old.'

Sylvie closed her eyes. 'I really, really don't want Hannah to be right,' she said, her voice almost a whisper. When she opened them, he was staring straight at her. 'He never meant to stay here – look at this empty place, Detective, he wouldn't put anything in it. Why did a single guy need this oversized, overpriced apartment?' When Martinson offered no explanation, Sylvie went on: 'Because it had French doors that you can walk right out of and be on your way, that's why. He must have really loved the floor plan, too, with the baby's bedroom so far distant back in the house, but so close up by those French doors.' She walked over toward the doorway to the dining room. Martinson followed behind. 'I wouldn't even have had to leave. He could have taken the baby even if I hadn't gone to the Grove, though he was always telling me to leave her alone. All he had to do was wait till I was in the kitchen. No curtains on the French doors – easy sight line.' She pushed against the heavy walnut swing door that completely closed off the kitchen from the dining room. 'The way this place is laid out, if he was quiet enough, I wouldn't have even known. In fact, he wouldn't have even had to be that quiet. There's no furniture to bump into when you want to move fast,' she pointed out.

'He was in Florida,' Martinson reminded her. And yet again he went over how they'd checked his registration at the hotel and how his call to her from the night before was on the hotel bill. And they'd double-checked that with the phone company.

'Unless it wasn't him on the phone at all,' Sylvie suggested.

'Did you have any suspicion at the time? Was his voice different in some way – muffled, say?'

'No,' she reluctantly admitted. 'All right, maybe he was in Florida, but then somebody must have helped him.'

'Who?'

'I don't know. Maybe one of those other blondes he picked up. Somebody who looked like me so that if people saw her, they'd think it was me. Look at all the people who claim to have seen me with the baby that day in spots where I wasn't. Maybe they really saw *her*, his helper, with the baby.'

'People get confused. They saw you two blocks over, two days ago, and the image gets merged into the day of the kidnapping.'

'But isn't it possible they saw somebody else?'

Martinson stared at her. She watched his eyes when he

finally moved them off her, saw how they roamed the room without seeing it, saw the eye movements turn quick and edgy, as though they pushed invisible puzzle pieces closer, pressed them up more tightly against one another. He looked at her again, though now he ran two fingers flat across his lips. She held a fingernail tight between her clenched teeth.

Martinson shook his head. 'This doesn't get us anywhere, Sylvie.'

'Yes, it does. We find this girl, she tells us how to find him, and then we find Cally. It gets us everywhere we want to go, Detective.' Her hand traced a gentle upward spiral as she spoke. 'Or,' she added, 'he got back on a plane under a different name and flew in. It doesn't take long to fly from Florida, does it?'

'Sylvie, listen to me. This doesn't help you.'

'What are you talking about? We know what happened now, we know he took her.'

She stared at his red tie, watching it rise with each slow, deliberate breath. She heard the rasp, like barely controlled anger, of air through his nose. It was the only sound between them for what seemed much too long a time. 'It doesn't make sense,' he admitted, and then she was crying, as suddenly as if his words had been a two-by-four slammed straight at her.

'Hey, this isn't the time to get sad, not when we're finally getting somewhere. We're figuring it out.' She nodded but couldn't speak for the deep fog that filled her all up. 'Do you want some more soda?' he asked, reaching for her mug. She shook her head – the mug was still nearly full. 'We're figuring it out,' he repeated, handing her the soda.

'I know,' she said, piecing through the words, picking them up the way you do when you're looking for just the right color bead to put in the necklace next, 'but I don't want this to be what it is.'

'I know,' he said quietly. 'I have real problems with it, too.'

She'd begun to drink from her mug but stopped. 'Why does it bother you?' He shook his head – little tiny shakes – turning from her, too, and she could see him dismissing her questions, hoping to put her off. 'Why?' she repeated, the word reaching for him now, ready to hook on.

'Because he's her father.'

'And?'

'And you have no custody order, and you have no restraining order against him. He has as much right to have her as you do.'

'No,' she said, the word a wail of pleading. She grabbed at his arm, catching up the harsh tweed of his jacket in her fingers. 'He took her by force from me, he snatched her away. He's a kidnapper. That's all, a kidnapper, plain and simple.'

Martinson put his hand over hers, pressing down on it, stilling it. He spoke quietly to her, but in the gray tones of one quoting from an informative pamphlet. 'You've acknowledged him openly as the father of your child. According to law, it's a domestic quarrel, nothing more. According to law, Peter has every right to have Cally with him.'

'Well, fuck the law,' she said, flinging her arm, and his, from her. She stalked across the room, then turned to face him. 'That can't be true.' She hurled the words at him, dead-aimed for his eyes.

'It is. A parent can be threatened by the other parent, sprayed with Mace, held at gunpoint, beaten. All kinds of things are done every day to get the other parent out of the way so the child can be taken. But not one of those things would constitute a kidnapping by law.'

'But if there were someone else, someone helping him,' she suggested.

'No. That doesn't matter. There've been cases of parents appearing with armed thugs to grab their kids. If she was acting on behalf of a parent and then she handed that baby over to that parent, it's not kidnapping. Assault, maybe, if she hurt anybody, but it doesn't look like she did. And he didn't assault you. We can't charge him with that, even.'

'Well, then charge her.'

'Who is she, and what exactly did she do?'

'Jesus Christ, she took my baby!'

'His baby,' Martinson said, though he had the decency to

163

turn his eyes away as he spoke the words.

'That's why he didn't want to get married, isn't it? If we were married—'

'No,' Martinson interrupted her. 'Even if you were married, it'd be exactly the same. A custody order's the only thing that's going to make a difference here. If you had custody, he'd be required to turn the baby over to you, and the police would go and collect her. But that's only if you knew exactly where she was. Custody order or not, nobody's going to chase him down; not the police and not the FBI.'

'Help me,' she pleaded with him.

'You're not hearing me, Sylvie. There's nothing a police officer can do for you anymore.'

'Help me find him,' she said, her hands twisting together, first suppliant, then fistlike, in front of her.

'I can't look for him, because he hasn't committed a crime.' He laid each word down as though it were a rough, heavy stone. 'Maybe there's the possibility of fraud or even obstruction over the case itself, but we can't initiate a nationwide manhunt based on that. If he turns up somewhere else in trouble, we might go get him. But even that's iffy. These things – obstruction – they're tough to make stick in court. So we may decide to let it go even if we know where he is. You know, this police department isn't really going to want to start announcing too loudly that they were royally duped by this guy and then on top of that, not be able to make a case against him. What I'll do, though,' he said, lowering his feet from the stool rungs and planting them firmly on the floor, 'is brief everybody about what I think is happening.' He'd taken his undersized notebook from his pocket and was searching through his jacket, shirt, and pants pockets for a pencil. She didn't move toward finding him one. 'I'll talk to Dolan, too, tell him how I see it, get him to see that this has to be what went on.'

'If you convince him that Peter took her, will he get back on the case?'

'No. It's domestic now. All it'll do is open up Dolan's thinking along those lines, for whatever that's worth. That's if he even takes me seriously. But I'll call him every few days, see if he's received any new info.' He put his pad back into his pocket. He hadn't written anything.

'That's not enough,' she said.

'Look, you know she's probably safe if he's got her. Isn't that worth something?'

'Why do I know she's safe?'

'He's her father. He adored her, you told me that.'

'I don't know if he did.'

'Come on,' he said.

'No, you tell me what I know about him, even one little bit of information I can trust, okay? I probably don't even know his real name, do I, or where he lived or worked, or what he wanted with me, *do I?*' Martinson shrugged. 'Can you tell me why he did this? We hadn't talked about splitting up, hadn't gotten into arguments about custody or anything like that before Cally disappeared. This isn't simple, I'm telling you. He wanted a baby for some reason and then took her when he got the chance. We don't know what plans he has for her. Or maybe that's his business – maybe I've finally got that much figured out. Maybe he makes blonde, white babies and sells them for a living. People would probably pay any price he asked for a blonde, white baby, don't you think?' Then she felt a terrible chill, as cold and battering as an Atlantic tide grabbing at her. Martinson was speaking to her, but she couldn't hear him, couldn't see him. And then he was moving her off the stool and she wanted to tell him, "No," but she thought she heard Cally and she wanted to tell her, "I'm here, hush, I'm here," but then she was on the floor, and Martinson was kneeling beside her.

'I think you passed out,' he informed her. He was holding her hand between both of his.

'I feel awful,' she said.

'Don't talk. Just relax.' She closed her eyes for a moment. 'Do you want some water?' he asked when she looked at him again. She nodded.

'Your feet slid right out,' he said, his hand tracing a long gentle curve for illustration. 'I got you before you hit bottom, though.'

'Thanks,' she said, raising herself slowly to sitting. She

165

sipped from the glass he handed her. 'Aren't you going to tell me to get a grip?' she asked him.

'I'll pass on that. But tell me again, why did you postpone getting married?'

She sighed. 'It had to do with converting,' she said, reaching for the memory as though she were reconstructing someone else's past. 'I was supposed to convert. He said he couldn't marry a non-Mormon. I needed to go through some kind of training program first.'

'Did you do that?'

'No. The timing was wrong for the program. They didn't have one here that I could get into. We talked about maybe going out to Salt Lake, where they had programs running all the time.'

'Did he seem to be a very religious man?'

She considered for a moment. 'The conversion was very important to him.'

'Did he go to church a lot?'

'Sometimes.'

'And where is the church?' She shrugged. 'You never went with him?' She shook her head. 'Why not?'

'I wasn't converted yet.'

'And non-Mormons weren't allowed in the church?'

'I guess not.'

'That sounds strange to me. Did he ever talk about his beliefs?'

'No.'

'Did you have any evidence that he was actually a Mormon? Some literature around the house, say, some special celebration, some talk of his missionary work?'

'No, I guess not. No – wait, he did talk about beliefs, or sort of beliefs, customs, maybe. He said in some societies – Mormons, Shakers – you could leave a child alone because it was such a close-knit community that everybody was always watching out for each other's kids.'

'He said Mormons and Shakers?'

'Yes.'

'You're sure?'

She thought for a moment. 'Yes. And there were others. I

forget their names, but Mormons and Shakers I definitely remember. It made me think of movers and shakers. That's one of the ways they teach kids with learning problems to remember stuff – make it sound like something more familiar.'

'Shakers don't have children, Sylvie. They're celibate. They're dying out because they have no offspring.'

Sylvie bent her head to one side. 'So you're saying . . .'

'I'm saying he made himself a Mormon for you, made himself something you wouldn't know much about, nor probably would anyone you might ask, so you wouldn't be able to argue with him about it. He said he couldn't get married for religious reasons. That's one of the things we tend not to question in this society – religious beliefs – we're likely to give it a wider berth than almost anything, including sex. He might even have been testing you with talking about Shakers, trying to see how much you knew about so-called exotic sects. He never took you to meet a minister or a counselor, did he, or anybody from the church?'

'I'm such a stupid person,' she said. 'I'm so incredibly stupid.'

'No,' Martinson said, and touched her hand, his fingers sliding once across the back of it, curving round it as it curved round the water glass, no more than that, but it eased something. Her next breath came more smoothly.

'He's just a con artist, isn't he? I fell for a stupid con artist.'

'It isn't that simple. This wasn't some stranger asking you for your credit card number over the telephone. This was your lover, your fiancé. The person you were going to trust most in the world. So he had all the advantages if he chose to play with that trust. And obviously he was very good at it.'

'It was all there, and I didn't pick up on any of it.'

'He's a clever man with a special skill and interest in deception. You shouldn't be blaming yourself for not seeing it. He was putting all his energy into making sure you didn't.'

'Maybe it isn't him,' she said, wanting to take it all back, not wanting Martinson to believe it. She was shaking, her whole body deserting her, going off on its own. She put her head down into her hands, and she was letting short, sad catches of breath

167

slip through the spaces between her fingers. 'I don't want it to be him,' she managed to say.

'I know.'

She ran a finger along the glass rim. She stopped for a moment and looked at him. 'I don't want it to be true,' she said.

'Of course we can't be absolutely sure.'

And she nodded, her shoulders rising high on the crest of a deep, deep breath. 'I'm sure,' she said, and he saw something different in her now, excitement rather than fear, it looked to him, just when he'd been thinking, What is this crazy buzz I'm feeling? but knowing, just as fast as he thought it, that it had to do with her, with her pale hair crossing over his hand as he grabbed for her when she started going down. And hell, she'd got these pieces lined up, worked it out, so there was that, too, that feeling he always got when he could see the end. The victory over chaos was how he thought of it, that moment when the information slipped together and started explaining itself backward. Only he knew it wasn't really that. He'd been slow this time – the solving was hers, not his, the victory all hers. This was something else, something, he was afraid, that was a whole hell of a lot cheaper and meaner than making sense of the world. It was triumph, not over the pieces of info that wouldn't fit before but did now, but over Peter himself. It was like he'd got the right to move in on her now, which, as any fool would tell him, he hadn't.

'Will you help me find him?' she asked.

'Strictly off the record, of course.'

The corners of her mouth rose in a gentle upturn. 'Of course,' she said.

Chapter 20

'How do you expect to locate him?' Hannah asked her daughter. 'Do you have any solid information as to where he is?'

'Not yet. We're still collecting information. It takes time.' Hannah shook her head. 'It takes time, Mother. We're looking at all the pieces, trying to narrow it more, that's all.' Sylvie poked her fork against the scallion omelette on her plate, checking to see if it would give under pressure. It didn't look like real food to her, but more like a stage-prop, the way it was all plumped up and shiny and much too yellow. 'I'm working on a bunch of stuff at once. I'm filing for custody and I'm going to try to get a birth certificate. Peter told me they mail them out to you automatically after about three months, but obviously that was a complete lie. The other thing I'm doing is calling all the places Peter had accounts, trying to get information.'

'That, at least, sounds reasonably concrete. Have you started on that?'

'Yes'

'And?'

'And there's very little to go on. I've gotten the account numbers from bills that have come in since he left, but that's not enough. Before the credit companies release any information they want his Social Security number, and I just don't have that. He gave a phony number to that place he worked for at the mall, so that doesn't help. I've tried telling places I call that the Social Security number they have is wrong, but they won't accept that unless I give them the right number. My calls get transferred to a manager who explains how they can't give out any information to me because my name's not on the account. They tell me to have him call in.' She laughed at the thought of this. 'I think once you get to the point of talking to the manager, you can't get anywhere – there must be some kind of lock that comes onto the computer file if they think an unauthorized person is trying to get information.'

'Why can't Martinson call all these places and say he's a police officer and demand the information?'

'Because there's no crime, I told you that.'

'It's a very bizarre world, Sylvie, when people can commit grotesque acts against one another but simply because they know each other or are related to them, it doesn't count as a crime.'

'I think it's more complicated than that.'

'Is it? I wonder. I wonder if it isn't just the power of sexual relations dominating our lives, yet again'

'Is this an academic lecture, Mother?'

'Think about it, Sylvie. He gets away because he's had sex with you, that's all. That's how he's made his mark, struck his signature, so to speak. I think we need to consider whether there's something you can get hold of in this power struggle. You can fight back with your sexual rights. Tell these people you're his wife.'

'I do that and it doesn't help.'

'Because you're the woman,' she said, hitting the counter sharply with her fist. 'But you better believe he'd be able to get the information on you, on his wife.'

'Mother, you may be right, but I have a baby to find, and that's all I care about right now. I do not actually care all that much whether the world is going to hell or not.'

'Then fight them on their own male terms. Have Martinson or some other man call and pretend he's Peter.'

'It's not going to help anyway, because we don't have the key information. Peter knew exactly what to withhold. You need those precious little Social Security numbers to break through their barriers. The places that'll talk to us if we give them a name and address don't have a damn bit of information to give us except balance due.'

'I want Martinson to do more,' Hannah said, and grabbed for the plate that held her uneaten lunch, grabbed Sylvie's plate, too, and marched them to the sink.

'I hadn't finished that,' Sylvie said as her mother scraped the eggs into the garbage.

'Oh, no,' Hannah said, and for a moment, Sylvie thought she was going to toss the plate and fork onto the floor. 'I'm sorry. I'll make you another one.'

'No,' Sylvie said, waving the offer away. 'I wasn't going to eat it anyway. I was just surprised that you took it.'

'You've got to push Martinson more; insist he do more,' Hannah said, abandoning the other omelette at the sink-side. 'The police have all kinds of ways to get information.'

'Look, there is no real case, I told you that. No crime except these vague obstruction things. He's helping me as much as he can. If he starts being the one doing the asking, he could lose his job.'

'So? We've lost our baby. What's a job compared to that?'

Sylvie shook her head. 'He's not a real happy man, I don't think. He has nothing but that job, you know.'

'So?'

Sylvie took in a deep breath. 'He's helping all he can, is what I'm saying.'

'These are criminal acts, giving false ID numbers, Sylvie. That's fraud.'

'Why are you telling *me* that? You don't think I know all that? Why do you always act as if I'm a complete idiot?'

'I know you know all that,' Hannah said. 'I'm only trying to understand this man and this horrendous situation he's gotten us into. An I want to know why they can't go after him for all he's done.'

'They could go after him if he was here, but they don't track people down and drag them back to Connecticut because they lie on a job application, believe me.'

'Well, damn the law, then. I feel so helpless against his lack of scruples.' Hannah said, her voice breaking in a way Sylvie was unused to. 'I have no way into him, no way to understand how he thinks. How can we possibly get anything concrete on him when he's lied and cheated and committed crimes to escape us?'

171

'I don't know. But I promise you,' Sylvie said, 'once we figure out what city he's in, I'll go door to door through it if I have to. Or through two or three cities. I'm not going to just let her go.'

Hannah closed her eyes for a moment.'Are you sure you don't want me to make you another omelette?' she asked, looking once again at her daughter.

'I'm okay,' Sylvie said.

'A cookie, maybe, or an apple?'

'Sure,' Sylvie said. 'That'd be nice. Cookie and apple, both.'

Later that afternoon when Martinson came over to help Sylvie brainstorm ways to locate Peter, he asked her, would she please not call him 'Detective' any more.

'Why?' she wanted to know. 'Isn't that what you are, a detective?'

'Yes, I am,' he said, feeling foolish and wondering why he was doing this. 'It just has a very hostile feeling to it.'

She opened her eyes wide at him, then repeated, 'Hostile?'

'Maybe that's not exactly the right word, but there's something about it that puts me on edge. It has to do with how you say it with the syllables all separated out, you know, "De-*tec*-tive". It sound like you're talking about something, not to somebody. Like you're addressing the whole New Haven Police Department all in one shot. Like when you said just now, "Listen, De-*tec*-tive." It always sounds like the beginning of a lecture.'

She nodded, but she was smirking, looking down, trying, he could see, not to laugh. 'So what do you prefer? "Mr Martinson," maybe? "Detective Martinson"?'

'Plain old "Martinson" would really be best. That other stuff is very artificial-sounding, I think.'

'I don't like to call people by their last names. *That* sounds hostile to me.'

'Forget it, then. "Detective" is fine,' he said, lifting his hand as if brushing the other words aside.

'How about I just try not to have it sound hostile?' she suggested.

'Great.' He was starting to feel like an incredible jerk. What

172

the hell difference did it make what she called him?

'Or how about "Marty"?' she asked him.

She had her lips pressed tightly together, holding in what looked to him like a major guffaw. 'Definitely not,' he said, and shook his head.

'That's what the officers call you, isn't it?'

'Yes,' he admitted, 'but I don't want you calling me that.'

'Why?'

'Look, I'm sorry I brought this up. You can call me absolutely anything you want, okay?' He tapped his pencil against the information they'd been compiling before he got sidetracked onto this.

'You have a first name?'

'Chad.'

She repeated it. It sounded flat, like the lid coming down on an old trunk.

'Forget it,' he said. "Detective" is fine, I told you.' He reached for his coffee cup, saw as he suspected, that he'd already drained it. He lifted the Styrofoam cup to his lips for a moment anyway, let his teeth sink partway into the giving white rim.

'Is that what I really call you – "Detective"?'

'When you call me something, yes, that's what it is you call me.' She nodded. 'So,' he said, tapping out three short signals on the counter with the pencil, 'let's get back to our list. We've chased down the credit card slips and utilities. How about a lease? That'd be a good thing to have.'

'Listen, Chad, I already told you, I don't think he left a paper behind in this house.'

'Stuff from an investment house?'

She was shaking her head. 'Chad,' she said, and the small word was bristling with reprimand.

'That sounds hostile, too. You might as well stick with the "Detective".'

'Detective, we are not going to come up with a paper trail on him.'

'Sylvie, we have to start somewhere. And you're going to have to face up to the fact that this is going to be very hard and very slow going, and if you don't want to follow up every single lead, no matter how slim, then you might as well tell me now and I'll get out of here.'

'Hey,' she said, cocking her head to one side. 'I'd say you're sounding pretty hostile right now. All I'm trying to tell you is that there's nothing here.' She gestured toward the apartment. 'Nothing. He didn't leave me little crumpled-up pieces of paper that just happen to be clues. There's nothing here that's going to help us find this bastard.'

'You telling me you want to give up?'

'No.'

'Then we're going to make a list and it's going to have at a bare minimum fifty different items on it that might take us somewhere. Do you understand that?'

'I understand you're being hostile, Detective.'

'Damn straight,' he said. 'I don't waste your time, you don't waste mine, understand?'

'Is making this list going to get him?'

'All I can tell you is, not doing it is not going to get him.'

She nodded. 'How about travel agencies? I could see if he used one to make his plane reservations,' she said after a short pause.

'Good,' he said, and his pencil was moving again.

It was an extensive catalog of information that they gathered on Peter, and it contained many more than the fifty items Martinson had originally set as their goal. It covered three pages and looked rather more like 250, maybe 300 entries, to Sylvie. It had the name of every magazine she'd ever seen him read, or even mention. The TV shows he watched. His favorite movies. His preferred ice cream flavor and brand. His shoe size. His favorite color. His style of dress. Places they had gone, comments he had made.

Peter had left nothing behind. Not a single piece of clothing with a label. Of course she'd seen labels in his clothes because she'd done his wash – but to recall them, well that was difficult. She didn't think there were store names at all, just clothing lines – familiar names that he could surely have gotten at the local Macy's. The cleaners? Martinson asked. She'd never taken anything of his to the cleaners. She didn't know.

'What good is all this?' she asked him when there really was absolutely nothing else she could come up with on him. 'Who cares what kind of pizza he likes?'

'What we're looking for is something that keys us into a certain region or state or city. Suppose he always talked about deep-dish pizza, said how much better it was than the thin New Haven crusts. That would mean that maybe he was from the Chicago area.'

'No, it wouldn't' she countered. 'It would just mean he'd visited some big city, that's all, and eaten that kind of pizza. They make that pan style in other places than Chicago, don't they?' He shrugged.

'You know what it really means?' she asked.

'What?'

'It means he's probably been to a Pizza Hut.'

'Look, I just meant that as an example.' He tossed the pencil down and neither of them tried to halt its rapid roll towards the edge of the counter. When it hit the floor he said, 'It's all Cally has.'

'Okay,' she protested, rising, walking from him toward the window where she leaned, palms pressed down on the sill, before she turned back and continued. Peter had told her he played tennis, and that he'd liked softball when he was a kid. He'd once said he'd teach Cally to catch when she was older. 'Too bad he wasn't into deep-sea fishing,' Martinson observed.

'Why?'

'Then we could have narrowed the search to ocean towns with Pizza Huts and those Häagen-Dazs ice cream stands he likes.'

He had a decidedly unencumbered life, they concluded. No magazine subscriptions, no books, no hobbies that he worked on, no prized possessions. No knick-knacks. No photographs. Disposable razors. Not even much in the way of clothes. 'Enough clothes, but just barely enough,' she said.

'And probably all new,' Martinson said.

She thought about it. 'Yeah,' she said. 'I think that's right. The latest stuff. No classic, slightly worn items. No frayed

175

elbows. What does that tell you?'

'That he bought it all for here. For this adventure. His other clothes, back home, may be very different. All his personal stuff – the books, the clothes – they're all somewhere else.'

'When he left,' Sylvie said, 'he was able to pack it all into a suitcase and a backpack. And there's nothing left behind at all.'

'How about a coat? Did he have one?'

'Yes.'

'New, too?'

'Yes. New and sharp, but casual, like all his stuff. You've seen it, it's one of those lined field jackets.'

'Oh, yeah,' he said. 'I'm thinking if he had a coat back where he lived, he wouldn't have needed to get another new one, would he?'

'Probably not. He'd just wear that one back and forth, I guess.'

'What was it lined with?'

'One of those wool flannels. A big plaid. Low-key, though. Beige and brown, I think. Funky but classy.'

'That kind of coat, that's more something people wear in the fall, isn't it? It wouldn't have been warm, would it?'

'No,' she said, 'not really. It was just those two thin layers. It was nowhere as thick as my coat, which I said to him, but he said he had a good heater in his car and he didn't plan on hanging around outside in the middle of winter anyway, so it didn't matter.'

'Right. He didn't plan on hanging around.'

'God, I'm stupid.'

'That was the only coat he had?' Martinson continued. She nodded. 'People around here usually have three, four coats don't they? One for September and October weather, one for November and December, and then the high-powered one for January and February.'

'I guess so,' she said. 'I guess I don't really put on my down jacket till I have to – New Year's or so. Before that I wear this black one I have, though it's getting really old. And I've got a bunch of lighter things – a jeans jacket, a hefty blazer, that sort of thing.'

176

'Right, just like everybody else who lives here, you collect coats for all the variations in seasons. I'm thinking maybe he didn't have a winter coat because he didn't need one where he came from – and where he knew he was going back to. And maybe he miscalculated, too about what would be a good one to have. That field jacket seemed like it had to be enough, given what *he* was used to in winter – or maybe he was hedging his bets and trying to opt for one that might work when he got back home. What do you think?'

'You're thinking he came from someplace warm, then?'

'Exactly. Someplace with very even temperatures so when he came out here, say, in October – and I'm just guessing when he came out here – he bought something appropriate for that time of year. To him, probably, it couldn't get much colder than it already was.'

'Well,' she said, smiling. 'This is almost as good as having him like deep-sea fishing, isn't it?'

'Yea, ma'am,' he said, grinning at her, near to laughing out loud.

Chapter 21

'No,' the clerk in City Hall explained to her. 'You don't just get a birth certificate for the asking. You have to have the certification letter.'

'What's that?' Sylvie asked.

'Every time a baby's born,' the woman explained in slow, drawn-out phrases, as though she had to go through this ten or twenty times a day and was by now extraordinarily bored by the recitation, 'the statistics clerk in the hospital issues a letter on the hospital letterhead certifying the time and date of the birth and the names of the baby and the parents. That's what we go by. Sometimes when the mothers don't stay very long in the hospital, the paperwork doesn't get done before they leave. Maybe that's what happened in your case. How long were you in?'

'She wasn't born in a hospital, she was born at home.'

'Oh, well, that's the problem, then. Did you have a doctor or midwife?'

'A midwife.'

'All right. Then she should have written something out.'

'I don't think she did. I don't have anything like that.'

'Well, maybe she just forgot. Check with her. I can't do anything for you till you have that.'

'Maybe I could call her from here?' Sylvie asked.

'Well, not here,' the woman said brusquely, then leaned around Sylvie to the next person in line. 'Yes?' she barked at him. 'Downstairs,' the woman said, turning back to Sylvie. 'There's a pay phone in the lobby.'

The queue for the phone was ridiculously long. People in the line were checking their watches, sighing, complaining. 'He's

179

been in there at least ten minutes, yes, he has,' a heavy woman in a coat with satin lapels said of the man who currently occupied the booth. Sylvie could see he had a stack of papers on top of the telephone directory that he was shuffling through and consulting as he spoke into the receiver. When the person next in line, a burly guy with dark, wet hair, knocked on the glass, the caller tried to turn his back to the man. The woman next to Sylvie was clicking her tongue, tapping one foot on the shiny floor. 'What if we got emergencies out here?' she shouted toward the booth. The other people in line shifted woodenly from one foot to the other, looking like an out-of-synch chorus line at a late-night rehearsal walking through their routine yet one more time. When the wet-headed guy started knocking on the glass again, this time moving round the booth, following the caller as he turned, knocking harder and harder on each successive rectangle of glass, Sylvie decided there must be a better way, and took off through the dark marble lobby and out onto Orange Street.

She drove directly to the midwife's office and gave her name to the receptionist. 'I need one of those forms that says when my baby was born,' she told the woman in a voice barely more audible than a whisper. The sight, just off to her right, of a room full of pregnant women was making her woozy.

'You didn't get one?' Sylvie shook her head. Even that little motion made her feel unsteady. 'Julia always writes those at the delivery.'

'She didn't this time.' The receptionist said she'd check with Julia, but she was with a patient, so Sylvie would have to sit down and wait.

She tried to sit still. To wait. To bury her eyes and thoughts in a magazine (not *American Baby*), turning pages, not reading, barely seeing the glossy images, but at least not seeing *them* sitting there, bellies full, counting down weeks or days or hours toward their babies. And then a woman came in to show off her infant, and everyone in the room, unwieldy in shape as they were, jumped up from their chairs to fuss over him. Sylvie felt her nipples tingle and swell, and she pulled herself up out of the chair and stumbled back toward the cloakroom. A nurse caught sight of her as she hung on the door frame trying to regain her equilibrium. 'Are you all right?' she asked her.

'I can't sit out there,' she said. The nurse led her back to a small room with a stool. Sylvie was crying. 'I miss my baby so much,' she said. The nurse took her hand and squeezed it.

'You're the one had her baby taken, aren't you?' Sylvie nodded. 'Oh God, I feel for you, I really do. What a nightmare you must be going through.' The nurse held tight to her hand while Sylvie struggled to make sense of her breathing. 'If you think you'll be okay alone for a minute, I'll go out and see if I can get Julia to stop in here and talk to you.'

Sylvie was in some kind of storage room. Samples of medications and instruments lined the shelves, and there were those cups for urine specimens, piles of charts, and pamphlets on pregnancy, osteoporosis, and methods of sterilization. The nurse had closed the heavy door as she exited, and Sylvie thought maybe she was about to lock her in there, that surely she'd just be forgotten. She could still hear the admiring coos of the women in the waiting room, could imagine them, too, still forming their tight ring around the infant, closing her out by enclosing her in storage where she was shunted away; separate from everything continuing and normal in life. Her breathing went so rapid and jagged again, she couldn't get hold of it, couldn't even find where one breath ended and another began. It was like when she was little and had stood before the revolving door at Macy's but hadn't been able to figure out how to step and move into the openings as they passed so as to become part of the moving circle. Then Julia was there, her large strong hand stroking across Sylvie's back, and she was talking to her just as she had in delivery, telling her to breathe, to count, to let it out slowly, and she was doing it, breathing again, riding the wave of her grief, just as she had ridden the waves of pain in labor.

Julia had called her the first night the information on the kidnapping had been in the newspaper. Peter had taken the call. 'Thanks so much,' she'd heard him say. And then, 'Yes,' in that tight voice he'd used on all the calls. He handled them all like he handled dinner-time telephone solicitations, communicating in tone, not actual language, his 'thank you, but we're not interested in what you have to offer, so bug off, why don't you?' He'd said to Sylvie, 'What the hell do any of them know about it?' and she'd agreed with him. How could anyone understand what she felt? Who could possible give solace?

But Julia might have helped. Julia's strength might have helped her – though even that wouldn't have changed the unalterable fact that Cally was gone. 'Julia, I need you to write that letter for me that says when Cally was born,' Sylvie said now.

'I did that,' she said. 'I gave it to Peter that day at the house.'

'I never saw it. I don't think it's anywhere in the house. Are you absolutely sure you gave it to him? Maybe you forgot this one time.'

'No,' she said, shaking her head. 'I know I did. I remember because I was touched by his reaction. He read it over, then he stroked it with his hand,' she said, demonstrating one hand gliding across the palm of the other. 'And then he kissed it.'

Sylvie took in a deep breath. 'He's a good actor.'

'What do you mean?'

And then she had to explain how the baby's father tricked her, how she'd been a dupe, how her baby'd been taken from her, not by a masked thief, but by her lover.

'I can't believe that,' Julia objected. 'I can't believe a person would do such a thing. Are you positive? Are you absolutely certain?'

'He's gone, Julia. He disappeared a week ago and said he was visiting a brother who doesn't exist. Where do you suppose he is, if he's not off hiding Cally?' Sylvie's voice had become shrill, the individual hardened words striking at Julia as though she were the enemy. 'It can't be coincidence, his leaving now. And he has this certification letter, too, I'm sure of it. I know it's nowhere in the house. Julia, it's like he and Cally never existed. He's taken every trace of himself away, and made it seem I imagined him. Maybe I did. Maybe I imagined Cally, too.'

'You didn't. I held her in my arms.' Julia took Sylvie's hand in hers. 'You have to believe in it, Sylvie.'

'I do,' Sylvie said. 'And I'm not going to stop believing in her, either.'

And then for all the good it would do her, Sylvie had Julia make another copy of the certificate. It was a simple letter, done up on her letterhead, and it stated the basic facts of Cally's origin. Sylvie looked it over, then said to the midwife, 'Anybody could have stationery made up like this, couldn't they, and then they could fill in any information they wanted, right?'

Julia looked at the document for a moment, then said yes, she was afraid that anybody bold enough and willing to lie to a printer could do it.

'Lying wouldn't be a problem,' Sylvie assured her, knowing that somewhere else, in some mild climate, her baby almost certainly already had a birth certificate and a new name.

Chapter 22

Sylvie took a chair next to the bank officer's desk. She began the usual way, asking whether Peter had provided their new forwarding address.

'A forwarding address,' the young woman repeated. 'No,' she said, running her fingernail down the smooth surface of the computer screen. 'I don't see any.' She was smiling at Sylvie, giving her one of those phony, trained-in, be-pleasant-to-the-customer mouth-shapes.

'My husband and I are moving to Florida, see,' Sylvie said, giving forth the lie she and Martinson had concocted, 'and I just want to be sure he gave you our new address there. He's already down there, see, and he says he hasn't gotten the statement yet. He's living down there now,' she said, and she could hear the repetition, the foolish, empty words, Unless she were a complete fool, a drunk, or a retard, the bank manager was bound to hear how false it sounded, too. This very thin woman who could surely only be ever so slightly older than Sylvie wore a flowered print dress with perky lace sleeves that stuck straight out from her shoulders. Sylvie, who was bundled in jeans, sweatshirt, and her down jacket – though it was nowhere near cold enough for that – realized she must look horribly misshapen and messy. Worthless, is what I look to her, Sylvie thought. No way is she going to take me seriously. Sylvie ran her fingers over her lips, covering them for a moment, so the absence of lipstick might not be so obvious. This was the first time Sylvie'd had to generate her lies face-to-face with somebody – up till now, she'd been able to hide herself inside her telephone voice. She was starting to feel much too warm. She unzipped her jacket, pushing it off behind her onto the chair.

185

The woman pushed a button on her keyboard, and eyes still on the screen, she pushed a few more, then waited, scanning the green letters before her. Sylvie went back to her story. 'We need to get it forwarded so we'll get our canceled checks. Otherwise, we'll never be able to balance the account. We're just hopeless when it comes to balancing,' Sylvie said, and added a laugh that nearly got away from her, threatening, as it did, to twist upward into a hysterical dark cloud around her head.

The woman's finger came down on one more key. 'Okay,' she said. 'Your husband closed out this account on the fourteenth, so neither of you should have written any checks after that because that would have really made a mess. Overdrafts make an incredible mess. Did any of you write any checks after the fourteenth?' Tracy – that was what the white letters on black plastic proclaimed the woman's name to be – turned toward Sylvie with raised, clearly judgmental eyebrows.

'Well, I did write this one check, because I didn't realize the account was already closed out, and the pharmacy told me about the insufficient funds and I realized the mistake right away. And then of course I didn't write any more, but I'm just worried maybe there was an old check that hadn't come in yet.'

'Well, with a checking account, he would have had to tell us if there were any outstanding checks first, so there shouldn't be a problem.'

'I know there shouldn't be any more checks, but people make mistakes, not that we did, but I worry. I wouldn't want to leave a trail of bad deeds behind me in this state.'

'Okay,' Tracy said when the screen had rewritten itself. 'The balance is at zero, and I don't see any checks that were presented. No flags for insufficient funds. Your pharmacist must not have tried to present that check again. Did you settle it with him privately?'

'I paid him cash.' That part was true. Hannah had handed her enough money to cover it.

Tracy nodded and pushed the terminal screen off left. Finished, Sylvie saw.

'No forwarding address?' she asked again, her voice sounding breathless, frantic, she knew.

'Nope,' Tracy said, clearly bored. She hadn't even bothered to swivel the screen back into view. 'You're on Livingston Street, right?' Sylvie said she was. 'Well, that's all the record shows. Livingston Street. But look, when you close an account there's just one more statement anyway, and that should have gone out to you already. It should have gone to your Livingston Street address.' The woman's oval pink nail clicked several times at a spot on the desk. 'You didn't get that yet?'

The statement had come to Sylvie's house. There'd been two canceled checks in the envelope, both written by her.

'No,' Sylvie said, shaking her head, the heat of the lies flaring off her cheekbones. 'Nothing's come to the house. That's why I'm wondering, did it go to the Florida address, maybe?'

'Well, I don't see how it could have, but I'll check on it, if you like.' Sylvie nodded with an eagerness that felt almost like frenzy to her. 'Do something, do anything,' she wanted to say. 'Don't just give me zeros again.' Tracy picked up the phone and her long finger pressed and lifted over the number pad. She smiled at Sylvie while she waited for the connection. 'Oh, hi, Diane, it's Tracy at Main. Could you check whether a statement has gone out to my customer? Terrific.' She read out the account names and numbers. The smile was turned toward her customer again. 'It was?' Tracy said into the phone. 'Good. Do you have the address it went to?' Another grin for her customer. 'That's what I thought.' She nodded at Sylvie. 'Do you have a Florida address on there as well? No?' Now she shook her head at Sylvie. 'Yes, I'll put it on file. Thanks, Diane, have a good day.' Tracy replaced the receiver in its cradle and swiveled her chair so that she faced Sylvie more head-on. 'It's the Livingston Street address, like I said. You'll get it in a day or so, but I really wouldn't worry about it, because all the activity on the screen is okay and, like I already said, too, he'd have had to account for all the checks anyway.'

'Okay,' Sylvie said, though she could barely control her voice around the word. What was left now? She couldn't do this lying business — not if she was going to get results. This was so

187

hopeless! How was she going to get any information from anybody about him?

Tracy was opening a file cabinet, taking out some blue cards. 'What I'll do is put in the new address anyway so that if anything comes up after today, it'll go there, okay?' She had begun to write in their names, copying them from the screen. 'Now, what's the new address?' she asked.

'I don't know,' Sylvie said, though that wasn't at all what she and Martinson had gone over. She was supposed to look in her purse, pretend to search for a slip of paper with the address, then say, 'I can't believe I left it at home. I'm never going to remember it. I'll have to call you when I get home, is that okay?'

'You don't know your new address?' Tracy asked.

'No,' she said. 'I don't have a new address.' Tracy's chair rolled back, away a few inches. Sylvie tried to close her eyes, tried to get a hold of herself but the tears washed boldly down her cheeks. Tracy wasn't smiling anymore. She stared at Sylvie, then seemed to look around, as if thinking of calling out for backup help. 'Look,' Sylvie said, motioning toward the box of tissues in the middle of Tracy's enormous desk. 'I don't know the address because I don't really know where he is.' Tracy pushed the tissue box over toward her. 'I'm trying to find him and this was the only thing I could think of. He took my baby.' Sylvie was shaking and she knew she shouldn't be saying all this, but she was, goddamn it, she was, and she wasn't stopping now. 'He took my baby and he took all my money when he closed out the account, and I can't find him and I can't find my baby,' and then she couldn't go on, she couldn't find the breath, and she was a complete mess; all she could do was hold a tissue up to her face and cry.

'My sister's ex took their kids,' Tracy whispered to Sylvie. 'Two little kids,' she said, 'three and four. Picked them up at nursery school and disappeared.' Tracy pulled a pile of tissues from the box and put them in Sylvie's hand. 'She almost went crazy thinking they were gone for ever. I dreamed their faces every night – those big brown gorgeous eyes. And they were always crying in my dreams. He took them out to his mother in

188

California, but we've got them back. You'll find your baby – you will.'

Sylvie shook her head. 'How?' she asked. 'He's been so careful. He hasn't left anything behind, not a single clue.' She was pulling a tissue apart into dusty little patches.

'Do what we did, go to all his relatives.' She moved closer, her voice hushed. 'You can't just call, because they lie. You have to go, show up there, surprise them at funny times, like dinner, or five-thirty a.m.'

'I don't know who his relatives are. I never met them. I haven't figured out any way to trace him.'

'Credit card bills, telephone calls?'

'There's nothing.'

'At least you know he's in Florida, that's a start.'

Sylvie shook her head. 'I made that up,' she confessed. 'I think he's someplace warm all year round, but big deal, what's that worth, given the size of the country?'

'How about his cancelled checks?'

'He took those or destroyed them, but I'm telling you, he wouldn't have left anything. He was very careful.'

'How long were you two together?'

'A year. Just barely,' Sylvie admitted as she rolled the fragmented tissue into a lumpy mass on the desk. Yes, Tracy. Of course she was a jerk, a total fool. She didn't need to be reminded she'd acted in haste.

'All right,' Tracy said. 'That's good. A year's hardly any time. Almost current, that's how I think of it. And he probably wasn't being as careful back before he met you, so we might just find something. I'll order a copy of his checks. Maybe there was something eighteen months ago, you never know.'

'The thing is,' Sylvie said, 'I don't think he lived here much before we met.'

Tracy turned back to her computer. Sylvie watched the screen fade, then fill again with letters and numbers. 'Way to go,' Tracy crowed, her pink fingernail highlighting a line on the screen. 'There's another account here that he closed out about a year ago. It was only open a couple of weeks before that.' The screen faded and re-formed yet again. Tracy was looking at the image, her eyes narrowed in concentration. 'Look at this,' she said after a moment, turning the terminal so Sylvie had a full view. 'See these two account numbers, how different they are from each other?' Sylvie nodded. One was a long stream of numbers with dashes and letters mixed in, the other, a short, clean string of numbers. 'This,' she said, clicking her nail against the screen, 'isn't our bank's numbering system. It's Freedom Bank's system. But see, four or five months ago we took them over, so we have their records. If the account had remained open over the change-over, new numbers would have been assigned to it, and it wouldn't be so obvious there were two different banks involved. But because he'd already closed that account out, it shows up this way.' She laughed at something else she saw on the screen. 'Look,' she said. 'He closed out the Freedom account the same day he opened this one. It didn't have anything to do with making it a joint account because he didn't add your name till two months later. When he closed the account, he withdrew everything, drove across town, and came here. Like he wasn't too keen, maybe, on someday somebody going in there and finding this other account.'

'Maybe he just thought Freedom was about to fold,' Sylvie suggested.

'No, I don't think so, because it wasn't. Freedom wasn't failing. It was just a merger, simple and clean. Our bank was getting bigger, is all. I think the guy was trying to cover his tracks. That's definitely what I think, when I see something like this.'

'Better interest rates?' Sylvie suggested.

Tracy looked at her straight on. 'You want to find some reason not to get him now?'

'No,' Sylvie said, shaking her head. 'I just don't want to get my hopes up, you know.'

'Well, it wasn't better interest rates because these are both checking, and they're neither of them interest-bearing. I'm betting my money that he had something to hide.' She turned toward Sylvie, smiling, though this time Sylvie saw the mischief in it, the shared mission. 'We're going to get him,' Tracy said, but so quietly Sylvie only barely made it out.

We're going to get him, Sylvie repeated silently to herself, confirming it. Her fingers were crossed so far over each other, the stretch was painful.

'Oh, wait a minute,' Tracy said. 'You can't get access to that account because it's in his name, not yours. Damn,' she said, and her fist hit the desk. 'And that's exactly where there might be something.' The manager sat back, pulled herself straighter in her chair. 'I can't authorize anyone other than the original owner of this account to have access to the records. Only signers can order access into an account,' she said. Sylvie stared at her. What was happening? She was responding like an automaton now, spouting rules like she was reading out of a test review booklet for manager school. 'You understand what the rules are, don't you?' Tracy asked her.

'Yes.'

'You understand I can't authorize this information?'

'Yes.'

'Okay. So we'll get your joint account and make do, that's all.' Sylvie's mind was racing. Maybe she could get Martinson to come in and pose as Peter. There had to be some way to get him, didn't there?

Tracy opened her file draw again and pulled out a long paper form. 'What we'll do,' she explained in a jarring, almost singsong voice, 'is ask for all the checks from your account. That kind of request needs your signature, of course, and it'll probably cost you a fortune to call up a year's worth of records. They charge by the check, you know.' Tracy was filling in the lines on the form. Her pen moved in firm, bold motions.

'That's okay,' Sylvie said, her voice an angry mumble. It wasn't okay; she wanted the other account.

After a few moments the manager turned the paper around and pushed it toward Sylvie. 'Here's a pen, and here's where I need your signature,' she said, pointing to a line she'd already marked with an X. 'Here's your account number,' she said, pointing higher up on the form where Sylvie saw the woman had actually filled in two numbers: the stubby short one and the long stringy one. Sylvie looked up at Tracy, whose face was solemnly blank. 'You copy numbers long enough, you can make small errors sometimes. It happens to everybody – tellers, managers – you just can't be one hundred percent protected all the time.' Sylvie nodded. 'And the terrible part is, mistakes are supposed to be caught by all the checking we do. Like this is supposed to go up to Hartford now and if there was a mistake on it, it would probably be caught, thank goodness, by the person processing the request. But even there, you can have a slip-up. Sometimes those people up on the night shift have looked at so many forms, they stop seeing what they're supposed to. Somebody up there is going to have to set up months and months of checks for copying both sides. Of course you can get into a sort of pattern, all dulled out, just putting the next batch through the copier, and maybe that's how security gets a little lax. I've worked up there, that's where I started when I was eighteen. And I know it's the most boring job imaginable. And most of the time I was sleepy, too, biding my time till a day job opened in the system. A lot of people I worked with, this was their second job on top of another eight hours. I've seen people put their heads down and start snoring up there.' She paused for a moment, her eyes full on toward Sylvie. 'I do want to make sure that I explained it all to you, that you understand my position and that I don't violate rules, right?'

'Oh, yes,' Sylvie said, trying not to smile.

'Okay. Now I fax this up there and we'll see what happens. You've got a good shot at it. You can call me tomorrow. I won't have gotten any copies by then, but I might know if anybody's flagged it, just in case I made any mistakes in filling out the form.'

'Thank you,' Sylvie whispered.

'We'll get the bastard,' Tracy said, and held out her hand. Sylvie took it, and held tight.

Chapter 23

'It might not mean anything,' Martinson told her. They had the whole packet of transactions that Tracy had come up with spread out on the kitchen counter. Sylvie'd found one check – from the old account in Peter's name – that had been cashed in Arizona.

'It means he maybe lives out there,' she told him.

'No, it doesn't. It means he wrote a check to "cash," well over a year ago, and somebody else happened to cash it out there.'

'Every single other check in that pack was cashed in Connecticut,' she argued. Martinson shrugged, held out his hands palms up. 'And isn't Arizona one of those warm places where people go to retire?' She picked up the copy of the check again. 'Tucson,' she read aloud. 'Don't people go out there and play golf all year round?'

'I guess so.'

'They do. It's one of those major retirement places with lots of sun. There was a big thing in the paper a couple of weeks ago about how there isn't very much water out there anymore, because it's gotten so overpopulated.' He tugged at the paper in her hand and she let it go. 'He lives in Tucson,' she said.

'It's too damn easy. He wouldn't make a mistake like this. He's too careful. Forget this.'

'It's the last check he wrote on that account. It's obviously why he closed the account.'

'No, he closed it because he was opening one with you.'

She leaned toward him, wanted, even, to point and press her finger against his chest, to insist, but she held back, saying only, 'No, he didn't add me for another two months. He changed banks because he wanted to hide this. He had second thoughts

193

when he realized somebody's name was going to be on the reverse side of this check. He wanted to cover his tracks.'

'No,' Martinson said, and pushed the check off to the side.

'Oh, come on, Detective! I finally come up with something and you're going to reject it. Why? What exactly is your objection? We've been looking for some kind of mistake and when I find it you claim he doesn't make mistakes. Where's the logic in that?'

'I'm not rejecting it, I'm just thinking about the possibilities. I don't want you to think it's all over, because chances are this is dead-end stuff. Or at best, a cold, frozen lead. This check is dated over a year ago.'

'Right, just a couple of days before he met me, *before* he was being Mr Careful.'

'Maybe, but what you've got here is the very smallest possibility that this will come up solid. And now you're high as a kite – I've never seen you like this, with your cheeks all flushed, all that jumping up and down the way you did when you found it.'

'Didn't you tell me that we have to look at everything?'

'Yes, and that's still true. I'm trying to be the realist, is all. I don't see him making this fundamental a mistake.'

'Okay, so maybe it's not quite so perfect as I thought, maybe Tucson isn't where he lives and it isn't where Cally is, but maybe there's someone there who knows him, who had contact with him and who can tell us where to go next.'

He lifted the paper and scanned it again. 'You know, even leading you that far would have been a pretty major mistake on his part,' the detective said. 'He wrote a check made out to "cash" that somebody presented in Tucson. That's all we know.

Sylvie took the paper back from his hand. The check had been endorsed by a Keith Blessing. Beneath that signature was another signature, that of Joanna Blessing. The check had been cashed at Western savings, Tucson, Arizona.

'There aren't any other checks in here made out to "cash" that are signed by other people. It could be,' Sylvie said, going slowly as though a gradual unfolding would convince more thoroughly, 'it could be that these are the people who have Cally.'

'I doubt it,' he said. 'Why would he be writing a check to them? If they had Cally, it's them who'd be writing to him, don't you think?'

She wished he hadn't said that. She closed her eyes, trying to blink away the image of people exchanging money while her child was passed, hand to hand, as though down an assembly line. 'It might be a friend, a sister, something like that,' she almost begged him, and was relieved to see him nod in assent.

'Or somebody he mail-ordered something from,' the policeman said.

'No,' she countered, 'that's not how those things work. If he was ordering something, the check would be made out to the company, not to "cash". I think this person, this Keith whoever, knows where Peter is.'

'Sylvie,' he protested. 'Let's suppose for just a second that you're right. What makes you think you'd get anything from this person? Why would he tell you where to find Peter?'

'Maybe he's been burned, too.'

'A year ago? That's an older lead than you've got. You'll be doing *him* a favor to tell him Peter was last seen in New Haven.'

'Peter liked Mexican food.'

'You said he liked steak. We've been over all that. Don't change the story to fit this check, Sylvie, please.'

'No, listen. His favorite food, like at home, or if we were going out, *was* steak, but he was always talking about how there was no good Mexican food out here. That they were always using tomato sauce when they should have been using chilies. And what about how he always said, *out here*. Where's Arizona?' she asked him.

'West,' he said. 'Next to southern California.'

'Okay, so you could call that *out there*, couldn't you. And you could say we're *out here*, right?' If it were Florida, wouldn't he say, *up* here?'

Martinson shrugged. 'Maybe, but there's still Texas, New

195

Mexico, and southern California and they're "out there," too.'

Sylvie felt as though this were a physical effort, like she was clutching Martinson under the arms and dragging him into believing. 'They do eat Mexican in Tucson, don't they?'

'Yes.' He gathered the other photocopies together, tapping them against the counter to even the edges, then set them off to the side. 'And steak,' he said.

She smiled at him, and she could feel how it really did seem like it went from ear to ear. It was the whole of her. 'Steak's a big thing there?'

He nodded. 'They grill it on wood fires. Mesquite wood, I think is what they use.'

'All right,' she said emphatically. She opened the refrigerator, took out a tall bottle from the rack on the door. 'Look at this,' she said, putting it down firmly on the counter. 'Authentic Mesquite Flavor,' she read from the label. 'It's disgusting stuff, vile-tasting. I always had to cut the steak in half before I cooked it so I didn't have to have it on my portion.' He took the bottle, looked at it for a moment, then put it down again. 'It *is* something, isn't it?' She whispered the words, then did a quick series of soft-shoe steps in place.

'I didn't say that. We have very little, Sylvie. A couple of guesses and hunches, but that isn't enough to believe in.' He put his hand on her shoulder, and she tried to stay still for a moment. 'I hate to be the doomsayer in all this because I have to admit, I like seeing you so up, so happy.'

'What do we do now?' she asked him, moving from his hand, twisting halfway round in a circle.

'We should try to contact these people.' He pointed at the Blessings' signatures on the check.

'This woman at the bank, Tracy, said we shouldn't telephone.'

'I know, but we don't exactly have a lot of choices right now. If we come up with the right questions, you'll do okay on the phone. I could try to run his prints – the ones we took for reference – through the Tucson files.'

'You can run the prints,' she said, 'but I'm still going to go out there.'

'Oh, no, you're not. You already said you get flustered when you do the face-to-face bit. You'll just end up blowing this thing.'

'I know how to do it now.'

'What does that mean?'

'Up till I got through to Tracy I was playing this real cool approach, using the detective model, like you've been telling me to and just asking for information. But that takes lying, and that takes worrying about being exposed in those lies. The way to do it is to tell the truth, Detective. People know the difference. They respond to real stuff that's happening to you. They feel it with you. They get caught off guard, they say "Okay, you need help, here it is." I'm going to go out there and say, "Do you know where this asshole is, because he took my baby?"'

'Because it worked with Tracy?' She nodded. 'Fat chance, Sylvie. You lucked out on that. You hit the one woman who happened to have a sister who'd had her kids swiped. Don't fool yourself that you'll get anywhere with sweet ideas of Girl Scout honesty.'

She turned away from him, knowing suddenly how right he was; how impossible it was, how impossible it had been from the moment she'd walked in and seen that empty crib.

'And technically,' he continued, 'you're not even supposed to leave the state, you know. You're a suspect in this case, remember. I think for now we should take it easy. I'll keep working at this end, trying to get the case against you dropped. That's what's really important right now. You need to sit tight, make some phone calls at most. You can't push these people, or they'll go cold on you.'

'Screw that. I'm not backing off,' she said. 'You can go keep track of the rights and wrongs on your little charts, Detective, if that's what turns you on, but I'm planning on looking for Keith Blessing.' She lifted his jacket from the end of the counter where he'd set it down. She flung it the short distance between them. 'Go already, okay?'

'Fine, no problem,' he said standing. When he got to the door, he turned toward her. 'Call me when you get there?'

All she did was take in a deep breath, didn't say a thing at all. Then he nodded, opened the door, and was gone.

Chapter 24

Hannah was concerned. The whole plan sounded hare-brained to her, she said. 'Won't they stop you?'

'Who?'

'I don't know – airport security. Don't they have lists of people who aren't supposed to leave the state? Don't they check for those things? You haven't thought this through, Sylvie. What if you end up in jail?'

Hannah's voice was rising, taking on that jagged edge that clutched and grabbed at Sylvie and tried to get in between her thoughts. But Sylvie knew her mother was right: She hadn't considered the possibility that she might be stopped. The suggestion set her insides awhirl. Maybe she ought to call Martinson, ask him what was likely to happen. Though what real good was there in that? If he said yes, it was true, she might get stopped, she wasn't going to *not* go, was she? She'd deal with it if it happened, that was all. 'I discussed it with Martinson,' she said, hoping to put her mother on hold on this issue. 'He says there's no problem. They can't keep a record of everybody in every city, you know.'

'I suppose not,' Hannah said. Sylvie was taking underwear out of her top drawer, putting it into the blue canvas suitcase that lay open on her bed. 'And if you do find Cally,' Hannah asked, 'what do you do then?'

Sylvie stared at her mother, her surprise at such a question evident in her tightened brows. 'I bring her back, of course.'

'I meant how. You can't just walk in and say, "Please—"'

'I'll deal with that,' Sylvie said, cutting her off. She was packing quickly, not worrying about how many , or what color, or if she'd be warm enough. Some underwear, some clothes, a

199

change of shoes . . . what else did she need? A toothbrush, a comb. The suitcase was filling up even more quickly than it had for the infamous trip to Puerto Blanco. She let her hands rest for a moment on the mound of clothes and cautioned herself: Slow down, this isn't the time to forget some important item. And then she thought maybe she should wait till she had an actual birth certificate, till custody was officially granted to her, but no, it was better to just get there, wasn't it? She didn't want to let them have time to . . . to what? she asked herself, but couldn't think what might happen next. But wasn't that open-ended feeling about Cally's fate reason enough to get out there fast? Who *could* know what might happen next? I've got to find out, she told herself. Settle it. She put the letter the midwife had written into the suitcase. The airline ticket she put into her purse, checking it yet again for departure time – God, this place was far away. It was going to take two planes and most of the day to get there. What she wanted, what she wished she had, was a gun, or something threatening, conclusive, and powerful that she could hold in her hand and say, 'Please . . .' and then he – they – whoever it was she was talking about, would have to surrender, to place the baby in her arms because 'please' was nothing, a whimper that wasn't going to be worth a damn. Well, she'd deal with it, like she said. She'd figure it out.

'Do you want the breast-pump?' Hannah asked, holding up an ugly thing that looked like a bicycle horn crossed with a baby bottle.

'My milk is almost gone,' Sylvie said as she took the pump from Hannah's hand and tucked it into the inner pocket of the valise. 'I can barely feel it anymore.' No, Sylvie thought, it *is* gone. The pumping that she did now was simply painful ritual. The chamber of the pump had stayed almost dry the last few days.

'She can be bottle-fed, you know that.'

'Of course I know it,' Sylvie said, her words jumbled in with not-to-be-shed tears. 'It just feels like she's draining away from me.' She turned and faced her mother. 'My body isn't falling for this trick with the pump. It knows how things are supposed to be, and this isn't it. My body knows she's gone. It knows more than that, too. It knows something's wrong. That she's not coming back, so the milk can go away. It's like I'm not entitled to it anymore.' The tears were hot below her cheeks.

'Sylvie, there's nothing mystical about it – you're not nursing, so the milk isn't in demand, and therefore it dries up. It's a purely physical cause-and-effect process, a natural supply-and-demand issue, that regulates lactation. It's not like your body can know where Cally is or what's happening to her.'

'You know,' Sylvie said, turning to her mother, 'I really don't care about scientific explanations right now. You can stop being academic with me, okay?' Sylvie saw Hannah's mouth tighten, her lips turn, ever slightly inward. 'You know what Martinson says?' she asked her mother.

'Oh, Martinson has the last word on breast-feeding now?'

'It's not breast-feeding, it's everything.'

'Oh, then, do tell. I want to hear this great philosopher's view of the world.'

'He says you can tell the weather just as well by listening to the wind as by analyzing the world's most sophisticated computer printouts.' Hannah shook her head. Sylvie lifted the hairbrush from the bed and slipped it between the clothing layers in her luggage. 'Don't you act on anything at all without trying to figure out why and how and wherefore and so what, first?' she asked her mother.

'I haven't found that impulsive behavior ever leads to sound solutions.'

'I didn't say impulsive. I'm talking about feelings.'

'Where has that gotten you?'

'It's gotten me Cally,' Sylvie said, defiant, chin jutting now. 'Tell me she isn't worth it.'

'I wouldn't presume to tell you that, you know that.'

'Maybe I've done some stupid things, misjudged, but I'm living my life, doing what I need to do.' Sylvie went to the closet and pulled a blue knit shirt off its hanger. Maybe she would find Cally, she thought. She'd find her safe, and she'd find her soon. In fact, maybe she ought to take a bunch of baby clothes with her. Or at least one little suit and one, or perhaps two or three diapers. It would be like carrying a good-luck token with her. It would be for hope. She realized she didn't even know what size to bring – how much bigger was Cally likely to be after these three weeks?

'Have you considered that this could be a wild-goose chase?' Hannah asked suddenly.

'Yes,' Sylvie said, and decided not to take the baby clothes. If she didn't find Cally, if this was a foolish, expensive, exhausting time-filler, then unpacking the clothes when she returned would be more than she could bear. 'And I'm doing it anyway.'

'And *I* think – *I* know – *you* should wait.' Hannah's emphasis was heavy over the pronouns. 'What do you expect to gain by grabbing her illegally?'

'I'll gain touching her, feeling her again.' She held a hand over her beast. The thought of her child snuggled in against her pulled all the breath out of her.

'You'll be arrested, Sylvie.'

'So I will.'

'Cally'll be taken away from you.'

'So she will. And I'll take her back again.' Sylvie changed her mind and put Cally's carrot jumpsuit down on top of her own clothes.

'What if – I don't know, what if the people who have her do something violent? You don't know what they're capable of.'

Sylvie barely had breath to form the words, but she went slowly through them, exploring them, feeling the truth of them: 'I've been hurt beyond hurting already.'

'I don't believe that,' Hannah said. 'Whoever has Cally can do more. Can't you wait? Can't you let the courts take care of it?'

It felt like a laugh, this tight thing in her chest that wanted unwinding, but it felt sharp, too, fearful, a cough, a crushing blow. 'Mama,' Sylvie said, 'if it were you, twenty years ago, if it were me, not Cally, what would you have done? Would you have waited till it was all legal and foolproof and safe? Would you have let weeks or days or hours go by while you waited?'

'I don't want to make it worse, to have you in jail, to have legal issues . . .' she said, her voice trailing off.

'I just want to know whether you, Hannah Pierson, would have gone after your baby.'

'It isn't a simple yes-and-no issue we're talking about here,' Hannah insisted.

'Okay, try explaining it to me then, in long form – essay style, if you want.' Sylvie sat down on the bed to wait for her mother to begin. Hannah picked up the little stuffed mouse, the one that used to sit on Cally's windowsill. Sylvie had placed it in her suitcase along with her clothing.

'There are always consequences to be considered,' Hannah said, smoothing down the blue fur. Sylvie nodded. 'If you were missing, if it were like this . . .' Her voice had gone husky, quiet. 'I wouldn't have waited.'

Hannah turned away for a moment, eyes closed. And then her eyes were back again on her daughter, and Sylvie put her hand out and Hannah came toward her, both arms reaching, needing, and she drew her child close against her.

Just before she left for the airport, Sylvie opened her wallet and took out a crumpled scrap of paper. She'd gotten the number that was written out in red marker so easily, she still couldn't believe it could possibly be the real thing. All she'd had to do was call Directory Assistance and ask for a Keith Blessing on Elm. 'I have nothing on Elm, but I do have a K. and J. Blessing on Larch,' the operator had responded.

'Oh, right, that must be it – 2740 Larch?'

'No, 368 Larch.'

'Well, then, *that* must be it,' Sylvie had said, not the least bit worried that it must be ridiculously obvious that she'd been pumping the operator for the address. What difference did it make if in the end she got the information she needed? And Martinson was right – it wasn't like you could call Directory Assistance and say your baby had been taken, cry a little, and hope that the operator, out of the goodness of her heart, would tell you all the addresses you'd ever wanted to know.

But in that moment when she'd let down the phone, it all felt much too simple, just like Martinson had warned. Could these people have anything on Peter if they were so very easy to locate? But then, just as quickly, she decided not to think about it. She dialed Directory Assistance again and asked for a number for Peter. Nothing. Not that she's expected it, exactly, but she felt shaken by it, shaken hard – like she'd jumped from up high on down to an ungiving concrete landing. It'd seemed like he should be out there, and that he should be listed. Could she be wrong about this whole Tucson thing? She tried a few more times, asked for a new listing, then tried the usual variations on his name, but still, it all came up zero. Another moment of conflict: Doubt about the soundness of a cross-country chase to pursue a wisp of a hint of a notion. Maybe she oughtn't to go, she thought, but then reminded herself it was possible, just possible (even Martinson admitted there was a chance, even if barely measurable), that these people actually had her baby. She had to go, and she had to go as soon as possible. She had to know.

The paper that she held in her hand was actually completely superfluous. She'd committed the seven digits to memory as the computer voice of Directory Assistance had chimed it out to her. She pressed the appropriate telephone buttons, heard the signal ring once, twice, then three times, heard the click of the lifted receiver, then the chirrupy answer – a woman, young, clear in voice, saying hello. 'Is this Mrs Blessing?' Sylvie asked.

'Yes, it is.'

'This is Janet from Babyland calling about our special offer for new parents.'

'Yes?' the voice had become suspicious, careful, but Sylvie was elated – the woman hadn't challenged the presumption that she was a new parent.

'I'd like to send you our special introductory card that gives you a twenty-five percent discount on all purchases made before your baby's six-month birthday.'

'What's the catch?'

'Nothing. We just want to get you to our store, so you'll see how special it is.'

'Well, I guess it's okay.'

'Good. We'll have that out for you real soon, then.'

'What's it good for?'

'You mean what can you buy with it?'

'Yes,' the woman said, and laughed. 'I didn't mean that to sound so negative.'

'Oh, that's okay,' Sylvie said. 'You can use it for anything in the store – clothes, furniture, toys, even diapers – and those are so expensive these days, aren't they?'

'Yes, they really are. I was kind of shocked, actually, by that.'

'So I'll be sending it out.'

'Thank you,' she said, and Sylvie replaced the receiver.

'Very impressive,' said Hannah, who'd been standing in the doorway. 'Maybe you have a future career ahead of you in acting.'

Sylvie smiled. 'It'd have to be limited to telephone acting, I'm afraid. I fall all to pieces when there are real people in front of me. I blush and stammer and cry.'

'Were you able to find out anything from this woman?'

'Only that she's a new parent and that her baby must be under six months.' Now Sylvie realized she might have asked for the baby's name, said she wanted to add it to the card, something like that.

'Did she say whether it was a girl or boy?'

'No.'

Hannah sighed. 'It isn't much, what you have.'

'No. They have a baby, and they have some kind of connection with Peter.'

'*Might* have a connection.'

'Yes, Mother.'

'And the connection might not be Cally,' Hannah pointed out.

'Right. And it might be, or maybe Peter buys and sells babies all over the place. Maybe this Blessing baby is one of his, but isn't Cally. But I might still find him through them. Or maybe these are just people who cashed a check of Peter's who happen to have a baby all their own. Legal, natural, all that good stuff.'

'Yes,' Hannah said. 'There are so many possibilities. It could be anything.'

'Maybe it's nothing, Mama,' Sylvie said. She zipped the suitcase, then brought the two zippers down toward the same bottom corner. 'Maybe it's a stupid wild-goose chase, like you said.'

'Anything's possible,' Hannah said, dreamy-like, it seemed to Sylvie, or maybe even a little hopeful.

'That's why I'm going,' Sylvie said, swinging the case off the bed.

PART 3

Chapter 25

It was warm in Tucson. She didn't need a coat, not even the lightweight jeans jacket she now pulled off and dropped across her suitcase. At least it isn't like Puerto Blanco, she thought, remembering how stifling the air had felt as they walked from the airport that day; so humid, so very hot, she hadn't thought she could possibly get enough air into her lungs, let alone actually enjoy her time there. But within a few hours, she'd gotten used to it, just like she'd gotten used to all sorts of other things in this life. You learned how to dress for the weather, somehow, wherever you were. This Tucson sun, though, she thought, was quite perfect – dry and warm, gentle on the bare skin of her arms where she'd pushed her shirt sleeves up above the elbows.

Sylvie signaled to a cruising taxi. Some kind of uniformed person stepped toward the curb, opened the door for her before the car had even come to a full stop, took hold of her two bags before she could grab them herself, and tossed them onto the back seat. She slid into the taxi and reached for the door, but he did that job for her, too, slamming it rather too firmly in her opinion. She hadn't tipped him, and might have worried over that for a moment or two, but truth was, she couldn't be dealing out dollar bills for unasked-for services just now. All the money for this trip had come from her mother, and she was going to be a very long time in paying it back. Hannah had been generous and gracious about giving her the funds, but her resources, though considerably better than Sylvie's, could hardly be considered limitless.

'What time will it be dark?' she asked the cabbie after she'd given him the name of her hotel.

209

'You've got about an hour of daylight left,' he told her.

Not enough time, she knew. All she'd be able to do this day was check in, get herself some good maps, and think about tomorrow. And find some cheap place for dinner, too.

'You here on business or pleasure?' the driver asked her.

'Business,' she told him.

'Too bad,' he said, and laughed such a big, hearty chuckle, she smiled to hear him.

He recommended a restaurant near her hotel. Told her, even, what to order. 'Get the carne seca,' he advised. 'They do the best in the whole town.' He also praised the blue corn tamales, though he thought they might not be in season. If they weren't he said, the Sonoran enchiladas were terrific. 'And, oh,' he concluded, rolling his head in remembered ecstasy (she was hoping he kept his eyes open), 'you *have* to have the mango chimichanga. You just have to. I take my whole family there and we eat like kings, all of us, for twenty dollars. If you have to be here on business, at least you'll have those pleasures.'

She was not able to do her cabbie's recommendations justice. She'd eaten so little since Cally had disappeared that her stomach had shrunk, or simply become intolerant, she wasn't sure which, so that a few forkfuls of food was all she could manage most of the time. It was enough, though, to see that this cuisine bore almost no resemblance to Mexican-style food back East, and that pleased her to the point of light-headedness. Tucson has to be it, she thought.

And tomorrow, she reminded herself, it would begin. She'd been given the name of the hotel she was now registered at by the Chamber of Commerce. They'd told her it was 'a hefty but acceptable walk' from there to 368 Larch. 'Nice pool there, too,' the woman had said to her on the phone. Not really all that expensive, either, she'd found when she made her reservation. So she was finished with taxis until she returned to the airport.

She did not unpack. Taking her clothes out of the suitcase and placing them in the drawers of the bureau seemed the wrong thing to do. When it came time to leave, she wanted to be ready to run.

She'd barely settled into the room – which really meant

210

taking off her shoes, stretching out on the bed, and going over the map she'd picked up at the airport – when the phone rang, startling her badly. It was Hannah, of course; no one else knew where she was. Their conversation was short, though filled with warnings from the older woman – not all about tracking down Peter either, but about walking alone at night through the city, about getting lost. Silly things, Sylvie thought, lying back on the bed, the phone propped against her ear by the pillow. 'You sound funny,' Hannah said. Sylvie pleaded exhaustion, and the conversation ended.

She couldn't sleep. She couldn't get the number 368 out of her head, or the image of the streets, still just straight black lines on a map, to go away. She had the directions learned by heart, for she could hardly walk about with a map spread out before her. Turn left in front of the hotel, walk three blocks, turn right, walk ten blocks, start looking. She knew where the nearest park was, and tomorrow she would find out where the grocery was, the pharmacy, dry cleaners, all of it – all places she might run into people with babies in strollers.

After realizing she'd begun to mumble the address half-aloud like a chant of some sort, she turned the light on and dialed Martinson's home number.

'Did I wake you?' she asked him, whispering into the phone.

'Just a bit,' he said 'but don't worry about it. I was trying to wait up for your call.' He wasn't whispering.

'Sorry. I wasn't really sure how we left it. Did I say I'd call?'

'Well, it doesn't matter. Tell me what's happening out there.'

'So far there's nothing to contradict that this is *out here*,' she said, 'though I suppose that's not worth much.'

'Not in a court of law, certainly.'

'No, well, I'm here, and tomorrow I'll go find these people. In person, no phone calls, like I said.'

'I'd feel better if you'd try to find out something on the phone first. You don't know what you're getting into there.'

'If I was going to call them on the telephone, I wouldn't have had to fly all the way out here. I'll be all right,' she insisted.

'And if you spook them?'

'I won't,' she said, believing it. 'I'll be okay, Detective.'

'Listen, you make an ID and get out of there. Don't do anything, don't give yourself away. Then call me tomorrow, right afterward. And I got the name of somebody on the Tucson force for you.'

'Police force?'

'Yes. A Detective Ortiz. A friend of mine here knows somebody on the force and he said this guy's really good. I called him, didn't tell him much, just said it was a domestic dispute, because they'll go nuts if they know you're planning to harass somebody for no cause, but I told him you might call if there's a problem. I'm faxing him the prints in the morning. He said he'd take care of it and you.'

'Detective, it's not *no cause*,' she complained.

'I'm talking legal terms here.'

'Sure.'

'Hey, think about it. I'm doing the best I can on this.' She didn't answer. 'Tell me you'll call him if there's trouble.'

'I'll call him,' she said, discharging him. She stared into the black headset, looking down into the silence.

'Daniel Ortiz is his name,' he finally said. 'Write it down.'

'I can remember a name.'

'Okay. Just take care, okay?'

'I will.'

And then she slept.

Chapter 26

In Tucson, Sylvie realized, there are no large trees to conceal someone who is spying. There aren't even any smallish trees that a person could lean up against so as to appear to be nonchalantly waiting for somebody else to show up. Occasionally, on her walk down toward Larch, she passed a wide-armed saguaro cactus, but noting the spines, she decided against that particular option.

Sylvie wasn't sure what to do. She started by walking past the house, but on the opposite side of the street. Walking briskly, as though headed somewhere, she passed a man coming out of his pale-colored one-story house. He carried a briefcase, got into his car, and headed, she assumed, off for work. He took no notice of her, which pleased her till she realized she'd been so intent on him during her near run down the block that she hadn't even looked over toward 368 to see if anyone was coming out of that house. She had to slow down and check out the landscape, she told herself as she headed back the other way.

Maybe Martinson was right and she should go find a telephone, call, ask, 'Can you tell me where to reach Peter Weston?' and get this over with. For all she knew, there was nobody at home now and there wouldn't be till six o'clock that night. Or eight o'clock. Or maybe as soon as they'd answered the call from Janet from Babyland, they'd taken off on a month-long vacation.

After two more strolls up one side of the street and down the other, Sylvie was starting to wonder how many times she could get away with this before someone came out and asked, 'May I help you?' or worse, called the police. She'd been staring into all the windows she passed, thinking she might catch a glimpse of Cally's round little face, though the only living creature she'd actually seen through the glass was a white cat sunning itself at a picture window. Okay, she said to herself, straightening up, stepping into the street to cross to the even-numbered side, it's time. She'd just go over there and ring the bell. And be done with it. And then I'll know, she thought. Then I can go home, already. Dead end, frozen lead number 297 or whatever they'd advanced to by now.

She stopped walking when she wasn't even halfway across the street, and turned back. Perhaps it would be better to catch them off guard, she told herself when she'd reached the safety of the curb. Not scare them with the mention of his name right off the bat in case they wanted to protect him. Wouldn't it be better to get them talking about something else first? One time a young couple had knocked on the door of the Livingston Street apartment asking if she knew of any apartments for rent. What the hell, she said to herself, I can work my way down toward 368 that way and make it look like I have some reason for being on the street. She headed for the house directly across from her and rang the bell. A dog barked, a woman answered. 'Hello,' Sylvie said. 'I'm sorry to bother you, but I'm wondering if you know of any houses for sale in this neighborhood. My husband and I are moving out here and we fell in love with this street and there's nothing on the market, but sometimes people know about these things before they're official.'

'Well, no, I don't know of any,' the woman said, pushing a small yapping poodle back away from the door with her foot.

'Mommy,' a child called from another room.

'I'll be right there,' the woman shouted over her shoulder. 'She's home sick today,' she explained. 'I can't help you on that, but I do wish you luck.' She smiled at Sylvie.

'Thanks,' Sylvie said, and nearly skipped back down the path. Hey, she said to herself, that was so easy. Keep the lies minimal, and it had to work.

When she reached the sidewalk, she counted the number of houses left before 368. Four. At the next house, no one answered. Easy victory there, she thought. At the one after that, a man in

214

a bathrobe came to the door. No, he said, he didn't know any houses, wasn't planning to put his up for sale, if that's what she was asking. 'You know, actually, I hadn't been thinking of that,' she said, and laughed. 'Do you want to put it up for sale?'

'Who are you really? A real estate agent? he asked with belligerence.

'No, I told you – I'm from the East. I don't even live here yet.'

'Sorry, but I'm just your basic average suspicious guy,' he said, softening his tone. 'I don't trust anybody's motives anymore. But look, let me take your name and I'll send you a postcard if I hear of anything.'

'Thanks,' she said, and when he handed her pencil and paper, she wrote out a false name, an address in a town in Upstate New York where she and her mother had once vacationed.

He read it. 'You live up on the lakes?' he asked. She nodded. She hoped he didn't know too much about it – she'd phonied up the zip code. 'I went to Cornell for a year, so I know that part of the world a little.' If he questioned the zip code, she'd just say she wasn't very good with strings of numbers, that she had this problem, attention deficit disorder. 'I hated all that snow – transferred down to the University of Virginia. Don't you hate the snow and the cold?'

'Yes,' she said. He'd slipped the paper into his robe pocket.

'It doesn't snow here,' he told her.

'I know. That's why we're coming out here. It's ice we especially hate.'

He nodded. 'I've been here seven years. I'd never go back.'

At the next house, a woman cracked her door only enough for Sylvie to see one of her eyes, her nose, and part of her mouth. The chain that held the door was shiny and thick. Sylvie started her speech, but the woman cut her off. 'I don't know anything,' she said, and closed the door. Sylvie heard the dead bolt slide to. No one answered at the last house before the one she needed to get to. And then she was walking up the front path of 368. Ready. Needing someone to answer.

It was a woman who opened the door; a pretty blonde woman with a tight, brand-new perm who looked only a little older than herself. She wore white running shorts and a tee-shirt that had a colorful hot air balloon on the front. Small-breasted, definitely not a nursing mother, Sylvie noted. Skinny and muscular through the belly, too, so if she had given birth, she either worked out all day or her baby must be pretty old by now. 'Yes?' the woman asked, and despite all the trial runs along the street, Sylvie, catching sight of the woman's blue eyes, couldn't remember how to begin, what she was meant to say here. 'Can I help you?' the woman asked.

'I'm from the East,' she began slowly, as though searching her memory for the lines from a nearly forgotten script. 'And my husband and I are moving here.' This wasn't going well at all – she could see the woman's eyes narrowing. 'The thing is,' she said picking up speed, 'we just love this street and there aren't any For Sale signs, but sometimes the people who live on a street know about other people moving before it's official, and I thought maybe you might.' She forced her mouth up into a smile.

'Oh,' the woman said, shifting her shoulders, relaxing a little, Sylvie thought, or at least she hoped that was what she was seeing. 'I can't think of anybody right off.' She put her hand to her lips and leaned forward through the doorway, actually scanning the street from end to end. Sylvie saw a stroller against the opposite wall. The back of the carriage had been let down for sleeping or for holding a very young baby. There was a rattle or teething toy of some sort tied to the front bar. 'I could give you the name of our real estate agent. She's really terrific, if you think that would help.'

'That'd be wonderful,' Sylvie gushed.

'Why don't you come in,' the woman said, motioning Sylvie into the tiled foyer, 'and I'll look up the telephone number for you.' She walked over to a mission desk and lifted a black address book from one of its drawers. 'If anybody knows anything, Martha will.'

'Thanks so much,' Sylvie said as the woman wrote the information out.

'Tell her Joanna Blessing gave you her name. That's me, of course,' she said, moving her shoulders that way again, almost as though she were doing a little bow, Sylvie thought. 'I've put my name down there, too, at the bottom. Martha's the best agent I've ever met. She always knows about houses before they're on the market and she usually knows of at least one person who's thinking of selling and just needs a little push. She'll know other good streets, too.' Joanna handed the paper over. Sylvie pushed it into her jeans pocket without bothering to look at it. She was trying to think of some way to bring the discussion around to the topic of babies when Joanna asked her where she was from.

'Connecticut.'

'That's where my baby was born,' Joanna said with animation.

Something was whirling fast, faster, deep inside Sylvie. 'So,' she said, catching hold of the word as it spun through her brain, 'did you just move out here, too?' She had real trouble getting her lips to move around the words.

'No. We've been here three years now. We like to say Lily's our little easterner. She was born out there, and then we adopted her.'

Lily, Sylvie said to herself. Her baby is a girl, and she realized while she was nodding her head, saying nothing, that her heart rate had shot way up. She'd be dismissed now, the well-glad-I-could-be-of-help stuff was about to start. 'You said she's adopted?' Sylvie managed to say, though her mouth was so dry, the words bumped and stumbled into one another. Joanna nodded. 'The reason I ask,' Sylvie continued, 'is that we're thinking of adopting.' She was actually glad in that moment that her breasts had finally shrunk down – a nursing mother was so awfully easy to identify. 'But you used an agency in Connecticut, even though you live out here?'

'Well, it's a very long story. We did infertility for more than two years, first. And then . . . Listen, I don't even know your name . . .'

'Marie,' Sylvie quickly volunteered. 'Emerson.' And so much for sticking close to the truth. God help me remember who I am, she said to herself, crossing her fingers, then uncrossing them, saying her new name to herself. She could feel this woman slipping away from her, closing the door between them, then sealing it shut forever. 'I just feel, I don't know, so hopeless these days,' Sylvie said, her hands nearly reaching, along with the words, for Joanna's attention. 'I mean with adopting. Didn't you feel all separate from the rest of the world?'

'Yes, I did. We both did,' Joanna said, the sharp defensive edge blurred a bit now.

'I feel so unnatural, you know what I mean? Like a freak, almost. And so lonely,' Sylvie added, though she knew that she might be pushing a little too hard now.'

'Listen, would you maybe want to come in and have some coffee and we can talk about this stuff?'

'I'd like that,' Sylvie said, 'if I'm not keeping you from something.'

Joanna paused, reconsidering. Sylvie knew now that she'd provided her with an all too easy way out. Yes, I want coffee, she should have said. Would that have been such an outrageous response to the question? *I want to come into your house. Now.* Why had she gone and blown her opportunity on an empty oh-so-terribly polite phase?

'I've got two cakes and a pie all started at once, if you can believe it,' Joanna began, 'but that's the sort of thing you have to do when you have a baby, even one like Lily who sleeps forever, because once they're awake, there's no time for anything else. I've got to get everything into the oven, but I'd love to have a real grown-up to talk to while I do it, so come on in.' And Joanna gestured for Sylvie to follow her.

It was like being spun round and round in that childhood game of statues, Sylvie thought, her head so dizzied, she couldn't keep her eyes fixed on Joanna, couldn't walk a straight line behind her. Once they'd reached the kitchen she clutched at a chair, pulled it out, and sat down before she was really invited. Joanna didn't seem to mind. 'I've got a pot of decaf going, but I've got regular and tea as well, if you'd prefer,' she told her guest.

'The decaf would be perfect.'

Joanna poured coffee, provided Sylvie with sugar and a spoon, then began consulting one of several cookbooks that were open before her on the counter. 'Later, when Lily goes down for her afternoon nap, I'm doing a chocolate mousse.'

'I'm impressed,' Sylvie said. 'I can't even make a single batch of cookies come out right. Are you having tons of people over for dinner tonight?'

Joanna laughed. 'No. Just Keith – that's my husband – and me. We have a special occasion that calls for four desserts.' She turned a heaping tablespoon of cocoa into a bowl.

'Something to do with the baby?' Sylvie asked, knowing it probably wasn't, but hoping it'd get Joanna talking about her again.

'No. It's to celebrate the night we met. We call it our Night of Endless Desserts. No appetizer, no soups and salad, no main course, nothing but dessert. Oh, and champagne. We have to have something to wash it down.'

'Sounds wild. I'm one of those people, when I go to a restaurant I always want to skip the dinner stuff and start with dessert.' Sylvie almost cringed to hear her own forced enthusiasm.

'Oh, me, too,' Joanna said. She was alternately putting the dry and wet ingredients for her cake into a stainless-steel bowl.

Joanna twisted the bowl into the base of the mixer, set the machine at its lowest speed, then slowly turned it up till the blades were a blur. 'See, how we met was we were on a double date at this elegant restaurant, only we weren't with each other. I was with the other guy and Keith was with the other girl.' She laughed. 'Right after we ordered dessert, I went off to the ladies' room, and when I came out, Keith was standing by the door, and he says, "I'm insane about you."' She looked at Sylvie, shaking her head at the memory. 'It almost blew me away. I mean, no small talk, just that: "I'm insane about you."' Joanna used a rubber scraper to transfer her cake batter from bowl to baking pan. 'And then, and I guess this is the totally evil part' – she paused, leaning back against the counter – 'we left.'

'Left the restaurant?' Sylvie had both hands round her coffee mug. She didn't even like coffee, but she took a few sips now.

Joanna nodded. She laughed quietly, a sound like purring, almost, and she did that funny little shoulder shift again. 'We didn't bother to go back and tell our dates. Keith said they'd figure it out soon enough on their own, which of course is true, but, still, definitely evil. Afterwards we laughed about them sitting there with those four different desserts, wondering what was taking us so long.' She opened the upper oven and slid the cake in. 'One down, two to go,' she said, closing one cookbook and reaching over for another. She was quiet for a moment while she ran her finger down through the wording of the recipe. 'This one's almost done. All I have to do is add the egg white.' She washed her scraper, then used it to fold the whites in with gentle, rounded motions. 'So, anyway,' she said as she poured this batter into a second pan, 'we always have four different desserts to mark that occasion.'

'Great story,' Sylvie said. She wanted to know about the baby, not courtship rituals, but she knew it might be better to let things move along like this at Joanna's natural pace. Sylvie sipped her nearly cool coffee. The pre-heat buzzer went off on the second oven and Joanna put the new cake in to bake.

'Keith is like that, he just goes for things he wants. One weekend, he said, "You know what would be really reckless?" Because we were talking about going skydiving, actually. And I said, "What?" and he said, "Getting married," so we did it. It was only six weeks after we met, and let me tell you, it definitely got the adrenaline going. He was right. Keith says when you know what you want, you *should* go for it, otherwise you end up spending your life planning and waiting, never doing anything.' Joanna had picked up a wooden spoon and was using it to stir a bowl that looked to Sylvie like it was filled with crushed raspberries. 'My mother's always on my back about how he doesn't do things the way my father did. "How can you stand it?" she's always saying, "having him travel like that, having him changing jobs, never knowing how long you'll be living where you're living."'

'My mother's after me about my husband, too,' Sylvie said. 'The same kinds of things bother her. She's one of those people who is really big on things being neat and predictable.'

Joanna nodded vigorously. 'The thing I found out from being with Keith is that I really like to live the way we do with never knowing what's going to happen next. And Keith has taught

220

me so much, I can't tell you.' Joanna was rolling out the pie-crust and Sylvie watched it grow into a bigger, thinner circle with each successive outward push of the rolling pin. 'One time, right after we first got married, he gave me a certificate for ten ballet lessons because I told him how when I was a kid I'd dreamed about being a dancer. So I went to the first class and I hated it – I actually cried when it was over because I felt so clumsy and everybody except me seemed to know what they were doing. I felt like everybody was laughing at me. But he told me this thing I'll never forget. He said: "Everything you do in life, you're always playing a role, and how well it works is how well you get into that role." So he said, "If you want to be a dancer, the key is to think of yourself as a dancer. First thing you do," he said, "is think about what they look like." So I did, I imagined them in my mind, and you know how they hold their chins a little high?' Joanna demonstrated. 'Well, I did that. In front of a mirror, I pulled my hair back and fixed it in a bun with a velvet ribbon around the edge. Then I put blush high up on my cheeks the way they do,' she said, drawing a finger across each cheekbone. 'Then I thought about how they move, how they glide. He told me that I should imagine that everyone *was* watching me, but that they were watching me because they knew I was an exquisite dancer.' She draped the circle of dough over her rolling pin, then eased it down into a pie tin. 'He said if I did something wrong, I should act like I was the only one in the room doing it right. He says, "What you do in your head, how you shape yourself, that's the only important piece."' Sylvie watched Joanna scoop the thick red berry mixture into the pie-crust, then lick off some of the bits that were left clinging to the wooden spoon.

'Did the dancer stuff work?'

'Like a dream. No, it was more like magic because it was as if I was transformed into a dancer.' She'd cut long strips of pie-crust, and now was weaving them across each other over the filling. 'I felt I was as good as – better, really – than all the rest of them. Because inside,' she said, tapping her chest, 'I was a dancer. Everybody complimented me. Then I started doing that in other parts of my life, like in my job, same as he does.

221

He's done so many different things in his life – he's been a teacher, an architect, he's worked for corporations, all sorts of things. He says people are so afraid to try new stuff, they never go anywhere, never see anything fresh. But he loves new stuff, he sort of thrives on learning the look and feel of a new job. He says, you keep your ears open, you dress for the part, just like with me being a dancer, and you're halfway there. He says if people come to you with problems, no matter what field it is, all you have to say to them is, "No problem, I'll put my best person on it." People don't even notice if you don't say anything that has content, so long as you sound sure of yourself. Doctors, lawyers, decorators, gutter cleaners, you name it, it's all the same, he says, it's all just believing in yourself. I know it's a sort of old-fashioned idea, but I think one of the main reasons I love him is because of how he's changed me, made me able to be so much more than I was.'

'And now you're working on being a mom, I guess,' Sylvie said, thinking, Time to move on to the real issue.

'Well,' Joanna said, smiling, 'I guess you could say that, but that doesn't feel like something I have to actually work on.'

'Would you want me to check on her?' Sylvie asked, her voice floating over the words like a bird banking into the wind, wings grazing treetops as she grazed oh so close to knowing. 'I mean, you're up to your elbows in flour right now.'

'Oh, no, Lily's not even here, Marie.'

'Not here?' No longer floating, heading for free-fall dive.

'No, my neighbor Gail, bless her heart, when I told her I was doing all this baking, she said she'd take her during her nap, then feed her, give me a little extra time that way.'

Sylvie felt cold all over. Was she deliberately hiding her? From what? Certainly not from her because Joanna couldn't have known she was coming, or at least Sylvie didn't think she could. Had Joanna perhaps become suspicious during their conversation and was now lying about the baby's whereabouts? Had she given Joanna any reason to become panicky? 'She's somewhere on this street?' Sylvie asked, filling in time.

'Yes. Just a couple of houses down.' She looked up at Sylvie. 'Hey, we haven't talked at all about adoption, have we?'

'No, but I want to,' Sylvie said, and she could hear the pathetic sound of longing in her own voice.

'And given that that's what I asked you in here for to begin with, it might be nice for me to get to it.' The phone rang, startling Sylvie.

'Oh, no, I hope that's not Gail already,' Joanna said, glancing at the clock over the stove. She wiped her hands on a dish towel and reached the phone on its third ring. It was Gail. She reported that the baby was awake and hungry. 'I feel like a real jerk,' Joanna told Sylvie when she'd hung up the phone. 'After all that talk about how I'm falling into the mother role so easily, I went and forgot to leave a bottle for her with Gail. I thought I left everything – a change of clothes, diapers, a blanket. There's just too much to remember, still.' Joanna took the baby bottle from the dishwasher and began to pour formula into it. 'Gail would have given her a bottle with milk because her baby's on that already, but I don't want to take a chance. The doctor wants her on formula, so she's getting formula. Sorry to cut us short,' she said as she closed up the bottle, 'but I know Gail's going to go nuts if she has to rock a hungry, screaming baby for very long.'

'Of course.'

'Maybe, when you move here, we can get together again?'

'No,' Sylvie said, 'before that.' She couldn't let this slip away through the politeness cracks, she wasn't going to become the victim of *Yes, whenever it's comfortable for you.*

'Oh, how quickly we forget,' Joanna said. 'Every day counts when you're waiting to have a baby, doesn't it? You don't put things off for weeks into the future if there's some possibility of help hovering out there, do you? Are you still going to be in town tomorrow?' Sylvie said she would be. 'Tomorrow morning, then?' Sylvie nodded and they passed through the doorway together and down the front steps. 'Come early,' Joanna suggested. 'I put her down at eight forty-five, usually. That'll guarantee us a full hour and I promise to stay on the topic.'

Walking down the street, Joanna kept a brisk pace, anxious, obviously, to reach the baby as soon as possible. 'Maybe tomorrow I can give you some ideas about what to do next, what not to do next,' she said, moving the hand with the bottle back and forth over the words as she spoke them. 'That sort of thing.' Joanna turned down the walk of the third house, leaving Sylvie out at the sidewalk. It was a house that Sylvie hadn't been to in the course of her phony real estate canvassing mission. 'Take care,' Joanna said over her shoulder as she mounted the steps and raised the knocker. The door was pulled open almost before the sound of the knock had completed and Sylvie saw another woman holding a baby, maybe her baby, but then before she could take a single step toward her, the three of them, Joanna, Gail, and the baby had disappeared behind the closed door.

Martinson didn't understand it. 'You didn't get an ID,' he said.

'I couldn't. She basically threw me out.'

'Why didn't you walk up the path with her, get a look at the baby's face?'

She was silent. God, she wished she had. 'I thought it would look too obvious, too pushy. I'd already gotten her to invite me back. I thought that would be enough.'

'All right. I'm the one told you to go slow. I guess we'll just have to deal with what we have. Did you see any adoption papers?' She said she hadn't. 'Maybe you should ask to see those tomorrow.'

'How can I do that? People don't show off adoption papers like photographs.'

'The thing is, Sylvie, if they've got papers, then this isn't even Cally.'

'Why, you don't think Peter's capable of forgery?'

'No, I know he is. But push her to see the papers. Say something like you've always wondered what adoption papers looked like. Maybe it'll turn out there aren't any papers and we can get a wedge in that way. Listen, you didn't give this Blessing woman anything to go on, did you?'

'What do you mean?'

'I mean when her husband comes home tonight, and she starts telling him about you, are they going to put it together and think something screwy's going on?'

'I tried not to. We talked about desserts. We never even got around to babies. That's tomorrow morning. But I was definitely a wreck the whole time. Maybe she picked up on that. Or maybe if she just says some stranger came by, he's going to be suspicious. I mean if he's already nervous.' And she'd said the thing about wanting to adopt. They'd figure it out from that, wouldn't they? They'd figure she was trying to pump them for information on their baby.

'I wish you hadn't left without an ID, because if they've got you figured out, they're not long for that address, and we don't have anything solid yet.'

'Well, I wish I hadn't left, either.'

'Let me call Ortiz again, see if he came up with anything on either of them. Maybe we'll get lucky and there'll be an outstanding warrant or something.'

'Call me,' she begged him.

'I'll call you if I get anything.'

'Just call me,' she said, 'whether you get anything or not.'

Chapter 27

Sylvie woke with a start, her hand clutched tightly around Cally's orange jumpsuit. She'd waited, mostly pacing her small room, for a call back from Martinson, till finally, at four twenty-five, when she knew he wouldn't call because he thought he'd wake her, and when she could no longer call him for fear she'd wake him, she'd tried to sleep. She'd taken the jumpsuit from her suitcase, lain down on the bed, and spread the small piece of clothing over her chest. In the quiet darkness that was lit only by the red glow of clock numbers, she imagined Cally in that outfit again, her round body filling it out, the big embroidered carrot cutting a charming, though slightly silly, swath across her body.

When she woke, the room was filled with light and the red numbers warned that it was already past eight o'clock. She rose quickly, no time, even, for a call to Martinson, showered, and changed her clothes.

This time, Sylvie told herself as she approached Joanna's house, I will identify her. I will hold her. And I will take her back. Her hand was shaking when she placed her finger on the front door-bell. I should have slept more, she thought. I should have eaten breakfast. But then, I probably should have done all sorts of things differently in my life.

'Great timing, Marie,' Joanna said when she opened the door.

'She's gone down to sleep?'

'Yes, not five minutes ago.'

'Here?'

'Yes. I thought you might want to see her when she gets up.'

'Oh, I do,' Sylvie said, and had to suppress an urge to hug Joanna.

'Did you eat breakfast yet?' Joanna asked when they reached the kitchen. Sylvie said she hadn't. 'Great. Keith went out and bought these this morning.' She put a plate of five muffins down on the Mexican-tile-topped table. 'Of course this used to be a true half dozen, but he's already been at it.'

Sylvie didn't think she'd actually be able to eat any of the muffins, her mouth felt so dry, but she was determined to try, to seem like a calm, normal, merely inquisitive person. 'So how'd your dessert party go last night?'

'Oh, it was wonderful, absolutely wonderful,' Joanna said as she put a plate before each of them. 'Keith brought home three different outrageous flavors of ice cream. We ate fabulously huge, delicious quantities.' She smiled. 'Now that I'm talking about it, though, I realize I'd be a whole lot better off eating dry toast this morning.'

'Muffins aren't all that bad,' Sylvie consoled her.

Joanna laughed. 'Relatively speaking, I suppose you're right. I'll have the toast tomorrow. I assume you want decaf again?' she said, and began pouring when Sylvie nodded. 'So, have you gone the infertility testing route yet?'

Sylvie had her hands clasped tightly together, keeping herself whole and concentrated that way. 'Oh, yes,' she said. 'You have to do that to adopt, don't you?' During Sylvie's brief stint at the gynecologist's office, she'd been aware that some women were undergoing fertility tests. She knew the visits were often lengthy and that the women sometimes experienced pain, and almost always seemed depressed. And she remembered, too, how each of the nurses had tried to avoid being the one to instruct husbands on sperm count collections. 'You did all the testing too, I take it?'

'Oh, yes. That and *in vitro*. And I definitely don't recommend that.'

'You did that?' Sylvie asked.

'I did. And it made me insane. You take sugar, right?' Joanna asked, pushing the white porcelain container toward Sylvie.

'Maybe you could tell me the name of the agency you used,' Sylvie said, her voice little more than a whisper. Her hand shook so badly, the silverware clicked out a crazed message

228

against the china bowl as she tried to lift out a teaspoon of sugar.

'It wasn't an agency,' she said. 'It was a private arrangement.'

A wave of nausea went through Sylvie. Private arrangement, was that what he called it? The bastard. 'And your baby,' Sylvie asked, 'how old is she?'

'Two months.'

Sylvie had to bite into her lip to keep it from shaking. 'And is that legal?' she asked. Her breathing was all out of whack.

'Is what legal?'

'A private arrangement.' Sylvie knew there was a clawing and scraping quality creeping into what she was saying. She tried to draw in a deep breath, to be who she pretended to be, a 'Marie' who wanted information about adopting a baby. 'I know that sounded awful, and I don't mean to question how you've done things, it's just that this whole business scares me. I don't understand how to do it.'

'I know exactly what you're going through, believe me. But it is legal. And please, you can say whatever you want to me.'

'Even talking about this, about adopting, makes me nervous,' Sylvie said, bringing a hand to her chest, as though her heartbeat needed stilling, which it did. 'It's so hard to find out information and we're starting to feel desperate.'

Joanna leaned back in her chair, both her hands circling her coffee cup. 'Nothing can make you so crazy as wanting a baby, can it?' she asked in a hushed, almost mournful tone.

'Nothing,' Sylvie said, her voice quiet as Joanna's.

'It can take over your life.' Sylvie nodded. 'The thing to remember is, there's lots and lots of ways to adopt. You don't have to go through those awful agencies. Ours was legal but it wasn't what you'd call regular or standard.' Hardly regular, Sylvie thought. 'Listen, I don't know how much you want to hear. I mean, I could tell you the whole history of us, but it's probably real boring to somebody else. I could just start with the adoption part.'

'No, tell me the whole history,' Sylvie said, probably too eagerly, she knew. Joanna had broken a cranberry muffin in half and she'd started eating it. Sylvie did the same to her

229

blueberry one, then broke off a tiny piece and put it into her mouth. The blueberry made the morsel moist enough to swallow.

'The thing that's really funny is that I never thought about having kids, you know what I mean? I'm not one of those people who always wanted a baby or anything. It was just one of the crazy kinds of games we used to play.' She sipped her coffee and Sylvie did the same. 'Baby roulette, we called it.'

'Baby roulette?'

'See, we'd make love two, three times a night, but we'd toss coins or play cards first to see which time we wouldn't use birth control.'

'Wild.'

'Yeah.' Joanna smiled. 'It was fun. See, the thing was, we didn't want a baby then, we just both like mixing risk into the brew. We even liked the worrying each month. Anyway, nothing happened, no pregnancy,' she said, dismissing the venture with a shake of her hand. 'After a while, we just stopped using birth control, because we couldn't believe it wasn't working. We started wanting it to work. I can't even tell you where the change came, but it did. After about six months, all we were talking about was how there was something wrong with us. I started feeling the way I used to when I failed a test in school and everybody else scored in the nineties. Like I was outside the secret knowledge, or something. Like everybody else had it figured out except me. We got books on fertility and we started trying all this weird stuff like cold baths and hot baths and different positions and fooling around with how deep the penetration was – have you done that stuff?' Sylvie nodded. She'd heard some of the doctors in her practice counseling women to strange acrobatics in the name of conception. 'I think that's all ridiculous, frankly. It made me feel more like a freak, if you want to know the truth. But I felt like we had to do it, we had to break through the failure, somehow. I bought one of those ovulation kits and did the bit with temperature and the chart, and when that didn't work, we went to a fertility place and they told me I had completely wrecked – "stunted", they said – fallopian tubes.'

'It's the same with me,' Sylvie interjected, hoping this wasn't too far-fetched as a coincidence. 'Stunted tubes.'

'Oh, wow,' Joanna said. 'This is amazing that we have the same diagnosis. You were absolutely meant to ring my door-bell yesterday. Did you just find that out recently?' Sylvie nodded, wishing she hadn't provided Joanna with this 'amazing' information which she probably couldn't wait to share with her husband. 'So have you thought about doing *in vitro*?' Sylvie nodded again. 'Listen, that's when it got really bad for us, really depressed us. I mean.' she said, looking at Sylvie, 'you think it's going to be the answer, that science is going to fix things up, and they show you all these fabulous-looking statistics on their success rates, but if you're in that twenty-two percent or whatever it is that it doesn't work for, it's pure hell. We just kept throwing thousands and thousands of dollars at them each time we did an *in vitro*, till we were up to our ears in debt. And this hormone they shoot you up with, Pergonal? It makes you completely crazy. I swear I was totally dysfunctional after two months on it. I cried all the time, sometimes I felt so crummy I didn't think I could get out of bed, and I wouldn't, I'd just pull the covers up over my head for two, three days at a time. I stopped going to work – I wasn't doing anything when I was there anyway, and I knew they were going to fire me any minute, so I just left. The clinic encouraged me to quit, too, telling me it would relax me more, but you know, being home, riding those Pergonal mood swings and having nothing to do but think about whether I was pregnant, was awful. But I did whatever that clinic told me. I was their little slave. I'd just lay down and do anything they said. I'd say, "Go ahead, stick catheters and needles and whatever other garbage you want up me, I don't care,"' she said, flinging a hand high in a gesture of resignation.

'Looking back, I can see how completely crazy it was, but I couldn't get out of it; I couldn't break out of the loop. I kept thinking, next month it'll work. Keith said it was like gambling: You think you have to earn your losses back, but all you're really doing is losing, losing, losing, with no hope in sight. All I can tell you about *in vitro* is, don't do it. Not if you've got these stupid stunted tubes, because the statistics are horrendous

231

with that. Of course, we didn't know that little detail till we were six months into it. Keith wanted to quit long before I did. The men do, usually. They're not on the hormone, so they stay more sane about it, I guess. But I wasn't ready to quit. I kept saying to him, "One more time, one more time. Begging him, like the way you see addicts begging people for money.' She shook her head. 'I could sort of tell I was losing him. I mean, before, we used to make love all the time, and then we almost stopped completely. He'd give me my Pergonal shot in the hip each night and we'd go to sleep. It was like we did that *instead* of sex.

'One time – we were out to dinner – he said the money was gone, that nobody was going to give us any more loans, that we could do one more *in vitro* run and that was it, and I completely fell apart right in the restaurant. I think he thought if we were in a public place when he told me, I'd be forced to handle it better, but I was too far gone by then. I felt like he'd betrayed me. Betrayed our baby, was what I said to him. I said he was giving up and not letting our child be born. I was screaming it at him. Everybody must have thought I was totally nuts, I was even talking about killing myself. I know this sounds crazy, but I felt I'd lose everything if I had to give up the trials. Keith was real calm, he just waited for me to run out of steam. Then real quiet, he said he wanted a baby but he wanted me most of all, and he wanted things back the way they had been with us making love and laughing and doing crazy stuff together. So I said I'd go off the Pergonal and stop, because deep down, I could feel the rightness of what he was saying, I could feel that I wanted the same thing.'

She sat back and paused, her finger tracing out the shape of a teaspoon that lay upon the table. 'So that's when I quit. I didn't even do that last trial. I knew I'd gone over the deep end and it was time to come back. We started adoption counseling that same week. Right here in town.' She reached for the other half of her muffin and began to break it into smaller and smaller pieces.

'But I take it that didn't work out, either. You didn't end up with an agency, you said?' Sylvie picked out another larger muffin piece with several blueberries embedded in it and popped it into her mouth.

'No,' she admitted. 'See, there's this power thing with these adoption people. They want to decide who gets babies. And it's totally ridiculous. I mean, if you can have a baby normally, you can be a murderer or a rapist or a satanist and nobody cares, but if you have one little thing smudging up your record, you can forget it if you want to adopt. They come to your house, they check how you live, check your credit, your employers, run you over the coals, believe me.' She stopped. 'I'm upsetting you,' she said, 'making it sound so hard.'

'Sylvie shrugged. 'Maybe a little.'

'But they probably won't come up with anything on you. With us, it was that Keith really was wild when he was younger, so they dug up garbage, things people said about him when he was only a kid. It was totally outrageous. You'll probably sail right through, but if you don't, what I think you should know is that there are all these other routes. That you shouldn't give up if that kind of thing happens. There are people who want to connect you with babies if you know where to look.'

'Legally?' Sylvie asked again. 'With papers and all?'

'Definitely. We have court papers. It was completely legal.' Sylvie wanted to say, 'Go get them, show me the papers,' but she held back. It would be better, she knew, if it were Joanna's idea to bring out the papers. 'And the thing is,' Joanna continued, 'that we ended up ahead of the game, because we got a surrogacy, not a straight adoption. With adoption, there's no way on earth you're ever going to get a blonde baby anymore. I don't know if that matters to you, but it is something to think about. You may not even end up with an infant that way. I mean, we were told we might have to take a four-year-old, and that wasn't what it was about for me. More coffee?' Joanna asked her, though Sylvie had barely brought the level down to half.

'No, thanks.'

'We did a match with the mother for physical characteristics so Lily's almost sure to resemble us — blue eyes, blonde hair, and all,' and Sylvie couldn't help it, her hand went up to her own yellow-white hair, and she pushed the long strands back over her shoulders. 'There just aren't very many babies like that in the world going begging,' Joanna continued. 'We arranged for artificial insemination with Keith's sperm.' Which meant what, Sylvie wondered. That the baby that was sleeping in the other room wasn't Cally, after all, but really, truly, the result of a private deal? And so what was Peter's connection? Maybe he arranged the Lily surrogacy, maybe that was his real business, and just maybe he added to his pot by making a baby or two on the side and kidnapping them for other 'private clients'? Joanna was continuing to explain: 'I don't know, I feel really good that Keith's her real father. I feel like we'll understand who she is better, and I think she'll have some feeling of belonging to us more. I wish she were biologically mine, too, but this is at least better than straight adoption. Also, you do know the mother this way and you can get medical information, so it's not such a great unknown where you're waiting while your child grows up to find out what the medical time bombs are.'

'Why'd you do it out there?' Sylvie asked.

'That's where the mother was that we found. There aren't hundreds of women wanting to be surrogates, so you have to take what you can get, fly where the people are, and she was a really good physical match, too. And just generally, statistically, there are more women willing to be surrogates out there – you know, the liberal Northeast mentality. It adds to the cost, of course, all the flying you have to do on top of the legal fees and the mother's fee. Keith used up all his vacation and personal leave on it. It seems endlessly long and difficult while it's happening.' She smiled. 'But then when it works out, it's all worth it. All the agony fades away. Have you thought about surrogacy?'

'We've talked about it, but we're not sure. Who'd you contact out there? Maybe I could talk to them.'

'With surrogacy you're kind of on your own. Keith followed up ads in newspapers, that kind of thing.'

'But you had a contact person.' She wanted to say his name, to get it out, over with.

'We worked with an attorney and the mother, that's all. There are agencies that deal with surrogacy, but they charge three and four times what you can do it for on your own, and then they have this same stupid veto power like the adoption agencies. You can use the National Surrogacy Foundation for leads, we tried them a little, but personally I think you're just paying for their laser printers and fancy offices. They don't do it any better than you can do it yourself. The way we did it, we felt like we were much more in control, and after the *in vitro* fiasco, we needed to have it be that way.' She reached for another muffin.

'I actually have the name of somebody who handles surrogacies,' Sylvie said. 'I don't know anything about him, which scares me.' Joanna gave a nod of understanding. 'Maybe you've heard of him – Peter Weston.' Joanna shook her head. No startled reaction, no anger, just a standard negative response.

'The name sounds vaguely familiar, but I almost always have that reaction when somebody asks me if I know somebody else. Daniel Meyers was the attorney – he's the only contact we had out there, except for the mother, and her name was never given to us and our name was never given to her. The court has the real names locked up in a safe, but they said it would be close to impossible to get access to it. I think you need a Supreme Court decision, or superior court, whatever it is, something like that. But, anyway, you should call this guy, this name you have, check him out, if you haven't already, because in this business, you need to follow up every lead. He may be the answer to your prayers.' She poured herself another cup of coffee. 'Want me to add some hot to yours?' she asked, the carafe poised above her guest's cup.

'No, thanks,' Sylvie said.

'You know, this whole surrogacy process is bound to get easier as more people do it, and this guy may be somebody who's figured out how to connect people effectively. Which is all it is, you know. You need an agent to handle all the rough edges that come along the way. And our attorney was reasonably good with that, but still, somebody who really specializes, who's familiar with the tricky spots, might be a real find. We almost lost Lily because the mother changed her mind. We were really glad we had a good attorney at that point, let me tell you. If you want, you could contact this Meyers. He seems very good.'

'The mother wanted to back out?' Joanna nodded. 'After the baby was born?'

'Right. And not just once, either. We were on this incredible emotional roller-coaster ride – I thought I was going to have to be committed. I didn't know what was happening from one minute to the next. I had all the baby clothes, the furniture, the whole bit. Keith kept flying out there, and she wouldn't give the baby up. She said the deal was off. We offered her more money and then she said fine, she'd hand the baby over in a week, but then I guess she thought if that tactic worked once, why not twice, so she backed out again and asked for more money. She delayed us almost six weeks. We had to go out there and go before a judge, and we had to have new papers drawn up each time. I cried every day, missing seeing her grow up.'

'It must have been hard.' Sylvie said, trying to force the sound of commiseration into her words. 'But it must have been hard for the mother, too, holding the baby, having the smell and touch of her.'

'I know, but she did agree. She signed all the papers. Anyway, I really think it was just about manipulation and money, not the baby at all.'

'Was it weird when you met her, talked to her, seeing her pregnant with what you knew was your baby?'

'I never actually met her, just my husband did.'

Sylvie's heart jolted and tumbled through its next round of beats. 'But after the birth – you said you went to court . . .'

'I didn't go, just Keith did. It was really only him that was actually required because he's the natural father. I was so sick by then, I really couldn't travel. I was down to a hundred and two pounds. Most women put on weight while they're waiting to have babies, I know, but I'd been losing it for over a year. I'm still not back up to my old weight but the thing is, the day he put her in my arms, I started eating again. The headaches stopped, the stomach pains, all the physical symptoms. And after last night, I probably added five pounds back.' She laughed. 'I still don't sleep, of course, because she's not making it through the night yet, but that kind of sleeplessness I don't mind. I've dreamed about that privilege for years.'

'I've been dreaming of it, too,' Sylvie said.

'Though you look really young to me, if you don't mind me saying that. I mean, you look like you could be a freshman in college.'

'I'm twenty-six,' Sylvie lied. 'We've been married five years.'

Sylvie heard a tiny cry, so tentative, it seemed to be within her own body, not coming from some other room in the house. 'The baby,' she said, standing.

Joanna laughed, looked at her watch. 'Oh, Lily,' she said with mock mournfulness, 'when will you ever grant me a long nap time?' And to Sylvie: 'Do you want to meet her?' The cry, again, coming clearly this time from the other side of the house, but still, Sylvie felt it inside her, felt it travel along the nerves of her arms, her back, felt it turn the blonde hairs on her arms straight up to attention.

'No,' Sylvie said, taking a step back, terrified, suddenly, of finding her, or of not finding her. 'It makes me too sad.'

'I know what you mean. I used to cry when I saw pregnant women.' The baby's cry was more vibrant now and seemed to move the air around Sylvie. She felt her nipples stiffen, and though she waited, breath held, for the rush of milk that would reveal her as a fraud, there was no flow. Her shirt was dry. The milk was distant memory, only.

Sylvie had moved toward the front door.

'You can call me if you want to talk more about it,' Joanna said as she followed her.

'I think I will,' Sylvie said as she turned the doorknob. She kept thinking that if she could let air in, it would ease the sound of her baby's call.

'I gave you the lawyer's name, right? Meyers. I could ask my husband if he can think of anything else, too, then I can call you. Where are you staying?'

'Arizona Inn,' she lied, giving out the name of one of the more expensive places she'd passed up.

'Oh, I love that place,' Joanna said, 'those pretty gardens and all that pink adobe. I told Keith, we're definitely having Lily's wedding there.'

'Please, don't bother your husband with my problems.'

'Oh, no, it's not a bother. He feels the same way I do. He wants to help people who are being locked out of getting babies.'

Please, she wanted to say, don't mention me. Don't talk to him about weird coincidences and people asking after details of his child's life.

'So call me if you have questions, and definitely, definitely call when you actually move here.'

The crying was strident now, insistent. Sylvie wanted to go to her, to step into the room, lift her, and run before it was too late. It's you, isn't it? she wanted to scream, but she stepped backward, down the stairs, no goodbyes, and she ran, unseeing, uncaring, in circles, in lines, running, far from the sounds of her.

No message from Martinson. And no answer at his home. At his office they told her he'd been in and gone out again. She'd forgotten about the time change. What the hell time was it out there? Where was he? She tried lying down on the bed – she knew she couldn't keep going on so little sleep, but she couldn't lie still, either. She called the main desk and told them she was going down to the restaurant and that they should call her there if any messages came in for her. In the restaurant, the hostess seated her and handed her a menu. A busboy filled her water glass and she propped the menu up in front of her and tried to read it, but the black letters danced too rapidly over the page, refusing to be pinned down to words. She found the laughter coming from a nearby table offensive, the constant jabber of the people at the next table unbearable, and she absolutely couldn't look at the table right in front of her, it was so intact, with its mother, father, and their three children growing up next to them. She left before the waiter got round to asking for her order.

238

Next she tried walking around the pool, then sitting, briefly, on a lounge chair and watching two women trying to ease themselves into the water. She started going over her meeting with Joanna as though it were a play script, reviewing and analyzing every word the two of them had spoken. She paced around the pool, saw, sometimes, when she was aware enough, as she rounded a corner, how she was stared at. And no wonder – she wasn't even in a bathing suit, she was probably talking to herself, stamping her foot, jumping up and down, acting generally like a fool. And why had she ever mentioned Peter's name? That was exactly the sort of thing Martinson meant when he asked, did she give anything away? Joanna hadn't had a reaction to the name, but her husband was the one most involved, the one who had been out on the East Coast. The one who would have had the contact with Peter if he was really the one running the operation. And now she was going to tell him somebody had come from out East, asking questions about adoption. About the legality of their 'arrangement.' What if he suspected – or knew – there was something screwy about the arrangement? How long would it take people to pack up necessary belongings and run? Couldn't they flee in a couple of hours?

She didn't wait for the elevator, but took the stairs two at a time, the hallway at a run. Martinson still wasn't at his desk, they told her. 'Where the hell are you?' she shouted against the well-spaced rings at his home number.

239

Chapter 28

Hannah thought she might go mad waiting to hear from Sylvie. She knew her daughter was supposed to try to see the baby again, so she'd spent all morning sitting at the kitchen table in her bathrobe staring at the phone and ripping paper napkins into soft, ragged spirals. When she started picking up the phone (just to make sure it was still working) she knew it was time – past time – to get dressed and out of the house.

She would drive, no particular destination necessary, she thought. She would turn on the radio and go out toward open country, it didn't matter where, so long as she was no longer perched on top of the telephone.

Even in her car, though, Hannah's mind wandered over to Sylvie and Cally, and to possible wild arguments she could engage in with FBI Agent Dolan. Hannah lost track of exit numbers, found herself traveling well above the speed limit, and several times had to admonish herself to pay more attention to the road. When the startling sound of held-down horns warned her that she was drifting distractedly between lanes, she was frightened by how completely oblivious she'd become of her surroundings, and of the apparent distance she'd traveled.

Hannah took the next exit, then followed the ramp straight ahead where it ran into the mall. Not an ideal place to find herself, but she knew she had to get off the road for a while and calm herself down. For that purpose, one parking lot was as good as another.

Hannah had been to the mall only once before, on the tail end of a date with a colleague from sociology. They were returning from dinner at a country inn when she'd remarked on the number of cars in the parking lot, and had declared it incomprehensible that people would spend their weekend evenings shopping. Her date had said, 'Malls are great entertainment, Hannah. They're the Main Street of the new, modern American village.' Hannah had laughed at his absurd words, then he'd driven right into the parking lot, told her it was a must-see, and in they'd gone.

He came there often, he told her, and that offhand comment, plus his rapt interest in the endless parade of people, all of them wanting things and more things and almost all of them stuffing food into their mouths, made her very uncomfortable with that man, though they'd been having a perfectly decent time up till that point. Now here she was, back in that once-again-full parking lot, watching people scurry toward the stores as if there were some kind of important, time-limited event for which they absolutely couldn't arrive late. Her stomach growled out a protest and she realized it'd been forever since she'd eaten anything, and knew that if she really wanted to be master of her body and soul again, she had to start by feeding herself, even if it did mean eating honky-tonk style. Hannah locked up her car and joined the flow of movement toward an arched opening that looked peculiarly like a green metal honeycombed beehive.

If they didn't play music in here, she thought as she took her cheese-filled baked potato to a table in the food court, it wouldn't be quite so disgusting. Unlike saccharine but innocuous elevator music, mall music seemed militantly determined to direct her mood. I refuse to feel upbeat just because you want me to, Hannah silently addressed the music. It wasn't only the music that aimed to manipulate, she thought, it was just about everything in the mall. She'd already passed at least a dozen signs with imperatives like 'Buy One Get One Free Today Only,' and she'd heard at least as many salespeople poised near store entrances greeting customers as though they'd shared some intimate past relationship together. This whole place, she thought, was a trap for people with gelatinous egos. And a perfect setting for someone like Peter, the king of the manipulative arts, to use his skills. Under his direction, people would surrender not only their wallets but their bodies and their lives. She looked around then, eyes grazing along the upper reaches of the place, wondering where that security office he had occupied might be, where his secret reality was hidden hard away from this fantasyland. Right now his former co-workers were still in there watching the mall, perhaps watching her. Damn him and damn all of them up there, making a living and a sport of invasion of privacy. She got up from the table without bothering to bus her tray and paper plate.

She wanted to see the cameras, understand where they were and what they saw, and so she started going into stores, looking for the snooping devices. When she came upon the first one, poised as it was over the inside door frame of a small boutique, she felt exhilarated, though she turned quickly away, aware that someone might be looking directly back at her face. At first, she thought many stores didn't have any cameras, but then she concluded some had simply hidden them better behind and inside pipes and boxes and vents and door frames and ceiling tiles. And no one, she thought, glancing round her at the people gathering merchandise into their arms the way earlier generations might have gathered sheaves of wheat, no one realizes they're being spied upon. What gives you that right? she wondered, then looked straight at one of the cameras, and said, loud and clear, 'Fuck you.' Two salesgirls came up to her and asked if she wanted help, and Hannah knew that the next step would be to get somebody down there to subdue her. She apologized and moved on.

What good exactly did that outburst do me? she asked herself when she had taken a seat on one of the benches where that long-ago date of hers had liked to sit and 'watch the prom.' She couldn't help laughing at what she must have looked like on video screen, a wild woman swearing into the camera, and she ran her hand through her hair, checking how it lay, which made her laugh even more, that she could be concerned about whether she looked good when she was cursing somebody out. She glanced up then to see if some member of the security force was lurking nearby observing her, but there was no one – or no one she could swear was actually watching her. If they were watching her, she knew it was by way of cameras, with maybe three or four of them huddled together up there deciding whether to call in reinforcements to nab her. She felt her pulse quicken, then thought, My God, I'm really losing my mind. Ten more minutes of this and I'll be a certifiable paranoid. She had to get out of there. Hannah headed toward a high-vaulted arch that looked at least something like the beehive where she'd come in. She paused for a moment and stared up at the intricate pattern of glass and metal that shaped out the roof. And again, she caught sight of something that might be a camera – a black rectangular box that she was nearly certain was moving, slowly, almost imperceptibly, but moving, doing its visual sweep of this entryway. What do you see? she wanted to ask it. What's it like for you behind that lens? Is it like watching a stage play, a movie? If those of us down here are the movie, what's the reality? And she could imagine then how Peter, as writer and director of his own movie, had jumped before the camera to meet with Sylvie, then rushed back to the security office to hear his performance reviewed. Was his whole life such a play? Certainly the parts with Sylvie were. Where is the booth from which you watch the play unfolding now? 'This is *my* reality you've gone and screwed up,' she said aloud, then turned and left the mall.

There were no messages from Sylvie on the machine when Hannah got back to the house. Maybe Martinson would have some news, she thought.

'Did you hear anything from her?' he asked when she reached him at the station.

She told him she hadn't. 'You didn't hear anything, either?'

'No. But I worked on it this morning. I sneaked a little time off from a robbery to check out this guy she's gone to see.'

'And?'

'And I don't have anything concrete, nothing solid at all.' His voice drifted over the words as though he explored the meaning of each one of them as he spoke.

244

'But you have something?' She could hear the pleading in her own voice.

'Mmm – maybe.'

'What?' she asked. She started taking off her coat, shifting it off her shoulder while she kept the phone tucked under her chin. She hadn't wanted to take the time to remove it when she'd first gotten into the house, but now she was feeling much too hot in her overheated study.

'I don't know yet. I'm feeling it through, still.'

'What exactly does that mean?' Why was he so damn evasive all the time? He reminded Hannah of doctors who became unaccountably vague when asked for details about the side effects of prescription drugs.

'It means that there are some interesting things to look at.'

'Look, Martinson, is there some reason you can't or won't tell me what these so-called interesting things are? Is it because the case is closed and you're not supposed to be working on it?'

'No, not exactly. I mean I'm *not* supposed to be working on it but I don't think the line's tapped, if that's what you're getting at. It's just that they're kind of interesting to me, and maybe they'll be interesting to somebody else later on, when they've jelled.'

'I'm interested now,' she insisted. 'I've got a deep personal interest in all of it.'

'Of course, that's why I mentioned it to begin with.' Then after a pause, as though deciding if she was actually entitled to the information, he said, 'First thing is, and it's the big downer here, there's nothing outstanding on him. No warrants, I mean.'

'No unanswered charges?'

'Exactly.'

'What about old charges?'

'Nothing that required fingerprinting, even. A bunch of traffic offenses. And here's something I thought was intriguing – he always went to court on them. Argued them instead of just paying them off.'

'Why is that so fascinating?'

'I don't know. See, that's what I mean. I get a feeling for some of these oddball things, but most other people don't respond the same way.'

'But you must have some reason for stopping at that particular piece of information.' She'd opened the box of paper clips that sat on her desk and, phone tucked between chin and shoulder, she'd begun linking the clips together.

'Well, going into court on traffic stuff isn't what most people do. Most people just want to be done with their violations and forget them. They stick the money in the envelope and send it off. They don't like taking time off from work, waiting all day in a courtroom till they're called, then maybe ending up no better, in terms of the fine, than if they'd just sent in the money anyway. Sometimes they can end up worse off.'

'But sometimes better.'

'Right.'

'So he likes to gamble?'

'Either that or he's a lawyer or a frustrated lawyer. Or maybe he just thinks he can outwit the system, that he's above it. Maybe it's just a general-purpose power trip to get in there and try to outwit the judge.' He paused, and she thought she heard him sipping what was probably his coffee. She wondered if he used those big tooth-marked Styrofoam cups at his desk, or if he actually kept a genuine coffee mug at hand. 'But then I still don't know where that leads us. It's just vague personality stuff. See, if he's really got anything to hide, why does he go into a court at all? That'd be risky, I think.'

'Unless he likes risks – can't stay away from them.'

'Possible.'

'So Sylvie's out there trying to confront some maniac who gets an adrenaline rush from risk? This definitely is not good news.'

'No,' he agreed, 'if we're guessing right. I've got a little more,' he told her, and she could hear him moving papers. 'My man out there, the one who checked him out. He called me back this morning, said he was having coffee with a couple of guys and he mentioned the case and the name and all, and one of them knew the name, because it's an unusual one – Blessing. It's one that'd stick in your mind longer than most.'

246

'And?'

'And so it turns out this one cop he's having coffee with adopted a baby a couple of years ago and one day he got a call from the woman at the agency who'd made the arrangements for them.'

'Wait, wait,' Hannah interrupted, letting go of the chain of clips and taking firm hold of the telephone receiver. 'There's an adoption agency in this guy's life?'

'Yes, ma'am.'

'And you're not sure this is interesting? Why didn't you tell me this part first?'

'You want to hear it or not?'

'Of course I want to hear it.'

'Well, this woman at the adoption agency is all distraught because some guy who wanted to adopt threatened her. So she calls this other guy she did an adoption for because she knows he's a cop. She asks him – but informal-like – what she should do.'

'Threatened her how?'

'Apparently the agency turned up something in their standard background check – he'd threatened a former employer with a gun. There weren't any formal charges against him, but the agency felt confident the incident had happened. So they nixed the adoption. When this woman dropped the news on our Blessing, he went nuts. He walked around her desk, pushed down on the arms of the chair – it was one of those adjustable jobs, a cheap one, I guess – and it sort of hit the floor from the pressure, scared the hell out of her. He put his face down close to hers and said something like, "Murderers have children if they want to, don't they?" And then he told her to forget she ever heard the information about the gun and suggested she think about it and call him back. That's when she called that cop, asked him what to do next, and he said he thought she could press charges if she really wanted to, but he told her it would be hard to make it stick, that the guy would more than likely claim he was distraught and she'd misunderstood and a judge would feel for him, not getting his baby and all. With no previous record, he'd probably walk away.'

'He tried to adopt a baby and couldn't.'

'So he might be looking to buy another somewhere, I suppose.'

'And he has a gun.'

'Or had a gun.'

'He gets violent.'

'Violent is too strong. Aggressive. When upset.'

'Great. Sylvie's there asking him questions like where he got his baby – isn't that likely to upset him?'

'We can't tell.'

'Come on, Martinson, she's completely vulnerable out there.'

'There's one more thing you might want to hear.'

'Is this going to make me even more crazy?' She didn't wait for him to answer. 'What?'

'I checked out his driver's license, that's standard. I did it on everybody out here, for instance.'

'You mean on me, too?'

'I had to.'

'On Peter?'

'Yes. Peter's checked out as far as it went. He got it with a birth certificate and a Social Security card. But all that's beside the point. I checked on Blessing's license. He got it with a Social Security card and a transcript from the University of Montana, which also seemed superficially fine and legal. Except that I got curious about that transcript. I asked myself, Why not a birth certificate? It seemed like he did everything a little different from most people. So I called the University of Montana and it turns out they list Keith Blessing's address as being in Missoula, Montana. In fact, I talked to Keith Blessing of Missoula about ten minutes before you called.'

'It's a different Blessing?'

'He says so. Says he's never been in Arizona. Hasn't left the state of Montana in his whole little lifetime.'

'I don't understand. Are you saying the one in Arizona has a faked transcript?'

'Seems like it. A faked transcript and a fake identity and a fake name. But it's a right fine transcript, I might tell you. He's got a three-point-nine average. Most people looking for new identities wouldn't go for a name like Blessing – too unusual, too likely to be remembered, like the way the cop remembered it, but then it looks like this guy got a little greedy, really got turned on by that three-point-nine, probably had some specialized job he wanted, or maybe it just fit his self-image, so he decided to take the risk. We already said he likes risks.'

'True,' Hannah commented. 'But how'd he get hold of the transcript to begin with?'

'He probably went through an alumni directory and found somebody the right age who was in the right field. Then maybe he called the guy's home, pretending to be checking current information for the alumni association. He could get a birth date or a Social Security number that way, which would probably be enough to get a transcript sent out to him. If the transcript office is picky and demands more information than what he's been able to come up with, he moves on to another university. It's not hard if you're comfortable with lying and fraud. But let me tell you the really interesting thing – the part that's, what you might say, the miracle of it. It's that both these guys, they're born on the same day, same year, and they've got the same name. But this one out in Montana, he tells me he's six-three, two hundred ten pounds, blue eyes, brown hair. But I've got a description here that was taken from a license and let's see, it reads, five-eleven, one hundred fifty-five pounds, blue eyes, blond hair.'

'For the one in Arizona?'

'Yes. And then I'm thinking,' he said, slow again, thinking, thinking, she could hear the thinking it was so slow and loud.

'Peter?' she asked him.

'Well, it's just a feeling, of course.'

'She's out there alone.'

'Well, I know that. But she's got Ortiz's name, and I've told her how to proceed, and she's got this number and my home number.'

'And she's what, two thousand miles away?'

'That's the thing. Two thousand miles, almost three thousand, you can't just pop over there. But I'm thinking I'm no good to anybody out here right now, so I'm just going to go to the airport and take the next thing headed west.'

249

'You're going out there?'
'Soon as I hang up this phone.'
'What'll you do out there?' she asked him.
'All I can,' he said, 'believe me.'

Chapter 29

No one was home. Sylvie rang the bell, waited, rang again. And again and again. Held it down, then pressed it in chains of endless repetitions, pausing only to listen for footsteps on the other side of the door. She brought the knocker down hard, and harder. She walked around the house, pounded on windows till her knuckles ached. No one was home.

The shades were drawn. They hadn't been earlier in the day. Or at least she didn't think they had been. 'They're gone,' she said, mumbling it sometimes, nearly shouting it others, while her hands tightened into fists. They've taken her, she thought as she circled the house. How could I have just left her there like that? Joanna had probably sped out of there with some basic necessities before Sylvie had even made it back to her hotel. How could she have let this happen – come so close then let her go again?

And then, as she rounded the front of the house, she saw her, Joanna, oh God, it was Joanna, pushing the baby carriage, a long way off, still, but coming toward her. Sylvie took a step back around the side of the house so that she was out of Joanna's line of sight, wiped the tears from her face, and worked on getting her tee-shirt tucked decently into her pants. She smiled, though it was an act near to violence to get the corners of her mouth to actually turn upward and stay there. She walked toward the street, lifted a hand to wave at Joanna, then headed down toward her.

She had no idea what she was going to say to Joanna because she was too focused on walking steadily, keeping her eyes on her. They hadn't fled. Maybe she hadn't talked to her husband about it yet, hadn't told him how she'd run out so strangely, so obviously upset.

'You're back,' Joanna said when they'd drawn close to one another.

'Yes,' Sylvie said, and she saw the baby was sleeping. Her face, half-covered by a cotton blanket, was turned against the carriage mattress. She could be anybody's baby, just like Martinson said. But she wasn't. She was Cally. Sylvie'd heard her calling. 'Does she still have a diamond mark on her bottom?' Sylvie asked, surprising herself with the directness of the question.

Joanna stared at her. 'What are you talking about?'

'Does she have a mark on her bottom?'

'Yes. How do you know about it?' Joanna had leaned over the stroller and adjusted the blanket higher across the baby's face.

'I know because she's my baby.'

Joanna pulled the stroller back toward herself. 'You're crazy,' she said.

'Her name's Cally,' Sylvie said. 'She's my baby, and she was kidnapped from my house. Stolen away. There was no surrogacy, no lawyer, no papers. She was stolen.'

'You're out of your mind,' Joanna said, and she turned the carriage, started to go down the street the other way, away from the house. Sylvie followed beside her.

'Listen to me, Joanna,' Sylvie pleaded. 'This man named Peter that I mentioned, he had the baby with me – it was *his* baby. There was no artificial insemination. We lived together and then he stole her from me – sold her, I have to assume, to you. But she's not your baby and she's not Keith's baby. Somebody lied to you real bad.'

'There are papers,' Joanna said. She hadn't slowed her pace.

'The papers are forged,' Sylvie said. 'She has the birthmark, doesn't she?'

They had reached the corner and Joanna stopped. 'You're her birth mother?' Sylvie nodded. 'But you can't have her back. You signed the papers.'

Sylvie shook her head. 'I never signed anything.'

'I have them. You did!' Joanna had stopped walking and had pulled the stroller in close against her body.

252

'Then show them to me.'

'They're in the vault.'

'I'll go to the vault with you, but I swear to you, I never signed anything.'

Joanna's face was red, her eyes wet and frightened. 'I knew this was never going to work. I knew you were going to come back. Keith said you were unstable, that you didn't really want to give her up, but it's too late, Marie. The court made its ruling.' Her eyes were darting between Sylvie and the baby. 'It's all done,' Joanna said, lifting the baby from where she slept. Sylvie saw the small limbs swing gently at open air, then settle quietly against Joanna's chest. Sylvie's empty breasts ached as she watched.

'Please,' Sylvie said, 'let's at least go back to your house, sit down, talk about it.'

'No,' Joanna said. 'I'm going to call the police.'

'Fine,' Sylvie said. 'Call Detective Ortiz. He knows about the case. He's in contact with the New Haven police. He knows my baby's been kidnapped. He'll come out, if you like.'

Joanna shook her head. 'It can't be true.'

'Call him,' Sylvie insisted, though she had no idea what Ortiz knew, or how much he'd back her up. Joanna stared at her. 'Let's go back to the house,' Sylvie suggested again. Joanna was shaking her head, but then stopped, closed her eyes for a moment, and Sylvie saw tears begin to flow over her cheeks. Joanna opened her eyes and nodded once. Sylvie put her hand on the stroller bar right next to the other woman's and began to turn the carriage around, to move it back toward the Blessing house. Joanna's feet seemed to lift only when the stroller got so far ahead of her that it dragged her forward like a recalcitrant puppy on a leash.

Once they were in the house, Joanna put the sleeping baby down in her crib. Sylvie watched from the hallway. She still hadn't really seen her baby's face. They walked together to the kitchen. 'I should call my husband,' Joanna said, and Sylvie agreed.

Sylvie was able to tell that the phone had been answered, for

Joanna began sobbing frantically. She was able to speak her husband's name, but nothing else would have been decipherable by the person at the other end. Joanna was pointlessly nodding her head at the phone, sobbing, listening to what he said, but saying nothing. Finally she handed the phone to Sylvie.

'Joanna needs you to come home,' Sylvie said.

'What's wrong?' came back the tense, brusque response.

'It's about the baby,' she said, and hung up without waiting for any more questions.

Sylvie walked through the kitchen while Joanna cried. She put up a pot of water, asked the other woman if she wanted anything. And, when the sobs had died, they sat in silence.

Sylvie heard the screech of the car on the street, the sharp turn of the wheels, as Keith pulled into the drive. She wanted to run to the windows, see him first, to know finally and irrevocably, but she couldn't make herself move, couldn't even feel her own limbs anymore. All she could feel was the perspiration running down her sides under her tee-shirt. She heard him try the door, then enter, shouting, 'Joanna! Where are you?'

Sylvie drew in a deep breath. *His* voice, yes, she was certain of that now.

'I'm here, in the kitchen,' Joanna quavered, rising briefly, holding herself up by leaning onto the table, then crumpling back down.

Sylvie stood up when he entered the room. His hair had been cut – or perhaps it was just that he wore it differently here – side-parted, conservative, businessman style – but that went with the different clothes, too. The khaki twills, navy blazer, and tie were rather a contrast to the funky clothes she was used to seeing on him. It wasn't what she would have called a deliberate disguise, just a change of costume. For this different role; for a different sort of woman, she supposed. But he was Peter, no mistake there.

He stayed in the doorway, staring at her, one fist clenched at his side. 'I thought it was you,' she said, and the words felt dry as dust across her tongue. 'On the phone,' she added.

'What do you want?' he snarled at her, and she laughed at

254

the absurdity of it – that he should have to ask.

'She says Lily's her baby, Keith,' Joanna said, her voice tentative as winter sunshine.

'Peter,' Sylvie corrected, though neither of them seemed to hear.

'I told you she was nuts,' he said to his wife.

'I was wrong,' Sylvie said, leaning toward Joanna. 'I said your husband wasn't the father, but he is.'

'I told you that,' Joanna said. He stood by her chair now, his hands on her shoulders.

'Joanna, she's confused. I told you, the shrink said she was desperate.'

'But it's not the way he said,' Sylvie continued, pushing her words in between them. 'She's his baby, but it wasn't artificial insemination. We lived together. And he traveled a lot. You were coming here, weren't you?' she said to him. 'And running back and forth to Florida to put in your alibi calls. The day he brought you Lily,' Sylvie said to Joanna, 'did you have one of your big blowout celebrations, or did he have to quick, take off again?'

Joanna put a hand down over one of her husband's. 'You did take off,' she said, her voice fading into the words.

'Of course I did. You knew I had to get back on the road after all the work I'd missed arranging the surrogacy.'

'Right, Joanna. He'd missed all that work because he spent half his time with me, in New Haven, Connecticut. In our bed.' She had her voice back, though it moved more quickly than she was used to, racing past her thoughts, speaking before she knew what it would be telling.

'This fantasy is sick, Joanna. I told you, she's had to build this whole elaborate story to explain what she's done. This is what she wishes was true.'

'Keith?' Joanna asked, her voice spiraling up into a pleading whine. She turned her head to look at him. 'Were you sleeping with her?'

'Of course not.' Sylvie saw Peter's hands working on Joanna's shoulders and neck, massaging almost, but something fiercer, too. 'Who are you going to believe?' he asked her. 'This crazy kid? She's got to come up with a story that makes it seem like it was all right to give her child up. Don't you remember what she put us through, changing her mind all the time? Why should we get swept along into her guilt?'

'What about the birthmark, the one you wanted to have a plastic surgeon remove?' Sylvie shot the question at him.

'What about it?'

'I can identify her that way. She's my baby.'

'Fine. I'm not arguing that point. She *was* your baby. But you signed her over.'

'That's a lie.' Sylvie snapped out the words like cards dealt crisply from a brand-new deck. 'You kidnapped my baby from me. You knew where she was, Peter, and you let me think she was abandoned or dead. Didn't it ever bother you that I was completely frantic with fear and guilt? Didn't it bother you at all?'

He spoke to his wife, not Sylvie. 'Don't hold me responsible for her delusions. You've just got to ignore all this raving.'

'Joanna,' Sylvie said, 'he told the police that he thought I killed the baby. He set it up so it looked that way.' She spun round to face him. 'And I'm sorry I resisted leaving her alone for so long. I know you had to wait forever, had to put Joanna off over and over, but I did it finally, didn't I? I took your advice, didn't wake her, and left her alone.'

'We should call a doctor, get her sedated. She's really flipped now,' Peter said to Joanna.

'Keith?' Joanna said again.

'I have papers,' he said. 'Nobody's going to take our child from us.'

'I never signed any papers.' Sylvie shouted the words at Joanna.

'That's funny – your signature's on them. And by the way, I also have her birth certificate.'

'And I have a letter from the midwife.' She sprang at him with the information. 'A copy of the one you never let me see that says I gave birth to Cally.'

'Terrific, but you see, I'm not contesting that you gave birth to her. I am saying that you gave up your parental rights to her. That means I have custody, and court papers to prove it,' Peter proclaimed, moving away from Joanna, around her, toward Sylvie. 'The police won't touch Lily if I show them the court order. But they will arrest *you* for interfering with custody. They won't come near the baby, as long as I'm the parent with custody.'

'What are you talking about? I never gave up my rights, I never went to court.'

'I'm calling the police,' he said, going to the wall phone.

'Do that. I already told your wife – you can ask for Detective . . .' and then Sylvie couldn't remember his name.

'Yes?' he said, turning to her. 'There's a special favorite detective of yours that I should ask for?'

Damn, she couldn't get the name at all. She looked at Joanna for a moment – she'd said the name to her earlier, maybe she remembered, but how foolish, she thought. Joanna wasn't on her side.

'Can't think of his name, Sylvie? What's the matter, brain a little fuzzy?' He looped circles in the air with one finger. 'Having trouble remembering things? How surprising. You're always so intellectually sharp, I can't imagine what could be wrong. Maybe you haven't had enough Pepsi yet today, is that it?'

'So call the police,' she said, sure he wouldn't.

He picked up the receiver, pressed three buttons. 'I have an emergency,' he said after what seemed like only a second or two. 'I have a court order for custody of my child, and the child's mother is in my home violating that order. She's indicated she intends to kidnap and she's threatening to harm the child. I'm afraid for my child's life.' He gave the address. Said he was Keith Blessing. And he hung up.

'I know that was fake. They answered too fast,' she said.

The kitchen table was between them and he leaned toward her, his hands flat on the tiled surface. 'Believe that, if you like,' he said. 'They answer fast in this town, and they'll get here fast, trust me.'

'You said your name was Marie,' Joanna protested.

'You understand now, Joanna, how she lies?' Peter asked.

257

'Every other word out of her mouth is a lie.'

'I told you that name and that story about wanting to adopt so you'd talk to me, not shut me out, Joanna. But all the rest is true, I swear it.' Sylvie stopped for a moment and listened for the siren. Nothing. She turned her eyes full on Peter once more. 'And what about your lies? Your name? Your whole life is one big lie. Why don't you just let me have my baby now, and then you can go get yourself some other toy.'

'Fortunately I keep the papers here in the house, and I'm getting them so I can show the cops. Don't move an inch while I'm gone. Tackle her if you have to,' he said to Joanna as he left the room.

'You can't go along with this,' she said to Joanna as soon as he was gone, and then Sylvie heard the cry, saw, too, by Joanna's face, by the stern intensity of her expression, that she hadn't heard. Sylvie felt that tiny seeking noise coming out of sleeping, the asking, reaching sound of her Cally, felt it inside her again. 'I'm going to the bathroom,' she said, then headed toward the baby's room, needing to get there before the real cries started, so she could, lift her, touch her. She was partway into the room before Peter caught up with her.

'Don't touch her,' he commanded, pushing in front of her, nearly knocking her over. He lifted the baby from the crib.

'Let me hold her,' Sylvie begged, her arms open for the pleading face that was Cally's, but he darted around her, the baby beneath his arm, as though he were making an end run with a football.

She followed him back to the kitchen and saw he'd handed the screaming infant to Joanna. 'She's hungry,' Sylvie said.

'Feed her,' Peter shouted at Joanna.

'I'll hold her for you while you make the bottle,' Sylvie said, but the woman spun round, turning her back on Sylvie.

'Stay away from her,' Peter said, taking hold of Sylvie's arm.

'Get yourself another baby, Peter,' Sylvie said, pushing against his hold. 'Give her back to me. Haven't I been through enough? You knew she was safe, you *knew*, and you let me think she was with a maniac, or that she might be dead, and you knew all along.'

Joanna was pouring formula into a bottle. She had the crying baby propped high on her shoulder.

'Let me hold her,' Sylvie implored. 'Let me feel that she's alive.' She tried to move toward them, but Peter still held her fast.

'What are we doing, Keith?' Joanna said, putting the can of formula down on the counter.

'What?' he asked, turning to his wife. 'You want to let Lily go, after all this shit we've been through? You want to give it all up?'

'Of course not.' Joanna had the crying child tucked tight against her. The abandoned bottle held only a fingerful of formula. 'I just want to understand this, to know what happened.'

'For Christ's sake, Joanna, get serious. You know what happened. Don't hold *me* responsible for someone else's lunacy.' He let go of Sylvie and walked back to his wife.

'Let me hold her, please,' Sylvie said, but neither of them acknowledged her repetitive pleadings.

'I'm telling you what happened, I'm telling you she's unstable. This is our baby.'

'Did you tell her these things she's saying, that the baby was dead?'

'No, of course not.' The baby's cries were piercingly sharp. Sylvie couldn't remember ever hearing her sound like that. She picked up the formula can and started to fill the bottle. 'Let me hold her while you talk,' Sylvie begged, coming closer to them.

'Fuck off,' Peter said. He moved – pushed really, it looked to Sylvie – Joanna and the baby further from her; set himself between them.

'She's crying from hunger,' Sylvie said, holding out the bottle, her voice heavy with pleading. 'Don't keep making her suffer for you.'

And then Peter was stalking off suddenly, and she spoke to Joanna. 'Joanna,' Sylvie said, her voice almost as low as a whisper. She wanted to keep Joanna here, not have her run off with Peter.

'What?' the other woman snapped back.

'I want to thank you for taking such good care of her,' she said. Joanna was going to bolt, too, Sylvie could tell, and she didn't know what Peter was up to, whether he was calling someone, maybe some goons, for all she knew, and Joanna kept turning her head toward where he'd gone. Sylvie needed to keep her here. 'She looks so healthy,' Sylvie said, though she'd barely seen her face, the way Joanna had her crushed up against her. 'And I know you love her, I know that.'

Joanna looked at Sylvie full face. 'She's my baby,' Joanna said, tears wetting her cheeks. She was having to raise her voice above the infant's vigorous cries.

'I know. And you should feed her now, that's what she needs and wants, that's what you need to do for her. Then when she's calm, you'll be able to think better.'

Joanna hesitated, then lowered the baby down into her arms. 'Let me have the bottle,' she said.

Sylvie moved in close to Joanna and handed the bottle across Cally. Sylvie felt the pinpricks of old love race through her dry breasts when she looked down at Cally's frantic, needing face; felt the milk wanting, trying, to be there. Joanna brought the rubber nipple to the baby's mouth, but she only cried louder, pushing against it with her tongue. Joanna looked at Sylvie in surprise, then tried again. 'She always takes it,' she said, but the baby pulled away, dodging the rubber thing as though it were an assault mechanism. 'Maybe she's not hungry.'

'No, she's hungry, but she's beside herself, she's forgotten what she wants. Just try again,' Sylvie advised her.

She wanted Joanna to talk to Cally, console her; do what had to be done to calm her. Her own hands hovered over the child, and her palms were hot with craving to touch her. And then Cally was turning away from Joanna, arching toward Sylvie, reaching her mouth toward the breast, bridging the gap between them, rooting at her shirt. Sylvie saw the dark spot forming, the wetness spreading, the milk, back again, and such tears on her own face, she could hardly see her, but it was Cally, that little face, not changed much, really, the mouth working over her shirt, the crying intermittent now, so frustrated. And she was feeling her against her own body, kissing her, kissing her

Cally, and she realized Joanna had backed away, that Sylvie had slipped her hands around the infant and Joanna stood before her, the bottle held upright in both her hands. 'My baby,' Sylvie whispered to Cally, and she had to take a seat – her legs could barely hold her she was shaking so wildly. Sylvie lifted her shirt, tugging her breast toward the open mouth, and the baby was there, latching on, drinking of her, the two of them, home again. The only sounds were her gulps and swallows.

'She remembers,' Sylvie said to Joanna, but the other woman only stared at them. 'And my milk remembers, too,' she said, and laughed.

'Hand her back,' Peter said, his voice so loud, Sylvie jumped, though Cally seemed not to mind. The baby's desperate guzzling noises filled the room.

Peter held a paper in his hand, and he shook it toward her. 'Court order,' he announced, pushing it so close to her face the black lettering was a fluid blur. He pulled the paper away before she was able to read a word of it. She wanted to be able to follow him across the room, to grab and twist the paper from his hand, but she couldn't. She was going to nurse Cally till she was sated. Once that was done, fine, she'd deal with him. She drew the baby tighter against her, bent low over her, let her continue to drink. 'Hand her back,' he repeated. She wasn't going to look at him. She heard a siren, a piercing noise, coming closer, closer. She turned her eyes toward him and he was smiling at her. The sirens were screaming at her now, coming down the street, this street, to this house. 'This isn't game time, Sylvie,' he said. She felt cold, gone all shivery. And then there was silence, no more screeching, only car doors, running feet, pounding on the door.

'Police,' she heard them say. Cally's eyes were closed, and she sighed in her sleep. Sylvie broke the seal of the baby's mouth over the nipple and pulled her shirt back down. Cally didn't wake.

Peter let them in. She heard them talking in the entrance hallway, but could barely make out the words. Behind her, Joanna was sniffling. And then they were there, two uniformed

261

officers, one as blond and thin as Peter, one his very opposite, a dark, heavyset Hispanic man. They stood there in front of her, and the light one rested his hand on his pistol. 'Ma'am,' he said, 'are you Sylvie Pierson?' She nodded. 'I'm sorry to have to tell you this, but you're going to have to hand that baby back to Mr Blessing because the court has said that baby belongs to him now.'

'I'm not going to hurt her, it's not true,' she protested.

'I know that, ma'am, but the court order says the baby belongs to him, not you. And I know this is hard for you, but we're here to enforce this court order, is all.'

'It's a forgery,' she insisted.

'It looks okay to me,' the officer told her. 'It looks like a legitimate court order. All we can do is enforce the law, ma'am, like we're sworn to do.'

'I never signed it.'

'Well, no, that's true, but Mr Blessing says you gave up your parental rights prior to the time of the order. In cases like that, as I understand it, you wouldn't need to be present.'

Peter was grinning. She wanted to lunge at him, tear at his face, but the officer had walked closer to her. 'Ma'am, I need you to hand that little girl over to me.'

'He stole her from me,' she said.

'We'll get it all worked out, once you hand her over.'

'I can't,' she said, pushing the chair back behind her, rising, backing away.

They were on either side of her, holding onto her arms, jarring her, pushing at her. Cally was startled, awake, looking at her, eyes wide in surprise. 'There's a detective,' she said. 'I can't think of his name, but he knows about it. Detective Martinson knows him,' she said.

'There's no Detective Martinson in Tucson that I know of,' he said.

'Not Tucson,' she said. 'New Haven. Call him. He headed up the kidnapping case. He knows she was taken from me. He knows Peter took her.'

'Who's Peter?' the officer asked.

'Keith, Peter, they're the same.'

'They're not,' Joanna said, her voice like a scream cutting through darkness.

'Look, we'll talk about all this out in the car, after you hand the baby back, okay?' Sylvie shook her head.

'You're making it hard on yourself, on everybody,' the blond one said. 'Mr Blessing says if you give the baby back, nice and easy, he won't press charges. On the other hand, you act like this, and he presses charges, we have no choice but to arrest you, take the baby, and we don't want to see her get hurt, like in a tug-of-war, you know what I mean?'

'What are you going to charge me with?' She was looking straight at Peter.

'Interference with custody,' he crowed.

'Charge me, then,' she challenged him. She turned toward the policemen. 'This is my child. He kidnapped her from me. I never gave up rights on her. There never was a surrogacy, I swear it. You have to call Martinson, please.'

'What's this about surrogacy?' the darker officer asked Peter.

'That's what she's raving about, that's why I'm telling you she needs to be sedated, probably.'

The Hispanic officer eased her back into a corner of the room. 'Let them have their baby,' he said, his voice gentle, confidential. 'We'll go down to headquarters, I'll check out this Martinson.'

Sylvie was crying. 'I can't let her go again.'

The officer had his hand on her shoulder. 'It'll be okay,' he said.

'No,' she said, 'it won't.'

She held Cally tighter against her, she couldn't help it. One cop reached his hands around Cally, and the other one started to peel Sylvie's hands back, away from her baby. 'Come on, Sylvie, be a good girl,' one of them said. Cally was squirming, protesting. 'We'll get it settled faster, get hold of your friend in New Haven much faster if you let her go and just come with us.' Cally was starting to howl.

'Don't hurt her,' she pleaded. 'Please, don't hurt her.'

The policemen exchanged glances. 'You going to come with us?' one of them asked.

Sylvie nodded and they let go their hold on Cally. Sylvie lifted her baby to kiss her once upon her tiny, sad, trembling lips and then let them have her; laid her crying baby down in a police officer's arms.

She remembered his name. They weren't two blocks from Larch and she remembered his name. 'Daniel Ortiz!' she shouted at them. 'Ortiz. Get Ortiz. Ortiz.'

'Ortiz knows about this?' the blond one asked, turning back to face her.

'Call him,' she said, 'he knows.' And then they were talking back and forth on their speaker or beeper or radio or whatever it was, asking for Ortiz, but it didn't help, she had a hollow place in her chest for her baby that was never, never going to fill and be healed ever again. She thought of all the things she might have done in those few moments when she had been able to hold her – feel out the shape and size of her fontanel, touch the bottoms of her smooth little feet, nibble at her ear, or blow the soft fair hair so it billowed up like milkweed. She hadn't done a single one of them. She'd had the chance and she hadn't done a single one of those things, she thought, and cried softly. She tried to keep her grief quiet, to keep it from seeping through the metal gridwork that separated her from the police officers, but she felt it shoot up and away from her, and knew that hers was as piercing and wild a howl as Cally's had been only minutes before.

They couldn't get hold of anybody. Nobody in New Haven knew where Martinson was. He didn't answer his home phone. She paced. They called again. He still didn't answer. Ortiz wasn't home either. His partner said yes, Ortiz *had* mentioned something about a call from New Haven but he didn't know anything about it.

'They'll run,' Sylvie told them. 'They'll take my baby and be gone. They're probably already gone,' she moaned.

She wanted them to book her, to get it over with and let her get out of there. *She* would go back there if they wouldn't. She could at least stand in the kitchen at 368 Larch, stalling for time. The police officers were moving no faster than dawdling children walking to school. What drugs are you on that put you into slo-mo? she wanted to say. They told her they didn't wish to book her if there was no reason. 'Book me,' she screamed at them. 'You can't just keep me prisoner here, you know.' Damn them, it was her baby, not theirs. And when the light one, Carvey, had disappeared from his desk and the dark one, whose name was Flores, kept playing with the redial button on his phone, she said, 'Send someone over to the house. Send anybody.' But Flores said he hadn't any actual reason to send anyone over there, as yet.

'Then I want a lawyer,' she said.

'When I charge you is when you need the lawyer. For now,' he counseled, 'you should just hang on.'

'No,' she argued. 'You said I had the right to a lawyer. You said that in the car coming over. So I want a lawyer now. I must be entitled.'

Flores shrugged his shoulders, raised his arms high in surrender. 'I'm trying to be nice about this. I'm hoping not to have to charge you with anything.'

She watched his hands flip idly through a stack of papers. 'I'm entitled to a lawyer,' she reiterated, and he picked up the phone.

She paced while they waited for the arrival of the public defender. 'Too bad Ortiz's kids are all grown,' Flores said from his perch on the corner of his desk. 'If there was a baby-sitter home there, she'd be able to tell us where he was.'

'Well, take a guess,' she said. 'Where does he usually go?'

Flores laughed. 'Well, I don't know, I'm not a buddy of his.'

'Call his partner, then,' she insisted, pointing at the phone.

The partner mentioned a few funky little restaurants in South Tucson, and he also said there were a couple of movies Ortiz had talked about wanting to see. 'But he could be anywhere in the whole city,' Flores pointed out to her.

'Call,' she said, pointing again.

'He's gonna be pissed if I pull him out of a thriller and tell him I've got this hunch about a baby.'

'You're stalling – trying to keep me here. Book me and let me go.'

He waited a minute before answering. 'You want me to book you before the lawyer gets here?'

'Yes.'

He shook his head, reached across the desk for the Tucson yellow pages, and opened it at the restaurant section.

They found him, third call. 'An easy shot,' Flores said to Sylvie while he waited for Ortiz to come to the phone at a restaurant where the owner said, 'Oh, yes, Detective Ortiz is our very favorite customer.'

Sylvie didn't like the sound of it from her end. The conversation was too soft and vague. Too many *uh-huhs*. No discussion of how soon Ortiz would join them. And then Flores was using words like *domestic*, and she knew nothing was going to happen. Cally would travel somewhere else to yet another new name. When Flores hung up, he was silent for a long time. She held her breath, waiting, hoping Ortiz had given them something more. 'He definitely knows the case,' he said after a time. 'The information he has is just what you're saying – fraud, phony kidnapping. He's been jerking the whole New Haven department around. But there's a catch, too, see.'

'I know,' she said. 'He's the father, so he can do any old thing he wants, break any laws he wants – right?'

'Well, I wouldn't put it that way, exactly.'

'How would you put it?'

'I'd say he has what he claims is a court order and if it's legit, we can't touch him in terms of the baby.'

'It's not legit.'

'I think you're right. Ortiz says any papers he has are likely to be forgeries.'

'So then we're okay, aren't we?'

'*Likely* is not the same as *is*, if you know what I mean. Monday you're going to have to try going to court, that's the best we can do for you. Martinson contacted him in case there was some threat against you, which there really isn't.'

'There's a threat against my baby.'

266

'Not a threat. They're not harming her. And as far as I know, he's the custodial parent.'

Sylvie'd been through this before. 'I'm getting out of here,' she said, jumping up from the chair.

'Oh, no, you're not,' he said, coming toward her. 'Now you're gonna get what you wanted. I'm booking you.'

He'd taken hold of her arm, high up, nearly at her shoulder. 'If you get near that place they'll charge you with trespassing or assault or something that forces me to keep you in here. Going out to that house isn't going to get you anywhere.'

The phone on his desk was ringing. With his free hand, he picked up the receiver. She tried prying his fingers up from her arm, but he held firm. The other officer, Carvey, came back into the room and Flores let her go. 'Yes, Mrs Blessing,' he was saying into the phone. Sylvie's pulse rate took a ferocious leap forward at the sound of the name. 'Yes, ma'am, we'll come back out, ma'am, of course.' He hung up the phone. 'Something broke loose over there,' he said, 'but I can't make out what she wants.'

'Time for another look-see,' Carvey said.

Chapter 30

When the police had first left the Blessing house with Sylvie in tow, Keith and Joanna seemed unable to move, unable to speak one to the other. There was the unmistakable sound of the patrol car doors being slammed to, the start of the engine, and yet they stood motionless, eyes meeting, then drawing apart. It was the baby who broke the silence, crying again as though she'd just remembered she'd never had a chance at Sylvie's second breast.

'Holy shit,' Keith finally said, the explosion of his voice startling Joanna as thoroughly as a physical blow. 'We've got to split. Go get packed. We can talk about where we want to go once we're in the car.' And then he moved off in long strides toward the bedroom.

'Shhh,' she cautioned the baby, though it didn't do the slightest good. She followed her husband then, shuffling along the arc he'd swept through moments before. She found him pulling a box down from a closet shelf. 'Tell me the truth,' she said to him.

'I did.' He hefted down another box, one she knew was filled with paper of some sort: household records, she'd always thought.

'What did you really do out there?'

He looked up at her for a moment. 'I got us a baby,' he said.

'It wasn't a surrogacy, was it?'

'It was a private surrogacy,' he said flatly.

'Which means what? That you've been living with that girl for the past year?' she asked, pointing back over her shoulder toward where Sylvie had once stood.

'No.' He was putting the boxes aside, coming to her. 'Joanna,'

269

he said, his hand sliding over her neck, entangling softly in her curls.

'What does it mean?'

'It means we have Lily.' He bent his head toward her, tried to kiss her, but she backed away.

'Tell me what you did, Keith, because I'm part of this. I need to know.'

He took a deep breath. 'I couldn't get a regular surrogacy,' he said. 'I tried, I swear to God. I tried, Joanna. You wanted this so much . . .'

'Me? And you *didn't* want it?' Joanna was trying to keep the baby quiet, jiggling her against her chest.

'Yes, of course I wanted it, *we* wanted it, both of us. Look, we can talk about this in the car. Right now, we really need to pack.' He pulled a suitcase from the closet and set it down on the bed.

'No,' she said, shaking her head. 'We really need to talk. I'm completely confused, Keith.' He was sorting through papers, not looking at her at all. 'I'm scared, Keith. You've got to help me with this.' She rocked back and forth as she spoke, trying to soothe the baby, trying to soothe herself. 'Keith,' she said, her voice more piercing now. 'If it wasn't a regular surrogacy, what was it? I need to know what you did to that girl. She told me some pretty terrible things.'

He nodded. 'I know she did. I told you she was unstable. Crazy people breed craziness wherever they go. She came here to undermine what we have, and damn it, she's being very successful.' He put his hands on Joanna's shoulders, the right one resting on the squirming infant's back. 'I know how hard this has been on you, but you need to pull yourself together now.'

'You slept with her?'

'Yes.' Joanna groaned. His hand tightened on her shoulder. 'Listen to me, it was only the once, I swear to you. We had an agreement, we had a lawyer, we completely discussed the surrogacy, we drew up the papers, everything was one hundred percent legal.' He'd stepped back from her as he spoke, his words delivered with precision and surety. 'She was a perfect match for you, she was in great health, but she just wouldn't go along with artificial insemination. She said it was degrading. What choice did I have? I could have said forget it, I know I could have, but there was no other surrogate mother out there for us. I searched everywhere. Now, maybe I did the wrong thing, I don't know, but it seemed right at the time, that's all I can say. She knew exactly when she was fertile – she had pains mid-month that her doctor said were a sure sign she was ovulating, so there was a very good chance that if we had sex once, just at that time, she would conceive. Which is exactly what did happen. And incidentally, it saved us two thousand dollars and two months' time to bypass the bureaucracy of a clinic doing an artificial insemination. And believe me, Joanna, there was nothing between us. We went to a motel room, a cinder-block room with a tufted bedspread and a print of Van Gogh's *Sunflowers* on the wall. She took a shower afterward, asked me to get her a can of Pepsi, and by the time I got back to the room, the TV was blaring out Tom and Jerry cartoons. I went out for dinner alone.' Joanna had sat down on the bed. 'People do it that way, it's one of the ways surrogacies are done. The lawyer knew about it. He said it didn't matter because the contract only covered from when there was a pregnancy anyway.'

'The lawyer said people do that, that it's common?'

'Yes.'

She shook her head. She's been thinking about putting Lily down in her crib, thinking she'd be better off out of this bad emotional stuff, but she just didn't want to let go. She looked at him full on and asked, 'Why didn't you tell me?'

'I had to make a decision for both of us. I thought it was the right one. And frankly, you weren't thinking clearly back then, as I'm sure you'll agree. Look, we need to pack, Joanna.' He took a second piece of luggage from the closet and held it toward her.

'Why?'

'Why what?' His voice was harsh.

'Why do we need to pack? Why are we running?'

'Because I don't want to deal with her if she comes back here.

271

I don't want her upsetting you. Look how she upset Lily.' He put the suitcase down and reached to take the baby from her arms, but she turned slightly, moving the infant beyond his hand. 'We have to get on with our lives, and that girl has to get on with hers. If we cut out of here for a while, she'll get tired of hanging around and go home.'

'I want to see the surrogacy papers.'

'I don't have them here.' He dismissed her request with a wave of his hand.

'Because there aren't any, are there?'

'Yes, there are, I told you that.'

'I know you did, but why haven't I ever seen them?'

'Because you never asked.'

'I didn't even think about them till today, but now that I have, I keep wondering why you didn't want to show them off to me, to show me the proof that she was finally ours. And why, when the police were here and Sylvie said something about surrogacy, did you tell them she was just talking crazy? If it was a surrogacy, if there was any kind of agreement, why didn't you explain it to the police?'

'Can we talk about it in the car?'

'No.' And then she was shaking so badly she worried whether the baby was safe in her arms.

He stared at her for a moment, then moved toward the other side of the bed, got back to taking things from the closet. 'I'm not going to subject myself to that shit with her and the police again, so make up your mind, Joanna. We go together or not, but I'm going.'

'What are you hiding from the police, Keith?'

'Enough already, Joanna. If you expect to keep Lily, I suggest you get your ass in gear and get moving.'

'They'll take her?'

'Damn straight.'

'Because it's not like you said, is it?'

He was pulling things out of drawers, tossing clothing and papers into his bag. 'You coming?'

'No, I can't believe this. You lived with her and then you took her baby.' She rubbed the infant's back as she spoke.

'I did what was best, Joanna. You needed a baby.'

'You never talked about a surrogacy with her, and you never went to a lawyer, did you? You got her pregnant and you kidnapped her baby from her, didn't you?' Joanna was crying, her low noises mixing in with the baby's attenuated cries. Joanna lowered the child into her arms and started kissing her, on the nose, the mouth, the cheeks, her tears washing over the infant's face. 'My poor Lily,' she sobbed. She looked up at him. 'And did you tell the police you thought she'd murdered Lily, murdered her own baby?'

He put aside the slacks he'd been about to pack and faced her. 'It's not like she's an intellectual giant, Joanna, surely you saw that? She's your basic mall rat, that's all. High culture to her is getting to choose which fast-food outlet to eat at.'

'She's Lily's mother, Keith.'

'Oh, Joanna, that's a biological accident, forget it. Did you look at her? Is this somebody you'd want to even hire as a baby-sitter for Lily? That girl would eat Pepsi and ice cream for breakfast, lunch, and dinner if she could pull it off. I spent all my energy feeding her decent food when she was pregnant so Lily would be healthy. I spoon-fed all the good stuff into her, goddamn it. She's a mall rat, one of those grazers, one of those kids who's looking to fill all her orifices. Remember that time we were at the mall and you pointed out to me how there were the boy herds and the girl herds prowling around looking at each other, practically panting for sex?'

'What does that have to do with our baby?'

'Do you remember saying that?'

'Yes.' Her voice was hard and flat.

'You're the one who gave me the idea. It was right after all that shit with the adoption agency screwing us over. You said you could read the sexual fantasies in their eyes when the herds passed each other.'

'Maybe I said that.'

'You said it.'

'And what's the point?'

He returned to his packing, putting one last pair of slacks atop everything else. 'The point is, she's one of those worthless

273

things shuffling through that mall, one hand in a bag of Mrs Fields cookies, one hand stroking over the different-colored sweaters and her eyes, her mind, looking at those boy-bodies. Joanna, when we were in the mall that day and you said that, I saw how we could do it; how we could get our baby. A short-term arrangement: I provided the cookies and tee-shirts and jeans and sweaters and sex, and she provided the baby. I figured it as a fair trade.'

'You didn't figure that quite right, though, Keith, because you never bothered to tell her about her part of the bargain.'

'No, but I figured she'd be glad enough to give it up and get back to the mall.'

'But she wasn't, obviously.'

'And I dealt with that. I always figured I'd take the baby if I had to. I got one of those old apartments with French doors. Easy in, easy out,' he said, laughing at the memory.

'I can't believe you're saying this.'

'Look, Joanna, she was a complete loner, the most needy thing you could imagine.'

'This is so cruel, Keith.'

'Joanna,' he said, pressing down on the valise, trying to get the overstuffed thing to close. 'She wanted what I had to give and I wanted what she had. And to me, that's what the world's all about. I didn't sleep with her much, if that's what's getting to you. Three, four times and we were finished. At that age, if they're fertile, they're fertile as hell.' Joanna turned away from him. 'Is that it, is it the sleeping with her you're angry about?' She shook her head. He pushed the zipper round the last bulge of clothing and papers. 'You coming?' he asked her. 'Because the only way we're going to keep Lily is if you get out of here. I've got a new ID, so we're all set on that. They'll never get to us. We make our move, now, fast, and we're home free. The new name's Kenneth Wilder. Definitely classier than Blessing. I thought that *wild* part was a nice touch, what do you think?'

'How many different names have you used in your life?'

'It doesn't matter.'

'And who am I? If Blessed's not your real name, it's not mine, either.' She shifted the baby in her arms.

'You get to choose a new first name, that's the fun of it. Your last name's Wilder, of course.'

'What am I supposed to do for ID?'

'That part's easy. Husbands can always vouch for their wives. We start at the bottom with a library card, then we move on, use that card to get something better. Eventually you get a credit card, a license. And hey,' he said, patting the baby's back, 'don't get so tense. You always liked moving before. The other times you always said it gave you a kick to start over.'

'We never changed names, we never did it with no notice.'

'The time we came here we did it in two days. The time we went to Sacramento we had maybe three days.'

'We weren't running.'

'You disappoint me, Jo. Where's my girl who's willing to try anything?'

'Were we running those times, too, Keith?'

He laughed. 'Kenneth,' he corrected her.

'There was no lawyer, no papers?' she asked, wistful almost.

'You coming?' he asked her as he pulled the suitcase off the bed. She shook her head. 'You wanted a baby, Joanna.' She didn't answer. He let the canvas case drop to the floor, then kicked its soft bulk ineffectually. 'What the fuck,' he said. He looked up at the ceiling. 'What the hell do I do now?' he asked of no one in particular.

Unlike Sylvie's earlier ride of the day in the squad car, on this trip the siren was screeching. She held onto the door handle with both hands as they took the corners. 'Is Cally all right?' she tried shouting at them, but they said they didn't know. She'd just have to wait.

Joanna came to the door, thinner, as though the water she'd lost through tears had made a visible difference in her weight from earlier that day. He's taken her, Sylvie thought when she saw Joanna, gray-faced and disheveled, backing away from them as they approached. The woman was weeping, one hand covering her mouth, not so much to muffle, Sylvie thought, as to support her faltering self. 'Where's the baby?' Sylvie asked as soon as she was close to the doorway.

'She's here,' Joanna said, and pointed back behind her. Carvey had taken hold of Sylvie's arm again.

'Let's check it out together,' he said. She started to twist against his hold, but he was moving forward, at least, and so she let herself be carried along with him.

'In the bedroom,' Joanna said as they passed by her, and the pace was much too slow, the way Carvey held back, moving one foot, then the other, but they finally made it, and Cally was there asleep, her breathing interrupted by that terrible hiccoughy catch that comes from crying too long and too hard. Carvey let go of her and Sylvie reached her arms in under her baby. She brought the little body close against her chest and Cally wriggled about for just a moment, then shuddered and slept on – the distraught crying all finished.

Flores and Joanna had come into the room. 'You should take her,' the woman said. 'He's gone. He lied.' Her sobs were so intense, Sylvie couldn't make out anything else she said.

'She says he told her he cooked up some business about a surrogacy,' Flores said, pointing with his head toward Joanna. 'She said to tell you she didn't know what he was doing. She thought it was all above board.'

'Where'd he go?' Carvey asked the crying woman. Joanna shrugged. 'Did he take luggage?' She shook her head.

'I love her,' Joanna said, one hand coming tentatively forward toward the sleeping baby's back, then drawing away. 'I love her but I can't do this to you.' She reached for a pile of baby clothes on the changing table and handed it to Flores. 'Here,' she said. 'Take it all out of here.' She was shaking her head. 'I don't know what I'm going to do, now.' Sylvie could feel the panic in Joanna's words, could hear the words break like a wine glass upon a tiled floor. Joanna glanced about the room, her eyes darting over the contents, and then she stooped and gathered baby paraphernalia into her arms. 'Take it,' she said, pushing diapers and infant clothing at Carvey.

Sylvie was kissing Cally, tracing out her fontanel, feeling how it had grown smaller, how the hair had thickened, and Cally opened her eyes and Sylvie saw how much firmer their focus was than she'd remembered, and how they were still that

276

same brilliant, piercing blue that had lit up her memory. Joanna was holding out a pair of tiny shoes, a hat, some sweaters.

'This is a lot more complicated than you ladies seem to think,' Flores interjected. 'I need to remind you that there's a court order, so we can't just stand here and let you hand this child over like this, Mrs Blessing.' Flores, then Carvey, put the baby clothes back down.

Sylvie held Cally closer to her. 'I'm her mother,' Sylvie said. 'Isn't that worth as much as him being the father?'

'But the point is, you don't have custody. We're talking law here, not what we think's right or wrong.'

Sylvie took a step toward Flores. 'But he doesn't have custody, either. You know it's all a lie.'

'She's right,' Joanna said. 'That paper was a forgery, I'm sure of it.'

'Look,' Carvey said, holding up his hands as though he might ask for the baby to be delivered back to him, but then dropping them down as he spoke. 'You'll have to work this out in the courts, that's all, that's the only way.'

'I can let her hold the baby, can't I?' Joanna asked.

'Well, yes, you can do that.'

'Well, that's all I want her to do.'

'We can't stop who you choose to hold the child.'

Joanna nodded. 'Well, thank you,' she said to Flores, walking toward him. 'Thank you for coming here.' She held a hand out to him, and he shook it. 'I'm sorry I bothered you.'

Carvey and Flores exchanged glances. 'Okay, ma'am,' Flores said after a pause. 'Is there any kind of problem here now?' Joanna shook her head. 'Then I guess we'll be leaving you,' he said.

Sylvie looked to see if they were waiting for her, but they were walking toward the front of the house, paying her no heed. Flores turned around. 'Good luck,' he said, then continued on his way.

'Let me just say goodbye to her,' Joanna said when they'd heard the front door shut. She bent over the baby and kissed her first on one cheek, then on the other.

277

'I'm sorry,' Sylvie said.

Joanna shook her head and turned away. 'Just love her for me, please.'

'Thank you,' Sylvie said, and then she walked slowly and carefully, so as not to shatter or alter anything that had been said or tacitly agreed to in that room. When she reached the living room picture window, she saw that the patrol car was gone. She went the rest of the way, through the house and down the streets, on a straight-line, swift-as-the-wind run.

Chapter 31

There was a message from Martinson when she got back to the hotel room: 'Stay where you are, I'm on my way.' The arrival time he'd listed was still five hours to the future.

Hell no, Detective, she thought. I'm not sitting here waiting for you, and she put Cally down on the bed just long enough to zip up her suitcase. We are out of here, Detective.

She dialed her mother's number but got her message machine. Why wasn't anybody where they were supposed to be when she wanted them? She waited through Hannah's overly enunciated phone announcement, then said, 'Stop worrying. We're free at last. See you soon. Love, Sylvie and Cally.'

Martinson was going to be furious when he arrived at the hotel and found she'd checked out, but she couldn't take the time to think about it. She wanted to be home, tucking Cally into her crib, and as long as she was in Tucson, Peter might find some way to stop her from leaving. It seemed to her like the faster she got to the airport and on to a plane and put distance between them, the better chance she had of shaking him. All he had to do was alert airport security to her trying to leave and her baby might be lifted right out of her arms – temporarily, maybe, but even that would be more than she could bear happening again. She sure as hell wasn't waiting for five whole hours.

She was able to get a flight right away. And she arranged for a message for Martinson after the first leg of his flight – he'd be arriving in Dallas in an hour and fifteen minutes. 'Sorry. Have departed AZ, see you in CT,' was what she sent. And then she went and hid in the restroom nearest her departure gate till the voice on the P.A. system announced that passengers traveling with infants could board.

She did not even look for Peter as she came out. Or not carefully. She just headed straight and fast for the gate. If he was there, he'd have had to buy a ticket to get this far. Which he might have, but somebody there, the airline personnel, somebody'd help her; they wouldn't just let him snatch her child from her arms. Wouldn't they go with the more reasonable, sane-sounding story? But which story, she mournfully asked herself, Peter's or hers, was actually even vaguely sane-sounding? Please, Joanna, she intoned to herself, eyes closed. Keep him there, talk him down. Make it all go away.

She boarded the plane, then watched everyone who came on and he wasn't one of them. Once the doors closed, and the plane lifted up, she wept, and though she told herself it was for joy and for freedom and for reunion and all the shared time stretching before them, it felt as sad and depressive as any weeping she'd ever done. These were tears for the truth of what had happened, she knew, for finally having to understand she had no lover, no husband or husband-to-be, no person who loved her or who had ever loved her. And worst of all, there was no father for her baby. They were in it alone, and there would be no way to tell the tale to Cally as she grew, no way to explain who she was without filling her with hatred and fear. 'You be strong,' she whispered to her baby. 'We both have to be.'

Martinson was waiting for her in Dallas. It'd been easy to intercept her, he said, once he'd gotten the message. All he'd had to do was meet incoming flights from Tucson, and hope, of course, that she had been booked through Dallas. He took her bag, slung it over his shoulder, where it bumped along on top of his weary tweed jacket. He searched out a store with diapers, a women's bathroom with a changing table, an icy-cold Pepsi, and they made the connecting flight – but only just.

It was while the plane was taxiing down the runway that he started to tell her that she couldn't let down her guard, that it wasn't over yet. He wasn't really looking at her, though she couldn't tell for sure, because she wasn't looking at him. She was looking at Cally, and she was kissing her still, all over her face, feeling almost like she could eat her. He said, 'You have to realize this man may never give up. You may be looking over your shoulder for the rest of your life.' He might track Sylvie, he said, if she tried to run. She knew all that. She knew she had a whole store-house of dreams awaiting her – dreams about his face at the window, his voice on the phone, his footsteps down the hall when she was in the shower. She knew how some people had to worry every time they sent their kids off to school in the morning. 'There's no point, really, in running,' she said to Martinson.

Martinson said something about how she'd have to check everybody out – school bus drivers, parents of friends, that kind of thing, if she really wanted to be sure. Sylvie looked at Cally's wispy hair, saw how it danced under her breath like honeysuckle leaves in a light summer breeze, and she told Martinson she could do it.

Sylvie had the window seat, and she had it tilted back as far as it could go. Cally slept on Sylvie's chest, the delicate in-and-out of the baby's breathing weaving in with her own. Cally's body, softened by sleep, felt weightier than Sylvie remembered, and she savored the firm pressure upon her heart. Sylvie imagined her Cally even larger, heavier, more of a real child, upright, their fingers entwined in unity. Now, though, Sylvie had one hand on her daughter's hair, the other on the small toes beneath white cotton baby socks. She couldn't sleep for the pleasure of it.

Martinson had his eyes closed, though she suspected he wasn't sleeping, either. 'Detective,' she whispered close by his ear. 'I'm not giving her up anymore.'

When he opened his eyes and turned to her, he said, 'I can believe that.' His hand settled across Cally, the tips of his fingers moving slowly over the infant's back. Sylvie's pinky stretched downward from the baby's head toward his hand, edging next to it. Two of his fingers wrapped around hers. When she drew in her next breath, a very deep one, she felt the baby's breath deepen as well. She felt the small fists move sideways across her chest, and then Martinson leaned his head down, bringing his lips to the baby's slowly opening hand.

When he lifted his head a moment later, she lowered Cally into the cradle of her arms, and together, they watched as the infant awakened.